GNU Octave
Beginner's Guide

Become a proficient Octave user by learning this high-level
scientific numerical tool from the ground up

Jesper Schmidt Hansen

BIRMINGHAM - MUMBAI

GNU Octave
Beginner's Guide

First published: June 2011

Production Reference: 2150611

Published by Packt Publishing Ltd.
32 Lincoln Road
Olton
Birmingham, B27 6PA, UK.

ISBN 978-1-849513-32-6

www.packtpub.com

Cover Image by John Quick (john@johnmquick.com)

Credits

Author

Jesper Schmidt Hansen

Reviewers

Piotr Gawron

Kenneth Geisshirt

Jordi Gutiérrez Hermoso

Acquisition Editor

Usha Iyer

Development Editor

Roger D'souza

Technical Editor

Dayan Hyames

Project Coordinator

Joel Goveya

Proofreaders

Lesley Harrison

Clyde Jenkins

Lynda Sliwoski

Indexers

Hemangini Bari

Tejal Daruwale

Monica Ajmera Mehta

Graphics

Nilesh R. Mohite

Production Coordinator

Kruthika Bangera

Cover Work

Kruthika Bangera

About the Author

Jesper Schmidt Hansen holds a Ph.D. in soft material science and is currently doing research in the field of nanofluidics and dynamics at Roskilde University, Denmark. He has been using GNU Octave on a daily basis for many years, both as a student and later as a researcher. The applications have varied from solving partial and ordinary differential equations, simple data plotting, data generation for other applications, dynamical system investigations, and advanced data analysis.

Firstly, I wish to thank the reviewers. They have been a great help and their many (at times overwhelmingly many) comments and hints have improved the manuscript considerably.

I have received encouragement and good ideas from everyone at the Department of Science, Systems and Models, Roskilde University. Especially, I want to thank Professor Jeppe Dyre from the Danish National Research Foundation centre "Glass and Time" for giving me the opportunity to finish the book in the last phase of the writing.

Also, I have found Octave's official mailing list very useful. Unlike many other user groups, there is a very constructive and helpful atmosphere here. I thank everyone who has submitted questions and all those that have replied.

I now realize that having a one year old child, a full time job, as well as writing a book is not really an ideal cocktail. I must thank Signe Anthon for her tremendous support and patience during the writing of this book. When I signed the contract with Packt Publishing, I was happy finally to be able to make a contribution to the open source community—Signe's contribution is just as big as mine!

About the Reviewers

Piotr Gawron is a researcher in the field of quantum information processing. His main research topics are quantum programming languages, quantum game theory, and numerical and geometrical methods in quantum information. He works in the Quantum Computer Systems Group of the Institute of Theoretical and Applied Informatics of the Polish Academy of Sciences in Gliwice, Poland. Apart from research in theoretical aspects of computer science, he has gained practical experience in FPGA development and real-time image processing for applications in UAVs working closely with the industry. He is administrator of www.quantiki.org , a portal for the quantum information community. He is a user and strong supporter of free software. He likes hard science-fiction literature, live-action role-playing, and French rock music.

Kenneth Geisshirt is a chemist by education and a geek by nature. He has been programming for more than 25 years—the last 6 years as a subcontractor. In 1990, Kenneth first met free software, and in 1992 turned to Linux as his primary operating system (officially Linux user no. 573 at the Linux Counter). He has written books about Linux, PAM, and JavaScript—and many articles on open source software for computer magazines. Moreover, Kenneth has been a technical reviewer of books on Linux network administration, the Vim editor, and JavaScript testing.

Jordi Gutiérrez Hermoso studied mathematics in Canada and Mexico, both pure and applied respectively. He has been programming since the age of seven, when he started to learn about computers while writing silly programs in BASIC. He has been a Debian user since 2001, his first and still preferred GNU/Linux distribution, to which he now occasionally contributes with GNU Octave packaging. Since 2005, he has been an enthusiastic Octave user and started getting more involved with its development in 2010. As of 2011, he resides in Mexico and works in BlueMessaging, where he's responsible for natural language processing and artificial intelligence. An Emacs user at heart, Jordi feels at home in a GNU environment and will gladly share .emacs configurations with anyone who asks.

I would like to thank my close friends and family for helping me get through difficult times and for celebrating the good ones with me. John W. Eaton, Octave's creator, deserves much recognition for starting and leading the project on which this book is based.

www.PacktPub.com

Support files, eBooks, discount offers and more

You might want to visit www.PacktPub.com for support files and downloads related to your book.

Did you know that Packt offers eBook versions of every book published, with PDF and ePub files available? You can upgrade to the eBook version at www.PacktPub.com and as a print book customer, you are entitled to a discount on the eBook copy. Get in touch with us at service@packtpub.com for more details.

At www.PacktPub.com, you can also read a collection of free technical articles, sign up for a range of free newsletters, and receive exclusive discounts and offers on Packt books and eBooks.

http://PacktLib.PacktPub.com

Do you need instant solutions to your IT questions? PacktLib is Packt's online digital book library. Here, you can access, read, and search across Packt's entire library of books.

Why Subscribe?
- Fully searchable across every book published by Packt
- Copy and paste, print, and bookmark content
- On demand and accessible via web browser

Free Access for Packt account holders

If you have an account with Packt at www.PacktPub.com, you can use this to access PacktLib today and view nine entirely free books. Simply use your login credentials for immediate access.

Table of Contents

Preface

Using a range of very different examples, this beginner's guide will take you through the most important aspects of GNU Octave. The book starts by introducing how you work with mathematical objects like vectors and matrices, demonstrating how to perform simple arithmetic operations on these objects and explaining how to use some of the simple functionality that comes with GNU Octave, including plotting. It then goes on to show you how to extend and implement new functionality into GNU Octave, how to make a toolbox package to solve your specific problem, and how to use GNU Octave for complicated data analysis. Finally, it demonstrates how to optimize your code and link GNU Octave with C++ code enabling you to solve even the most computational demanding tasks. After reading GNU Octave Beginner's Guide, you will be able to use and tailor GNU Octave to solve most numerical problems and perform complicated data analysis with ease.

What this book covers

Chapter 1, Introducing GNU Octave briefly introduces you to GNU Octave. It explains how you can install GNU Octave and test your installation. This first chapter also discusses how to customize the appearance and the behavior of GNU Octave as well as how you install additional packages.

Chapter 2, Interacting with Octave: Variables and Operators shows you how to interact with GNU Octave through the interactive environment. Learn to instantiate objects of different types, control their values, and perform simple operations on and between them.

Chapter 3, Working with Octave: Functions and Plotting explains GNU Octave functions and shows several examples of the very useful functionalities that come with GNU Octave. In this chapter, you will see how you can perform two- and three-dimensional plotting, control the graph appearance, how to have multiple plots in the same figure window, and much more.

Chapter 4, Rationalizing: Octave Scripts looks at how you can rationalize your work using scripts. It will teach you how to control the programming flow in your script and how to perform loops using different statements. At the end of the chapter, you are shown how you can save your work and load it back into GNU Octave's workspace.

Chapter 5, Extensions: Write Your Own Octave Functions takes a closer look at functions and teaches how you can write your own GNU Octave functions. You will learn how to control and validate user input to the function. The important concept of vectorization is discussed and an example of this is given in the last part of the chapter.

Chapter 6, Making Your Own Package: A Poisson Equation Solver teaches you how to make your own GNU Octave package from a collection of related functions. The package will be able to solve one- and two-dimensional Poisson equations and is therefore relevant for many problems encountered in science and engineering. In this chapter, you will also learn how to work with sparse matrices in GNU Octave.

Chapter 7, More Examples: Data Analysis shows you examples of how GNU Octave can be used for data analysis. These examples range from simple statistics, through data fitting, to Fourier analysis and data smoothing.

Chapter 8, Need for Speed: Optimization and Dynamically Linked Functions discusses how you can optimize your code. This includes vectorization, partial looping, pre-instantiation of variables, and dynamically linked functions. The main part of the chapter shows how to use GNU Octave's C++ library and how to link this to the GNU Octave interactive environment. Special attention is paid to explaining when and when not to consider using dynamically linked functions.

What you need for this book

If you use Windows, you basically only need to have a full version of GNU Octave installed on your computer. For GNU/Linux, you may need a plotting program like gnuplot, a Fortran and C/C++ compiler like gcc, and the GNU make utility; fortunately these are standard packages on almost all GNU/Linux distributions. In *Chapter 1*, it will be shown how you install GNU Octave under Windows and GNU/Linux.

Who this book is for

This book is intended for anyone interested in scientific computing and data analysis. The reader should have a good knowledge of mathematics and also a basic understanding of programming will be useful, although it is not a prerequisite.

Conventions

In this book, you will find several headings appearing frequently.

To give clear instructions of how to complete a procedure or task, we use:

Time for action – heading

1. Action 1
2. Action 2
3. Action 3

Instructions often need some extra explanation so that they make sense, so they are followed with:

What just happened?

This heading explains the working of tasks or instructions that you have just completed.

You will also find some other learning aids in the book, including:

Pop quiz – heading

These are short multiple-choice questions intended to help you test your own understanding.

Have a go hero – heading

These set practical challenges and give you ideas for experimenting with what you have learned.

You will also find a number of styles of text that distinguish between different kinds of information. Here are some examples of these styles, and an explanation of their meaning.

Code words in text are shown as follows: "For example, the inverse of sine is called `asin` and the inverse hyperbolic of sine is `asinh`."

A block of code is set as follows:

```
# flush the output stream
fflush(stdout);

# Get the number of rows and columns from the user
nr = input("Enter the number of rows in the matrix: ");
nc = input("Enter the number of columns in the matrix: ");
```

Any command-line input or output is written as follows:

```
octave:35> projectile = struct("mass", 10.1, "velocity", [1 0 0],
"type", "Cannonball");
```

New terms and **important words** are shown in bold. Words that you see on the screen, in menus or dialog boxes for example, appear in the text like this: "Now go to the Octave-Forge web page, find the `msh` package, and click on **Details** (to the right of the package name)."

Specific commands entered in Octave are referred to using the relevant command numbers:

```
octave:5 > A = [1 2 3; 4 5 6]
```

```
A =

   1   2   3
   4   5   6
```

Warnings or important notes appear in a box like this.

Tips and tricks appear like this.

Reader feedback

Feedback from our readers is always welcome. Let us know what you think about this book—what you liked or may have disliked. Reader feedback is important for us to develop titles that you really get the most out of.

To send us general feedback, simply send an e-mail to feedback@packtpub.com, and mention the book title via the subject of your message.

If there is a book that you need and would like to see us publish, please send us a note in the **SUGGEST A TITLE** form on www.packtpub.com or e-mail suggest@packtpub.com.

If there is a topic that you have expertise in and you are interested in either writing or contributing to a book, see our author guide on www.packtpub.com/authors.

Customer support

Now that you are the proud owner of a Packt book, we have a number of things to help you to get the most from your purchase.

Downloading the example code

You can download the example code files for all Packt books you have purchased from your account at `http://www.PacktPub.com`. If you purchased this book elsewhere, you can visit `http://www.PacktPub.com/support` and register to have the files e-mailed directly to you.

Errata

Although we have taken every care to ensure the accuracy of our content, mistakes do happen. If you find a mistake in one of our books—maybe a mistake in the text or the code—we would be grateful if you would report this to us. By doing so, you can save other readers from frustration and help us improve subsequent versions of this book. If you find any errata, please report them by visiting `http://www.packtpub.com/support`, selecting your book, clicking on the **errata submission form** link, and entering the details of your errata. Once your errata are verified, your submission will be accepted and the errata will be uploaded on our website, or added to any list of existing errata, under the Errata section of that title. Any existing errata can be viewed by selecting your title from `http://www.packtpub.com/support`.

Piracy

Piracy of copyright material on the Internet is an ongoing problem across all media. At Packt, we take the protection of our copyright and licenses very seriously. If you come across any illegal copies of our works, in any form, on the Internet, please provide us with the location address or website name immediately so that we can pursue a remedy.

Please contact us at `copyright@packtpub.com` with a link to the suspected pirated material.

We appreciate your help in protecting our authors, and our ability to bring you valuable content.

Questions

You can contact us at `questions@packtpub.com` if you are having a problem with any aspect of the book, and we will do our best to address it.

1

Introducing GNU Octave

This chapter will introduce you to GNU Octave. We shall briefly discuss what GNU Octave is, its strengths and its weaknesses. You will also see GNU Octave in action; however, before this it must, of course, be installed on your computer, and we will quickly go through the installation procedure.

More specifically, in this chapter you will:

- Get a quick introduction to GNU Octave.
- Learn how to install GNU Octave on Windows and GNU/Linux.
- Give GNU Octave a few commands to see it in action.
- Customize GNU Octave.
- Install additional packages.
- Learn a few tricks of the trade.

GNU Octave exists for Mac/OS X, Solaris, and OS/2, but we will limit ourselves to go through the installation procedures for Windows and GNU/Linux. I strongly recommend that you install the most recent version of GNU Octave (which will be version 3.2.4 or higher). Many features described in this book are not supported in the version 2-series, especially, as the plotting facilities improved significantly in recent versions.

So what is GNU Octave?

In brief, GNU Octave is a multi-functional tool for sophisticated numerical analysis. GNU Octave provides you with:

1. A large set of build-in functionalities to solve many different problems.
2. A complete programming language that enables you to extend GNU Octave.
3. Plotting facilities.

This book will cover these features.

GNU Octave uses an interpreter to compile and execute a sequence of instructions given by the user at run-time. This is also how, for example, PHP and Python work. This is in contrast to pre-compiled programming languages such as C where the program is first compiled and then executed manually. Just like Python, you can give GNU Octave instructions in a prompt-like environment. We shall see many examples of this later. The following image shows a screenshot of GNU Octave in action—do not worry about what the plots are, for the time being.

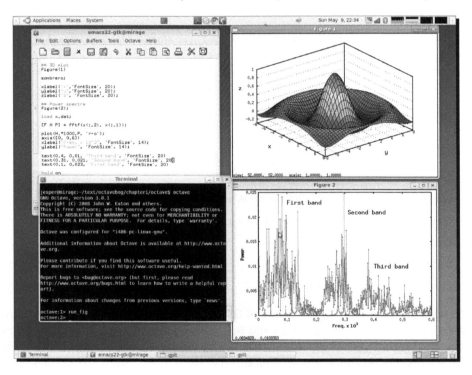

GNU Octave is named after the chemist Octave Levenspiel and has nothing to do with music and harmonic waves. The project was started by James B. Rawlings and John G. Ekerdt, but it has mainly been developed by John W. Eaton, who has put a lot of effort into the project. GNU Octave is an official GNU project (hence, the GNU prefix), and the source code is released under the GNU General Public License (GPL).

In simple terms, this means that you are allowed to use the software for any purpose, copy, and distribute it, and make any changes you want to it. You may then release this new software under GPL. If you use GNU Octave's own programming language to extend the functionality, you are free to choose another license. I recommend you to have a look at the license agreement that comes with GNU Octave at `http://www.gnu.org/software/octave/license.html`.

In the remainder of the book, GNU Octave will simply be referred to as Octave for convenience. However, if you wish to sound like an Octave guru, use the "GNU" prefix!

Applications

As mentioned previously, Octave can be used to solve many different scientific problems. For example, a Copenhagen-based commercial software and consulting company specializes in optimization problems, especially for packing containers on large cargo ships. This can be formulated in terms of linear programming which involves solving large linear equation systems and to this end, the company uses Octave. Pittsburgh supercomputing center also used Octave to study social security number vulnerability. Here Octave ran on a massive parallel computer named Pople with 768 cores and 1.5 TB memory and enabled researches to carry out sophisticated analysis of different strategies before trying out new ones.

In the research community, Octave is used for data analysis, image processing, econometrics, advanced statistical analysis, and much more. We shall see quite a few examples of this throughout the book.

Limitations of Octave

Octave is mainly designed to perform numerical computations and is not meant to be a general purpose programming language such as C or C++. As it is always the case, you should choose your programming language depending on the problem you wish to solve. Nevertheless, Octave has a lot of functionality that can help you with, for example, reading from and writing to files, and you can even use a package named **sockets** for accessing a network directly.

The fact that Octave uses an interpreter means that Octave first has to convert the instructions into machine readable code before executing it. This has its advantages as well as drawbacks. The main advantage is that the instructions are easy to implement and change, without having to go through the edit, compile, and run phase and gives the programmer or user a very high degree of control. The major drawback is that the program executes relatively slowly compared to pre-compiled programs written in languages such as C or Fortran. Octave is therefore perhaps not the first choice if you want to do extremely large scale parallelized computations, such as state-of-art weather forecasting.

However, as you will experience later in the book, Octave will enable you solve very advanced and computationally demanding problems with only a few instructions or commands and with satisfactory speed. The last chapter of this book teaches you some optimization techniques and how you can use C++ together with Octave to speed things up considerably in some situations.

Octave is not designed to do analytical (or symbolic) mathematics. For example, it is not the best choice if you wish to find the derivative of a function, say $f(x) = x^2$. Here software packages such as Maxima and Sage can be very helpful. It should be mentioned that there exists a package (a package is also referred to as a toolbox) for Octave which can do some basic analytical mathematics.

Octave and MATLAB

It is in place to mention MATLAB. Often Octave is referred to as a MATLAB-clone (MATLAB is a product from MathWorks™). In my opinion, this is wrong! Rather, Octave seeks to be compatible with MATLAB. However, be aware, in some cases you cannot simply execute your Octave programs with MATLAB and vice-versa. Throughout the book, it will be pointed out where compatibility problems can occur, but we shall stick with Octave and make no special effort to be compatible with MATLAB.

The Octave community

The newest version of Octave can be found on the web page `http://www.octave.org`. Here you will also find the official manual, a Wiki page with tricks and tips, latest news, a bit of history, and other exciting stuff. From this web page, you can join Octave's mailing lists (the help-list is especially relevant), which only require a valid email address. The user community is very active and helpful, and even the developers will answer "simple" user questions. You can also learn quite a lot from browsing through the older thread archives.

There also exists an Usenet discussion group `http://groups.google.com/group/comp.soft-sys.octave/topics?lnk`. Unfortunately, this group seems quite inactive, so it could take a while for help to arrive.

There exist a very large number of additional packages that do not come with the standard Octave distribution. Many of these can be downloaded from the Octave-Forge `http://octave.sourceforge.net`. Here you will find specially designed packages for imaging processing, econometrics, information theory, analytical mathematics, and so on. After reading this book and solving the problems at the end of each chapter, you will be able to write your own Octave package. You can then share your work with others, and the entire Octave community can benefit from your efforts. Someone might even extend and improve what you started!

Installing Octave

Octave is primarily designed to run under GNU/Linux. However, you can also run Octave under Windows with only a few glitches here and there. The installation procedure, runs very smoothly under Windows. Let us start with this.

Windows

Installing Octave on Windows is straightforward. The steps are as follows:

1. Go to the Octave-Forge web site. Here there is a hyper link to a Windows installer. Download this installer onto your desktop or any other destination you may prefer.

2. Double-click on the installer icon.

3. You will see a greeting window. Click on the **Next** button.

4. The next window shows you the license agreement, which I recommend that you read. Click the **Next** button.

5. Now, you will have the opportunity to choose where Octave will be installed. The default path is usually fine. When you are happy with the installation path, click on **Next**.

6. The following window asks you to choose between different versions of the FFTW3 and ATLAS numerical libraries that Octave uses for Fourier transforms and linear algebra computations. These different versions are specially designed for different CPU architectures. You can also choose any additional packages you want to install, as shown in the following screenshot. Let us not worry about the details of the FFTW3 and ATLAS libraries at the moment, and just choose the generic versions for now.

7. Choose to install all additional packages by ticking the Octave-Forge box. Click on **Next** and Octave will get installed.

8. After the installation, you can change the menu folder if you wish. If you want, you can also check the README file, and if not, simply uncheck the box to the left of where you are asked whether you want to see the README file. Click **Next,** and you are done!

 This installation guide has been tested on 32-bit Windows 2000, Windows XP, and Windows 7.

Notice that Octave's interactive environment (the Octave prompt) may be launched when the installer exits. To close this, simply type:

```
octave:1> exit
```

or press the *Ctrl* key and the *D* key at the same time. We shall write this combination as *Ctrl + D*. By the way, *Ctrl + D* is a UNIX end-of-file indicator and is often used as a shortcut for quitting programs in UNIX-type systems like GNU/Linux.

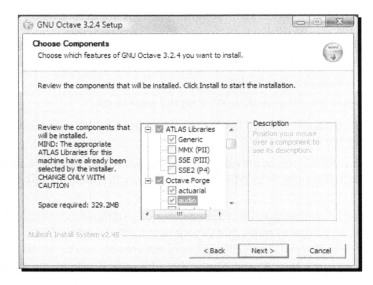

Alternatively, you can run Octave under Windows through Cygwin, which is similar to the GNU/Linux environment in Windows. I will not go through the installation of Cygwin here, but you may simply refer to the Cygwin web page `http://www.cygwin.com`.

 If you install Octave version 3.2.4 under Windows, I strongly recommend that you leave out the **oct2mat** package. This package may prevent the plotting window to update properly. For instance, when you plot a graph, it will not appear in the plotting window. This is not an issue under GNU/Linux.

GNU/Linux

On many GNU/Linux distributions, Octave is a part of the standard software. Therefore, before installing Octave, check if it already exists on your computer. To do so, open a terminal, and type the following in the terminal shell:

```
$ octave
```

If Octave is installed (properly), you should now see Octave's command prompt. Now just exit by typing the following:

```
octave:1> exit
```

Alternatively, you may use *CTRL + D*, that is, press the control key and the *D* key at the same time.

If Octave is not installed, you can often use the distribution's package management system. For example, for Ubuntu, you can use the Synaptic Package Manager, which is a graphical tool to install and remove software on the computer. Please refer the following screenshot. In case of Fedora and CentOS, you can use YUM.

 Make sure that your package manager also installs a plotting program with Octave, for example, gnuplot.

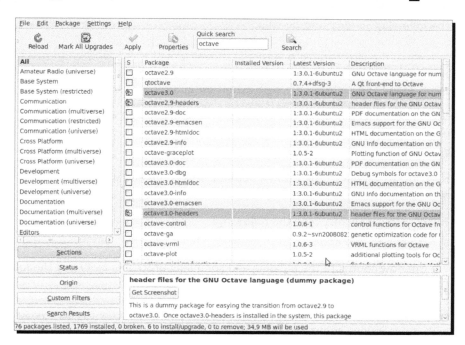

Building Octave from the source under GNU/Linux

If you wish, you can also build Octave directly from the source code. However, I only recommend this if Octave is not available through the system's package manager. In order to build Octave from source, you will need (at least) the following:

- The GNU make utility
- Fortran and C/C++ compilers (GNU Compiler Collection (known as GCC) version 4.1 or later suffice)
- gnuplot (to be on the safe side)

Fortunately, these software packages usually come with most GNU/Linux distributions. If not, you should be able use the package manager to install them.

Time for action – building Octave from source

Perform the following actions step-by-step:

1. Download the latest stable release of Octave from `http://www.gnu.org/software/octave/download.htm` and save it to any directory. The file will be a compressed and archived file with extension `.tar.gz`.

2. Open a terminal and enter the directory where the source was downloaded. To unpack the file, type the following:

   `$ tar zxf octave-version.tar.gz`

3. Here `version` will be the version number. This command will create a directory named `octave-version`.

4. To enter that directory type the following:

   `$ cd octave-version`

5. We can now configure the building and compiling processes by typing the following:

   `$ ./configure`

6. If the configuration process is successful, then we can compile the Octave source with the following command(this will take a while):

   `$ make`

7. Before doing the actual installation, you should test whether the build was done properly. To do so, type the following:

   `$ make check`

8. Some of the tests may fail. However, this does not mean that the build was unsuccessful. The test is not mandatory.

9. To install Octave on the computer, you need to have root privileges. For example, you can use the following:

```
$ sudo make install
```

10. Now type in the root password when prompted. That is it!

What just happened?

As you can see, we just performed the standard UNIX installation procedure: `configure`, `make`, `make install`. If you do not have root privileges, you cannot install Octave on the computer. However, you can still launch Octave from the `bin/` sub-directory in the installation directory.

Again, the preceding installation will only install Octave and not the plotting program. You will need to have this installed separately for Octave to work properly.

 I recommend that you have Emacs installed under GNU/Linux, because Octave uses this as the default editor. You will learn how to change the default editor later.

Checking your installation with peaks

It is time to take Octave for a spin! There are different ways to start Octave's interpreter. One way is to execute an Octave script, and another way is to enter Octave's interactive environment, which is what we will do here.

Time for action – testing with peaks

1. You can enter the interactive environment by typing `octave` in your shell under GNU/Linux, or by double-clicking the Octave icon in Windows. You should now see the Octave prompt:

```
octave:1>
```

2. You have already learned how to exit the interactive environment. Simply give Octave the command `exit` or press *Ctrl + D*, but we do not want to exit just yet!

3. At the prompt, type as follows:

```
octave:1> surf(peaks)
```

4. You should now see a three-dimensional surface plot as depicted on the left-hand side figure shown next. If not, your installation has not been successful. Now, put your mouse pointer over the figure window, hold the left mouse button down, and move the pointer. If the plotting program supports it, the figure should now rotate in the direction you move the pointer. If you click on the figure window using mouse button three (or the scroll wheel) you can zoom by moving the pointer side to side or up and down.

5. Let us try a contour plot. Type as follows:

```
octave:2> contourf(peaks)
```

6. Does it look like the following figure on the right? If not, it can be because you are using Octave version 3.2.4 and have the package **oct2mat** loaded. Try typing

```
octave:3> pkg unload oct2mat
```

7. Now retype the previous command.

8. Click somewhere on the window of the right-hand side figure with button three. A cross and two numbers appear in the window if you are using gnuplot with Octave. The cross is just the point where you clicked. The two numbers show the x axis and y axis values.

Octave can use different plotting program, for example, gnuplot or its own native plotting program. Therefore, your figures may look a bit different, depending on that program.

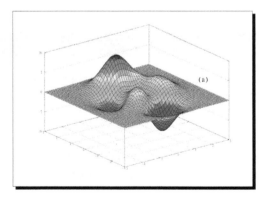

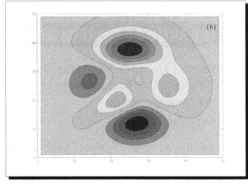

What just happened?

The figure to the left shows a graph of a mathematical function, which is a scalar function of two variables y and x given by:

$$f(x,y) = 3(1-x)^2 \exp(-x^2 - (y+1)^2) - 10\left(\frac{x}{5} - x^3 - y^5\right)\exp(-x^2 - y^2)$$
$$-\frac{1}{3}\exp(-(x+1)^2 - y^2). \tag{1.1}$$

The function value (range) is evaluated in Octave by the command `peaks`, which is the nick name for the function f. The graph is then plotted using the Octave function `surf`. As a default, Octave calculates the range of f using 50 x and y values in the interval $[-3; 3]$. As you might have guessed already, the `contourf` Octave function plots the contours of f. Later we will learn how to label the axis, add text to the figures, and much more.

Did you notice the phrase "Octave function" previously? An Octave function is not necessarily a mathematical function as Equation (1.1), but can perform many different types of operations and have many different functionalities. Do not worry about this for now. We will discuss Octave functions later in the book.

Notice that the interpreter keeps track of the number of commands that have been entered and shows this at the prompt.

Customizing Octave

When the Octave interpreter starts, it reads several configuration files. These files can be changed in order to add system paths, the appearance of the Octave command prompt, how the editor behaves, and much more. The changes can be global and affect all users of Octave that run on a particular computer. They can be targeted to work with a specific version of Octave, a specific project, or a user. This is especially useful on multi-user platforms, such as GNU/Linux.

The configuration files are named either `octaverc` or `.octaverc`, depending on where they are located and how the configurations affect Octave. They basically consist of a sequence of Octave commands, so you can also give the same commands to the interpreter from the Octave prompt. This can be a good way to test new configurations before implementing them in your `octaverc` or `.octaverc` files.

The names `octaverc` and `.octaverc` are, of course, not supported by MATLAB. However, most commands are. It is therefore just a matter of copying the content of the octave configuration files into MATLAB's `startup.m` file.

Under Windows, the user does not have a home directory equivalent to the home directory under GNU/Linux. I therefore recommend that you create a home directory for Octave. You can then command Octave to go to this directory and look for your configuration file here, whenever you start the interpreter.

If you are using GNU/Linux you can skip the following "Time for action" section.

Time for action – creating an Octave home directory under Windows

Let us assume that the Octave home directory is going to be `C:\Documents and Settings\GNU Octave\`. We can actually create this directory directly from Octave; so let us go ahead.

1. Start Octave and give it the following commands:

```
octave:1> cd C:
octave:2> cd "Documents and Settings"
octave:3> mkdir "GNU Octave"
ans = 1
```

2. The response **ans = 1** after the last command means that the directory was successfully created. If Octave returns a zero value, then some error occurred, and Octave will also print an error message. Instead of creating the directory through Octave, you can use, for example, Windows Explorer.

3. We still need to tell the interpreter that this is now the Octave home directory. Let us do this from Octave as well:

```
octave:4> edit
```

4. You should now see an editor popping up. The default editor under Windows is Notepad++. Open the file `c:\octave-home\share\octave\site\m\startup\octaverc`, where `octave-home` is the path where Octave was installed, for example, `Octave\3.2.4_gcc-4.4.0`. Add the following lines at the end of the file.

```
setenv('HOME', 'C:\Document and Settings\GNU Octave\');
cd ~/
```

Be sure that no typos sneaked in!

5. Save the file, exit the editor, and restart Octave. That is it.

Downloading the example code

You can download the example code files for all Packt books you have purchased from your account at `http://www.PacktPub.com`. If you purchased this book elsewhere, you can visit `http://www.PacktPub.com/support` and register to have the files e-mailed directly to you.

What just happened?

The first three Octave commands should be clear: we changed the directory to `C:\ Documents and Settings\` and created the directory `GNU Octave`. After this, we opened the global configuration file and added two commands. The next time Octave starts it will then execute these commands. The first instructed the interpreter to set the home directory to `C:\Document and Settings\GNU Octave\`, and the second made it enter that directory.

Creating your first .octaverc file

Having created the Octave home directory under Windows, we can customize Octave under GNU/Linux and Windows the same way.

Time for action – editing the .octaverc file

1. Start Octave if you have not already done so, and open the default editor:

   ```
   octave:1> edit
   ```

2. Copy the following lines into the file and save the file as `.octaverc` under the Octave home directory if you use Windows, or under the user home directory if you use GNU/Linux. (Without the line numbers, of course.) Alternatively, just use your favorite editor to create the file.

   ```
   PS1 (">> ");
   edit mode "async"
   ```

   Exit the editor and restart Octave. Did the appearance of the Octave prompt change? It should look like this

   ```
   >>
   ```

> Instead of restarting Octave every time you make changes to your setup files, you can type, for example, `octave:1> source(".octaverc")`. This will read the commands in the `.octaverc` file.

What just happened?

`PS1(">> ")` sets the primary prompt string in Octave to the string given. You can set it to anything you may like. To extend the preceding example given previously, `PS1("\\#>> ")` will keep the command counter before the `>>` string. You can test which prompt string is your favorite directly from the command prompt, that is, without editing `.octaverc`. Try, for example, to use `\\d` and `Hello give a command, \\u`. In this book, we will stick with the default prompt string, which is `\\s:\\#>`.

The command `edit mode "async"` will ensure that when the `edit` command is given, you can use the Octave prompt without having to close the editor first. This is not default in GNU/Linux.

Finally, note that under Windows, the behavior will be global because we instructed Octave to look for this particular `.octaverc` file every time Octave is started. Under GNU/Linux, the `.octaverc` is saved in the user's home directory and will therefore only affect that particular user.

More on .octaverc

The default editor can be set in `.octaverc`. This can be done by adding the following line into your `.octaverc` file

```
edit editor name of the editor
```

where `name of the editor` is the editor. You may prefer a notepad if you use Windows, or gedit in GNU/Linux. Again, before adding this change to your `.octaverc` file, you should test whether it works directly from the Octave prompt.

Later in the book, we will write script and function files. Octave will have to be instructed where to look for these files in order to read them. Octave uses a path hierarchy when searching for files, and it is important to learn how to instruct Octave to look for the files in certain directories. I recommend that you create a new directory in your home directory (Octave home directory in Windows) named `octave`. You can then place your Octave files in this directory and let the interpreter search for them here.

Let us first create the directory. It is easiest simply to enter Octave and type the following:

```
octave1:> cd ~/
octave2:> mkdir octave
```

It should be clear what these commands do. Now type this:

```
octave3:> edit .octaverc
```

Add the following line into the `.octaverc` file:

```
addpath("~/octave");
```

Save the file, exit the editor, and restart Octave, or use `source(".octaverc")`. At the Octave prompt, type the following:

```
octave1:> path
```

You should now see that the path `~/octave/` is added to the search path. Under Windows, this path will be added for all users. The path list can be long, so you may need to scroll down (using the arrow key) to see the whole list. When you reach the end of the list, you can hit the *Q* key to return to Octave's command prompt.

Installing additional packages

As mentioned earlier, there exists a large number of additional packages for Octave, many of which can be downloaded from the Octave-Forge web page. Octave has a superb way of installing, removing, and building these packages. Let us try to install the **msh** package, which is used to create meshes for partial differential solvers.

Time for action – installing additional packages

1. Before installing a new package, you should check which packages exist already and what their version numbers are. Start Octave, if you have not done so. Type the following:

   ```
   octave:1> pkg list
   ```

2. You should now see a table with package names, version numbers, and installation directories. For example:

   ```
   Package Name | Version | Installation directory
   --------------------+-----------+-----------------------------------
   combinatorics | 1.0.6   | /octave/packages/combinatorics-1.0.6
   ```

3. If you have chosen to install all packages in your Windows installation, the list is long. Scroll down and see if the **msh** package is installed already, and if so, what the version number is. Again, you can press the *Q* key to return to the prompt.

4. Now go to the Octave-Forge web page, find the **msh** package, and click on **Details** (to the right of the package name). You will now see a window with the package description, as shown in the following figure. Is the package version number higher than the one already installed? (If not, sit back, relax, and read the following just for the fun of it.) The package description also shows that the **msh** package dependents on the **spline** package and Octave version higher than 3.0.0. Naturally, you need Octave. However, the **spline** package may not be installed on your system. Did you see the **spline** package when you typed `pkg list` previously? If not, we will need to install this before installing **msh**. Go back to the main package list and download the **msh** and the **spline** packages to your Octave home directory. (By the way, does the **spline** package have any dependencies?) The downloaded files will be archived and compressed and have extensions `.tar.gz`. To install the packages, make sure you are in your Octave home directory and type the following:

   ```
   octave:2> pkg install splines-version-number.tar.gz
   ```

(If you need it.)

```
octave:3> pkg install msh-version-number.tar.gz
```

5. Make sure that you have downloaded the package files into the Octave home directory.

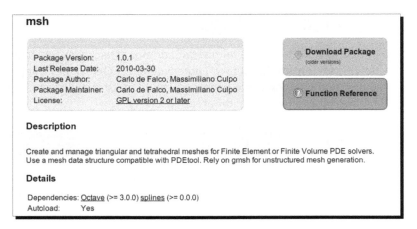

6. To check your new package list, type the following:

```
octave:4> pkg list
```

Package Name | Version | Installation directory
---------------------+------------+----------------------------
combinatorics | 1.0.6 | /octave/packages/combinatorics-1.0.6
msh | 1.0.1 | /home/jesper/octave/msh-1.0.1
splines * | 1.0.7 | /home/jesper/octave/splines-1.0.7

7. You can get a description of the msh package by typing the following:

```
octave5:> pkg describe msh
---
Package name:
        msh
Short description:
    Create and manage triangular and tetrahedral meshes for Finite
    Element or Finite Volume PDE solvers. Use a mesh data structure
    compatible with PDEtool. Rely on gmsh for unstructured mesh
    generation.
Status:
        Not loaded
```

8. From the status, you can see that the package has not been loaded, which means we cannot use the functionality that comes with the package. To load it, simply type the following:

```
octave:6> pkg load msh
```

9. You should check that it actually has been loaded using `pkg describe msh`. Naturally, you can also unload the **msh** package by using the following command:

```
octave:7> pkg unload msh
```

 If you are using a multi-user system, consult your system administrator before you install your own local packages.

What just happened?

The important points have already been explained in detail. Note that you need to install **splines** before **msh** because of the dependencies.

You may find it a bit strange that you must first load the package into Octave in order to use it. The package can load automatically if you install it with the `-auto` option. For example, command 3 can be replaced with the following:

```
octave:3> pkg install -auto msh-version-number.tar.gz
```

Some packages will automatically load even though you do not explicitly instruct it to do so when you install it. You can force packages not to load using `-noauto`.

```
octave:3> pkg install -noauto msh-version-number.tar.gz
```

Uninstalling a package

Unistalling a package is just as easy:

```
octave:8> pkg uninstall msh
```

Note that you will get an error message if you try to uninstall **splines** before **msh** because **msh** depends on **splines**.

Getting help

The `pkg` command is very flexible and can be called with a number of options. You can see all these options by typing the following:

```
octave:9> help pkg
```

The help documentation is rather long for `pkg`. You can scroll up and down in the text using the arrow keys or the *F* and *B* keys. You can quit the help anytime by pressing the *Q* key. The previous example illustrates the help text for `pkg`. Help is also available for other Octave commands. You may try, for example, `help PS1`.

The behaviour of the Octave command prompt

Often you will use the same commands in an Octave session. Sometimes, you may have forgotten a certain command's name or you only remember the first few letters of the command name. Octave can help you with this. For example, you can see your previous commands by using the up and down arrow keys (Try it out!). Octave even saves your commands from previous sessions.

For example, if you wish to change the appearance of your primary prompt string, then type the following:

```
octave:10> PS <up arrow key>
```

Now only the previous commands starting with `PS` show up. Instead of using the arrow key, try to hit the tabulator key twice:

```
octave:11> PS
```

(Now press *TAB* key twice)

```
PS1 PS2 PS4
```

This shows all commands (and functions) available having `PS` prefixed.

Summary

In this chapter, you have learned the following:

- ◆ About Octave, it's strengths, and weaknesses.
- ◆ How to install Octave on Windows and GNU/Linux.
- ◆ To test your installation with `peaks`.
- ◆ How to use and change the default editor.
- ◆ To customized Octave. For example, we saw how to change the prompt appearance and how to add search paths.
- ◆ To use the `pkg` command to install and remove additional packages.
- ◆ About the help utility.

We are now ready to move on and learn the basics about Octave's data types and operators.

2

Interacting with Octave: Variables and Operators

Octave is specifically designed to work with vectors and matrices. In this chapter, you will learn how to instantiate such objects (or variables), how to compare them, and how to perform simple arithmetic with them. Octave also supports more advanced variable types, namely, structures and cell arrays, which we will learn about. With Octave, you have an arsenal of functionalities that enable you to retrieve information about the variables. These tools are important to know later in the book, and we will go through the most important ones.

In detail, we will learn how to:

♦ Instantiate simple numerical variables i.e. scalars, vectors, and matrices.

♦ Instantiate text string variables.

♦ Instantiate complex variables.

♦ Retrieve variable elements through simple vectorized expressions.

♦ Instantiate structures, cell arrays, and multidimensional arrays.

♦ Get information about the variables.

♦ Add and subtract numerical variables.

♦ Perform matrix products.

♦ Solve systems of linear equations.

♦ Compare variables.

Let us dive in without further ado!

Simple numerical variables

In the following, we shall see how to instantiate simple variables. By simple variables, we mean scalars, vectors, and matrices. First, a scalar variable with name a is assigned the value 1 by the command:

```
octave:1> a=1

a = 1
```

That is, you write the variable name, in this case a, and then you assign a value to the variable using the equal sign. Note that in Octave, variables are not instantiated with a type specifier as it is known from C and other lower-level languages. Octave interprets a number as a real number unless you explicitly tell it otherwise[1].

You can display the value of a variable simply by typing the variable name:

```
octave:2>a

a = 1
```

Let us move on and instantiate an array of numbers:

```
octave:3 > b = [1 2 3]

b =
   1    2    3
```

Octave interprets this as the row vector:

$$\mathbf{b} = [1\ 2\ 3] \tag{2.1}$$

rather than a simple one-dimensional array. The elements (or the entries) in a row vector can also be separated by commas, so the command above could have been:

```
octave:3>  b = [1, 2, 3]

b =
   1    2    3
```

To instantiate a column vector:

---

[1]*In Octave, a real number is a double-precision, floating-point number, which means that the number is accurate within the first 15 digits. Single precision is accurate within the first 6 digits.*

$$\mathbf{c} = \begin{bmatrix} 1 \\ 2 \\ 3 \end{bmatrix} \qquad (2.2)$$

you can use:

```
octave:4 > c = [1;2;3]

c =

   1
   2
   3
```

Notice how each row is separated by a semicolon.

We now move on and instantiate a matrix with two rows and three columns (a 2 x 3 matrix):

$$\mathbf{A} = \begin{bmatrix} 1 & 2 & 3 \\ 4 & 5 & 6 \end{bmatrix} \qquad (2.3)$$

using the following command:

```
octave:5 > A = [1 2 3; 4 5 6]

A =

   1   2   3
   4   5   6
```

Notice that I use uppercase letters for matrix variables and lowercase letters for scalars and vectors, but this is, of course, a matter of preference, and Octave has no guidelines in this respect. It is important to note, however, that in Octave there is a difference between upper and lowercase letters. If we had used a lowercase a in Command 5 above, Octave would have overwritten the already existing variable instantiated in Command 1. Whenever you assign a new value to an existing variable, the old value is no longer accessible, so be very careful whenever reassigning new values to variables.

 Variable names can be composed of characters, underscores, and numbers. A variable name cannot begin with a number. For example, a_1 is accepted as a valid variable name, but 1_a is not.

In this book, we shall use the more general term array when referring to a vector or a matrix variable.

Accessing and changing array elements

To access the second element in the row vector b, we use parenthesis:

```
octave:6 > b(2)

ans = 2
```

That is, the array indices start from 1. We saw this `ans` response in *Chapter 1*, but it was not explained. This is an abbreviation for "answer" and is a variable in itself with a value, which is 2 in the above example.

For the matrix variable A, we use, for example:

```
octave:7> A(2,3)

ans = 6
```

to access the element in the second row and the third column. You can access entire rows and columns by using a colon:

```
octave:8> A(:,2)

ans =

   2

   5

octave:9 > A(1,:)

ans =

   1    2    3
```

Now that we know how to access the elements in vectors and matrices, we can change the values of these elements as well. To try to set the element A(2,3) to -10.1:

```
octave:10 >   A(2,3) = -10.1

A =
   1.0000     2.0000      3.0000
   4.0000     5.0000     -10.1000
```

Since one of the elements in A is now a non-integer number, all elements are shown in floating point format. The number of displayed digits can change depending on the default value, but for Octave's interpreter there is no difference—it always uses double precision for all calculations unless you explicitly tell it not to.

You can change the displayed format using `format short` or `format long`. The default is `format short`.

It is also possible to change the values of all the elements in an entire row by using the colon operator. For example, to substitute the second row in the matrix A with the vector b (from Command 3 above), we use:

```
octave:11 > A(2,:) = b

A =
   1    2    3
   1    2    3
```

This substitution is valid because the vector b has the same number of elements as the rows in A. Let us try to mess things up on purpose and replace the second column in A with b:

```
octave:12 > A(:,2) = b

error: A(I,J,...) = X: dimension mismatch
```

Here Octave prints an error message telling us that the dimensions do not match because we wanted to substitute three numbers into an array with just two elements. Furthermore, b is a row vector, and we cannot replace a column with a row.

 Always read the error messages that Octave prints out. Usually they are very helpful.

There is an exception to the dimension mismatch shown above. You can always replace elements, entire rows, and columns with a scalar like this:

```
octave:13> A(:,2) = 42

A =
   1   42    3
   1   42    3
```

More examples

It is possible to delete elements, entire rows, and columns, extend existing arrays, and much more.

Time for action – manipulating arrays

1. To delete the second column in A, we use:

```
octave:14> A(:,2) = []

A =
   1   3
   1   3
```

2. We can extend an existing array, for example:

```
octave:15 > b = [b 4 5]

b =
   1 2 3 4 5
```

3. Finally, try the following commands:

```
octave:16> d = [2 4 6 8 10 12 14 16 18 20]

d =
    2    4    6    8   10   12   14   16   18   20

octave:17> d(1:2:9)

ans =
    2    6   10   14   18

octave:18>   d(3:3:12) = -1

d =
    2    4   -1    8   10   -1   14   16   -1   20    0   -1
```

What just happened?

In Command 14, Octave interprets [] as an empty column vector and column 2 in A is then deleted in the command. Instead of deleting a column, we could have deleted a row, for example as an empty column vector and column 2 in A is then deleted in the command.

```
octave:14> A(2,:)=[]
```

On the right-hand side of the equal sign in Command 15, we have constructed a new vector given by [b 4 5], that is, if we write out b, we get [1 2 3 4 5] since b=[1 2 3]. Because of the equal sign, we assign the variable b to this vector and delete the existing value of b. Of course, we cannot extend b using b=[b; 4; 5] since this attempts to augment a column vector onto a row vector.

Octave first evaluates the right-hand side of the equal sign and then assigns that result to the variable on the left-hand side. The right-hand side is named an expression.

In Command 16, we instantiated a row vector d, and in Command 17, we accessed the elements with indices 1,3,5,7, and 9, that is, every second element starting from 1. Command 18 could have made you a bit concerned! d is a row vector with 10 elements, but the command instructs Octave to enter the value -1 into elements 3, 6, 9 and 12, that is, into an element that does not exist. In such cases, Octave automatically extends the vector (or array in general) and sets the value of the added elements to zero unless you instruct it to set a specific value. In Command 18, we only instructed Octave to set element 12 to -1, and the value of element 11 will therefore be given the default value 0 as seen from the output. In low-level programming languages, accessing non-existing or non-allocated array elements may result in a program crash the first time it is running[2].

As you can see, Octave is designed to work in a vectorized manner. It is therefore often referred to as a vectorized programming language.

Complex variables

Octave also supports calculations with complex numbers. As you may recall, a complex number can be written as $z = a + bi$, where a is the real part, b is the imaginary part, and i is the imaginary unit defined from $i^2 = -1$.

To instantiate a complex variable, say $z = 1 + 2i$, you can type:

```
octave:19> z = 1 + 2I
```

```
z = 1 + 2i
```

When Octave starts, the variables i, j, I, and J are all imaginary units, so you can use either one of them. I prefer using I for the imaginary unit, since i and j are often used as indices and J is not usually used to symbolize i.

[2] *This will be the best case scenario. In a worse scenario, the program will work for years, but then crash all of a sudden, which is rather unfortunate if it controls a nuclear power plant or a space shuttle.*

To retrieve the real and imaginary parts of a complex number, you use:

```
octave:20> real(z)

ans = 1

octave:21>imag(z)

ans = 2
```

You can also instantiate complex vectors and matrices, for example:

```
octave:22> Z = [1 -2.3I; 4I 5+6.7I]

Z =
  1.0000 + 0.0000i     0.0000 - 2.3000i
  0.0000 + 4.0000i     5.0000 + 6.7000i
```

Be careful! If an array element has non-zero real and imaginary parts, do leave any blanks (space characters) between the two parts. For example, had we used $Z=[1 -2.3I;$ $4I 5 + 6.7I]$ in Command 22, the last element would be interpreted as two separate elements (5 and 6.7i). This would lead to dimension mismatch.

The elements in complex arrays can be accessed in the same way as we have done for arrays composed of real numbers. You can use `real(Z)` and `imag(Z)` to print the real and imaginary parts of the complex array Z. (Try it out!)

Text variables

Even though Octave is primarily a computational tool, you can also work with text variables. In later chapters, you will see why this is very convenient. A letter (or character), a word, a sentence, a paragraph, and so on, are all named text strings.

To instantiate a text string variable you can use:

```
octave:23 > t = "Hello"

t = Hello
```

Instead of the double quotation marks, you can use single quotation marks. I prefer double quotation marks for strings, because this follows the syntax used by most other programming languages, and differs from the transpose operator we shall learn about later in this chapter.

You can think of a text string variable as an array of characters, just like a vector is an array of numbers. To access the characters in the string, we simply write:

```
octave:24> t(2)

ans = e

octave:25> t(2:4)

ans = ell
```

just as we did for numerical arrays. We can also extend existing strings (notice the blank space after the first quotation mark):

```
octave:26> t = [t " World"]

t = Hello World
```

You can instantiate a variable with string elements as follows:

```
octave:27> T= ["Hello" ;   "George"]

T =

 Hello
 George
```

The string variable T behaves just like a matrix (a two dimensional array) with character elements. You can now access these characters just like elements in a numerical matrix:

```
octave:28> T(2,1)

ans = G
```

But wait! The number of characters in the string "Hello" is 5, while the string "George" has 6 characters. Should Octave not complain about the different number of characters? The answer is no. In a situation where the two string lengths do not match, Octave simply adds space characters to the end of the strings. In the example above, the string "Hello" is changed to "Hello ". It is important to stress that this procedure only works for strings. The command:

```
octave:29 > A = [1 2; 3 4 5]

error: number of columns must match (3 != 2)
```

leads to an error with a clear message stating the problem.

Higher-dimensional arrays

Octave also supports higher-dimensional arrays. These can be instantiated like any other array, for example:

```
octave:30> B(2,2,2)=1

B =
ans(:,:,1) =
   0   0
   0   0

ans(:,:,2) =
   0   0
   0   1
```

The previous command instantiates a three-dimensional array B with size 2 x 2 x 2, that is, $2^3 = 8$ elements, by assigning the element B(2,2,2) the value 1. Recall that Octave assigns all non-specified elements the value 0. Octave displays the three dimensional array as two two-dimensional arrays (or slices). We can now access the individual elements and assigned values like we would expect:

```
octave:31 B(1,2,1) = 42

B =
ans(:,:,1) =
   0   42
   0    0

ans(:,:,2) =
   0   0
   0   1
```

Pop Quiz – working with arrays

1. Which of the following variable instantiations are not valid

a) a=[1, 2, 3]

b) a=[1 2 3]

c) a=[1 2+I 3]

d) A=[1 2 3; 3 4 5]

e) A=[1 2; 3; 4]

f) A=[1 2; 3 4 5]

g) A=ones(10,10) + 5.8

h) A=zeros(10,1) + 1

i) A=eye(2) + [1 2 3;4 5 6]

2. A matrix **A** is given by

$$\mathbf{A} = \begin{bmatrix} 1 & 2 & 3 & 4 & 5 \\ 6 & 7 & 8 & 9 & 10 \\ 11 & 12 & 13 & 14 & 15 \\ 16 & 17 & 18 & 19 & 20 \\ 21 & 22 & 23 & 24 & 25 \end{bmatrix} \tag{P.1}$$

What are the outputs from the following commands?

a) `A(3,1)`　　　b) `A(1,3)`　　　c) `A(:,4)`

d) `A(1,:)`　　　e) `A(1,1:3)`　　　f) `A(1:4,5)`

g) `A(1:3,1:3)`　　h) `A(1:2:5,1:2:5)`　　i) `A(1:3,:)=[]`

Structures and cell arrays

In many real life applications, we have to work with objects that are described by many different types of variables. For example, if we wish to describe the motion of a projectile, it would be useful to know its mass (a scalar), current velocity (a vector), type (a string), and so forth. In Octave, you can instantiate a single variable that contains all this information. These types of variables are named structures and cell arrays.

Structures

A structure in Octave is like a structure in C—it has a name, for example projectile, and contains a set of fields[3] that each has a name, as shown in the following figure:

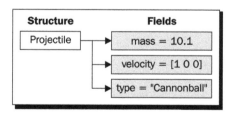

We can refer to the individual structure field using the `.` character:

structurename.fieldname

where `structurename` is the name of the structure variable, and `fieldname` is (as you may have guessed) the field's name.

---

[3] *or members in C terminology*

To show an example of a structure, we can use the projectile described above. Let us therefore name the structure variable `projectile`, and set the field names to `mass`, `velocity`, and `type`. You can, of course, choose other names if you wish—whatever you find best.

Time for action – instantiating a structure

1. To set the projectile mass, we can use:

```
octave:32>projectile.mass = 10.1

projectile =
{
mass = 10.100
}
```

2. The velocity field is set in a similar fashion:

```
octave:33>projectile.velocity = [1 0 0]

projectile =
{
mass = 10.100
velocity =
   0   0
}
```

3. We can also set the text field as usual:

```
octave:34>projectile.type = "Cannonball"

projectile =
{
mass = 10.100
velocity =
      1    0    0
type = Cannonball
}
```

and so on for position and whatever else could be relevant.

What just happened?

Command 32 instantiates a structure variable with the name `projectile` by assigning a field named `mass` the value 10.100. At this point, the structure variable only contains this one field.

In Commands 33 and 34, we then add two new fields to the structure variable. These fields are named `velocity` and `type`. It is, of course, possible to keep adding new fields to the structure.

Instead of typing in one structure field at a time, you can use the `struct` function. (In the next chapter, we will learn what an Octave function actually is):

```
octave:35> projectile = struct("mass", 10.1, "velocity", [1 0 0],
"type", "Cannonball");
```

The input (called arguments) to the `struct` function is the first structure field name followed by its value, the second field's name and its value, and so on. Actually, it is not meaningful to talk about a structure's first and second field, and so you can change the order of the arguments to `struct` and it would not matter.

Did you notice that appending a semi-colon after the command suppresses the response (or output) from Octave?

 You can suppress the output that Octave prints after each command by appending a semi-colon to the command.

Accessing structure fields

You can access and change the different fields in a structure by, for example:

```
octave:36>projectile.velocity(2) = -0.1

projectile =
{
mass = 10.100
velocity =
    1    -0.1     0
type = Cannonball
}
```

In case you have many cannonballs flying around[4], it will be practical to have an array of projectile structures. To instantiate an array of two such projectile structures, you can simply copy the entire projectile structure to each array element by:

```
octave:37> s(1) = projectile;
```

```
octave:38> s(2) = projectile;
```

Notice that to copy a structure you just use the equal sign, so you need not copy each structure field. For accessing the structure elements, you use:

```
octave:39 s(2).type
```

```
ans = Cannonball
```

Octave has two functions—one to set the structure fields, and one to retrieve them. These are named `setfield` and `getfield`:

```
octave:40> s(2) = setfield(s(2), "type", "Cartridge");
```

```
octave:41>getfield(s(2), "type")
```

```
ans = Cartridge
```

You need to assign the output from `setfield` to the structure. Why that is so will be explained in *Chapter 5*. The above example only showed how to instantiate a one dimensional array of structures, but you can also work withmultidimensional arrays if you wish.

You can instantiate nested structures, which are structures where one or more fields are structures themselves. Let us illustrate this via the basic projectile structure:

```
octave:42 > projectiles = struct("type1", s(1), "type2", s(2));
```

```
octave:43 > projectiles.type1.type
```

```
ans = Cartridge
```

Here `projectiles` has two fields named `type1` and `type2`. Each of these fields is a structure, given by `s(1)` and `s(2)` (Commands 37-41).

As you can probably imagine, the complexity and variety of extended structures can become quite overwhelming and we will stop here.

---

[4]*A rather undesirable situation, of course.*

Cell arrays

In Octave, you can work with cell arrays. A cell array is a data container-like structure, in that it can contain both numerical and string variables, but unlike structures it does not have fields. Each cell (or element) in the cell array can be a scalar, vector, text string, and so forth. I like to think about a cell array as a sort of spreadsheetas shown in the figure below:

Cell array		
cell {1,1} 10.1	cell {1,2} 1 0 0	cell {1,3} "Cannonball"
cell {2,1} 1.0	cell {2,2} [0 0 0]	cell {2,3} "Cartridge"

Time for action – instantiating a cell array

1. To instantiate a cell array with the same data as the `projectile` structure above, we can use:

```
octave:44> projectile = {10.1, [1 0 0], "Cannonball"}

projectile =
{
    [1,1] = 10.1
    [1,2] =

1   0   0
    [1,3] = Cannonball
}
```

   The numbers in the square brackets are then the row indices and column indices, respectively.

2. To access a cell, you must use curly brackets:

```
octave:45> projectile{2}

ans =
    1   0   0
```

3. You can have two-dimensional cell arrays as well. For example:

```
octave:46>  projectiles = {10.1, [1 0 0], "Cannonball"; 1.0, [0 0 0], "Cartridge"}

projectile =
```

```
{
    [1, 1]  =   10.100
    [2, 1]  =   1
    [1, 2]  =

            1   0   0

    [2, 2]  =

            0   0   0

    [1, 3]  =   Cannonball
    [2, 3]  =   Cartridge
}
```

4. To access the values stored in the cell array, simply use:

```
octave:47> projectiles{2,3}

ans = Cartridge
```

What just happened?

Command 44 instantiates a cell array with one row and three columns. The first cell contains the mass, the second cell the velocity, and the third cell the string "Cannonball", analogous to the structure we discussed above. Notice that the cells in the array can contain different variable types, and the cell array is therefore different from a normal array.

To access the value in a cell, you use curly brackets rather than the usual parenthesis, as shown in Command 45.

You can also work with two-dimensional cell arrays. Commands 46 and 47 show an example of this. Note that to insert an additional row into the cell array, you use semi-colons—just like a numerical array.

Have a go hero – working with structures

Instantiate a structure with the variable name train that contains the following field names and values:

Field	Value
type	"Freight"
weight	60.0
wagon_index_array	1 to 10

Use the `setfield` function to change the weight to 90.0. Set the second element in the `wagon_index_array` field to 23.

Getting information

In this section, we will learn how to obtain information about the variables that have been instantiated. This is particularly useful when you have forgotten the names, sizes, or when you have loaded data from files (more on the latter in Chapter 4).

Time for action – using whos

We are working with quite a few variables now. We can list them all with `whos`:

```
octave:48>whos
```

Variables in the current scope:

Attr	Name	Size	Bytes	Class
====	====	====	=====	=====
	A	2x2	32	double
	B	2x2x2	128	double
	T	2x6	12	char
	Z	2x2	64	double
	a	1x1	8	double
	ans	1x9	9	char
	b	1x5	40	double
	c	3x1	24	double
	d	1x12	96	double
	projectile	1x3	42	cell
	projectiles	2x3	83	cell
	s	1x2	83	struct
	t	1x11	11	char
	z	1x1	16	double

Total is 81 elements using 648 bytes

What just happened?

As seen above, whos prints out five columns. The first column can have values g or p, which means that the variable is global or persistent. We shall return to what these qualifiers mean in *Chapter 5*. In our case, all the variables are what are named local, which is not stated explicitly by the command whos. A local variable is characterized by being visible and therefore accessible to a given workspace (or scope). In the example above, we have just a single workspace—the top-level workspace—wherein all our variables can be accessed. In fact, we can say that the local variables above define our current top-level workspace.

The second column simply lists the variable names. The sizes of the variables are given in column three in the form: number of rows times number of columns. For example, the scalar variable a (from Command 1) has size 1 x 1, meaning that it has one row and one column. The projectile cell array has one row and three columns, as we know from Command 44.

It is seen from column four that the scalar variable a takes up 8 bytes of memory and is of class double (column five). The fact that the class is a double means that Octave uses double precision for the variables, as mentioned earlier. Recall from Command 26 that the variable t is the text string "Hello World". This string is composed of 11 characters including the blank space, which can be seen from the output above.This is unlike C, where the end of the string is indicated with '\0' and is a part of the character array.

The variable s is a two dimensional array of structures (Commands 37-41) and the variable projectiles is a cell array with same basic "building blocks" as the structure array s. From the table, we observe that it takes up the same memory, so we do not save memory space using one or the other. By the way, does the number of bytes in the structure array s agree with the sum of bytes of the fields?

Below the table, we can see that we use a total of 648 bytes of memory for the variables.

You can call whos with an argument, for example, whos("A"), if you only wish to retrieve information about A. Also, whos has a little brother who. who lists the local variables, but does not list other information.

Size, rows, columns, and length

Rather than listing all available information about a variable, you can get information about its number of rows and columns. We will use this extensively throughout the book. The size of A is retrieved by:

```
octave:49> size(A)

ans =

   2   2
```

since A is a 2 x 2 matrix. In general, `size` returns the number of rows and columns. You can retrieve these individually if you prefer:

```
octave:50> rows(A)

ans = 2

octave:51> columns(A)

ans = 2
```

What happened here should be straightforward to understand.

In Octave, you can also retrieve the length of a variable. We need to understand what that means exactly. If the variable is a vector or text string, the length is the number of elements in the array. If the variable is a higher-dimension array, the length is defined as the maximum number of elements in any of the dimensions. Let us see two examples:

```
octave:52> length(c)

ans = 3

octave:53> length(T)

ans = 6
```

The output from Command 53 is the number of columns in the text array. This is returned rather than the number of rows since the variable T has 6 columns but only 2 rows.

Identifying the variable type

Octave can tell you whether a variable is interpreted as a vector, matrix, string, complex number, cell array, and much more. Let us check if Octave actually agrees that the variable a is a scalar:

```
octave:54>isscalar(a)

ans = 1
```

Octave returns 1, meaning true (or yes). What about the row vector b?

```
octave:55>isvector(b)

ans = 1

octave:56>ismatrix(b)

ans = 1
```

That is a bit strange! b is a (row) vector which is recognized by Octave as seen from Command 55, but why does it interpret b as a matrix as well? A matrix is just an array of elements (a way of organizing numbers).Thus b can be thought of as a matrix with one row and three columns. What will the command `ismatrix(a)` return? Try it out!

You can check the type of any variable with the istype family. Simply use:

octave:1>is <Tab><Tab>

at the command prompt to see the complete list.

Instead of using the istype, you can use `typeinfo`. For example, instead of Command 56 we could use:

```
octave:56>typeinfo(b)

ans = matrix
```

Deleting variables from the workspace

You can delete variables using the `clear` command. For example, if you wish to delete the variable A:

```
octave:58> clear A
```

You can also use the wildcard *, for example, to delete the variables `projectile` and `projectiles`, and any other variable name beginning with p, you can use:

```
octave:59> clear p*
```

If you do not specify any variables, the `clear`, command will delete all the variables, so be very cautious when using the command, because there is no way to retrieve the variables once you have cleared them from the memory (unless you have saved them somewhere else, of course). Try to use `whos` (or `who`) to see if the variables were cleared by Commands 58 and 59.

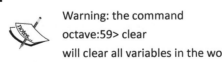

Warning: the command

octave:59> clear

will clear all variables in the workspace.

Pop Quiz – understanding arrays

What are the outputs from the following commands when **A**, **x**, and **y** are given in Equation (P.2)?

$$A = \begin{bmatrix} 1 & 2 & 3 \\ 4 & 5 & 6 \\ 7 & 8 & -9 \end{bmatrix}, \quad x = \begin{bmatrix} -1 \\ -2 \\ -3 \end{bmatrix} \text{ and } y = \begin{bmatrix} 1 & 2 & 4 \end{bmatrix}.$$ (P.2)

a) `size(A)`   b) `row(A)`   c) `columns(A)`

d) `ismatrix(x)`   e) `isscalar(A)`   f) `length(A)`

g) `length(x)`

A few things that make life easier

Imagine that you wish to generate a sequence of numbers in the interval -2.1 to 0.5 (including -2.1 and 0.5) with an incremental spacing of 0.2. This is rather tedious to do by hand and is very error prone, because it involves typing a lot of digits. Fortunately, Octave provides you with a very convenient way to do this (note that we now assign the variable b a new value):

```
octave:60> b = [-2.1:0.2:0.5]

b =

 Columns 1 through 7

   -2.1000   -1.9000   -1.7000   -1.5000   -1.3000   -1.1000   -0.9000

 Columns 8 through 14

   -0.7000   -0.5000   -0.3000   -0.1000    0.1000    0.3000    0.5000
```

If we had done this by hand instead, we should have typed in:

```
octave:61> size(b)

ans =

    1     14
```

14 numbers. You can also use negative increments if the interval starting value is larger than the end value. If you do not provide an incremental value, Octave assumes 1.

An important point is that if we have chosen an increment of, say 0.4, in Command 60, Octave will give us a number sequence starting from -2.1, but ending at 0.4.

Often you will find yourself in situations where you need to generate a certain sequence of numbers in a given interval without knowing the increment. You can of course calculate this, but Octave has a functionality to do just that. Let us generate a sequence of 7 numbers in the interval above (that is, from -2.1 to 0.5):

```
octave:62 > b = linspace(-2.1, 0.5, 7)
```

```
b =

  -2.1000    -1.6667    -1.2333    -0.8000    -0.3667     0.0667     0.5000
```

Octave calculates the increment needed, also ensuring that both points in the interval are included.

As we shall see later, the functions `ones` and `zeros` are very helpful in cases where you want to generate an array composed of elements with a certain value. For example, to create a 2 x 3 matrix with elements all equal to 1, use:

```
octave63:> ones(2,3)
```

```
ans =

   1   1   1
   1   1   1
```

Likewise, to create an array (row vector in this case) with zero elements:

```
octave64:> zeros(1, 4)
```

```
ans = 0   0   0   0
```

`ones` and `zeros` also work with multi-dimensional arrays.

You can just as easily create a diagonal matrix with `eye`:

```
octave65:> eye(4)
```

```
ans =

Diagonal Matrix

   1   0   0   0
   0   1   0   0
   0   0   1   0
   0   0   0   1
```

Notice that we need not specify both the number of rows and the number of columns in Command 65, because a diagonal matrix is only defined for square matrices.

Basic arithmetic

Octave offers easy ways to perform different arithmetic operations. This ranges from simple addition and multiplication to very complicated linear algebra. In this section, we will go through the most basic arithmetic operations, such as addition, subtraction, multiplication, and left and right division. In general, we should think of these operations in the framework of linear algebra and not in terms of arithmetic of simple scalars.

Addition and subtraction

We begin with addition.

Time for action – doing addition and subtraction operations

1. I have lost track of the variables! Let us start afresh and clear all variables first:

    ```
    octave:66> clear
    ```

    (Check with whos to see if we cleared everything).

2. Now, we define four variables in a single command line(!)

    ```
    octave:67> a = 2; b=[1 2 3]; c=[1; 2; 3]; A=[1 2 3; 4 5 6];
    ```

    Note that there is an important difference between the variables b and c; namely, b is a row vector, whereas c is a column vector.

3. Let us jump into it and try to add the different variables. This is done using the + character:

    ```
    octave:68>a+a

    ans = 4

    octave:69>a+b

    ans =

       3   4   5

    octave:70>b+b

    ans =

       2   4   6

    octave:71>b+c

    error: operator +: nonconformant arguments (op1 is 1x3, op2 is
    3x1)
    ```

It is often convenient to enter multiple commands on the same line. Try to test the difference in separating the commands with commas and semicolons.

What just happened?

The output from Command 68 should be clear; we add the scalar a with itself. In Command 69, we see that the + operator simply adds the scalar a to each element in the b row vector. This is named element-wise addition. It also works if we add a scalar to a matrix or a higher dimensional array.

Now, if + is applied between two vectors, it will add the elements together element-wise if and only if the two vectors have the same size, that is, they have same number of rows or columns. This is also what we would expect from basic linear algebra.

From Command 70 and 71, we see that b+b is valid, but b+c is not, because b is a row vector and c is a column vector—they do not have the same size. In the last case, Octave produces an error message stating the problem. This would also be a problem if we tried to add, say b with A:

`octave:72>b+A`

`error: operator +: nonconformant arguments (op1 is 1x3, op2 is 2x3)`

From the above examples, we see that adding a scalar to a vector or a matrix is a special case. It is allowed even though the dimensions do not match! When adding and subtracting vectors and matrices, the sizes must be the same. Not surprisingly, subtraction is done using the - operator. The same rules apply here, for example:

`octave:73> b-b`

`ans =`

`   0   0   0`

`is fine, but:`

`octave:74> b-c`

`error: operator -: nonconformant arguments (op1 is 1x3, op2 is 2x3)`

`produces an error.`

Matrix multiplication

The * operator is used for matrix multiplication. Recall from linear algebra that we cannot multiply any two matrices. Furthermore, matrix multiplication is not commutative. For example, consider the two matrices:

$$\mathbf{A} = \begin{bmatrix} 1 & 2 \\ 3 & 4 \end{bmatrix} \text{ and } \mathbf{B} = \begin{bmatrix} 1 & 2 & 3 \\ 4 & 5 & 6 \end{bmatrix}. \tag{2.4}$$

The matrix product $\mathbf{AB}$ is defined, but $\mathbf{BA}$ is not. If $\mathbf{A}$ is size $n \times k$ and $\mathbf{B}$ has size $k \times m$, the matrix product $\mathbf{AB}$ will be a matrix with size $n \times m$. From this, we know that the number of columns of the "left" matrix must match the number of rows of the "right" matrix. We may think of this as $(n \times k)(k \times m) = n \times m$. In the example above, the matrix product $\mathbf{AB}$ therefore results in a 2 x 3 matrix:

$$\mathbf{AB} = \begin{bmatrix} 9 & 12 & 15 \\ 19 & 26 & 33 \end{bmatrix}. \tag{2.5}$$

Time for action – doing multiplication operations

Let us try to perform some of the same operations for multiplication as we did for addition:

```
octave:75> a*a

ans = 4

octave:76> a*b

ans =
    2    4    6

octave:77> b*b

error:  operator *:  nonconformant arguments (op1 is 1x3, op2 is 1x3)

octave:78> b*c

ans = 14
```

What just happened?

From Command 75, we see that * multiplies two scalar variables just like standard multiplication. In agreement with linear algebra, we can also multiply a scalar by each element in a vector as shown by the output from Command 76. Command 77 produces an error—recall that b is a row vector which Octave also interprets as a 1 x 3 matrix, so we try to perform the matrix multiplication (1 x 3)(1 x 3), which is not valid. In Command 78, on the other hand, we have (1 x 3)(3 x 1) since c is a column vector yielding a matrix with size 1 x 1, that is, a scalar. This is, of course, just the dot product between b and c.

Let us try an additional example and perform the matrix multiplication between **A** and **B** discussed above. First, we need to instantiate the two matrices, and then we multiply them:

```
octave:79> A=[1 2; 3 4]; B=[1 2 3; 4 5 6];

octave:80> A*B

ans =

     9    12    15
    19    26    33

octave:81> B*A

error: operator *: nonconformant arguments (op1 is 2x3, op2 is 2x2)
```

Seems like Octave knows linear algebra!

Element-by-element, power, and transpose operations

If the sizes of two arrays are the same, Octave provides a convenient way to multiply the elements element-wise. For example, for **B**:

```
octave:82> B.*B

ans =

     1     4     9
    16    25    36
```

Notice that the period (full stop) character precedes the multiplication operator. The period character can also be used in connection with other operators. For example:

```
octave:83> B.+B

ans =

     2     4     6
     8    10    12
```

which is the same as the command B+B.

If we wish to raise each element in B to the power 2.1, we use the element-wise power operator `.^`:

```
octave:84> B.^2.1

ans =

   1.0000      4.2871     10.0451
  18.3792     29.3655     43.0643
```

You can perform element-wise power operation on two matrices as well (if they are of the same size, of course):

```
octave:85> B.^B

ans =

        1         4        27
      256      3125     46656
```

 If the power is a real number, you can use `^` instead of `.^`; that is, instead of Command 84 above, you can use:

octave:84>B^2.1

Transposing a vector or matrix is done via the `'` operator. To transpose B, we simply type:

```
octave:86> B'

ans =

   1    4
   2    5
   3    6
```

Strictly, the `'` operator is a complex conjugate transpose operator. We can see this in the following examples:

```
octave:87> B = [1 2; 3 4] + I.*eye(2)

B =

   1 + 1i    2 + 0i
   3 + 0i    4 + 1i

octave:88> B'

ans =
```

```
1 - 1i      3 - 0i
2 - 0i      4 - 1i
```

Note that in Command 87, we have used the `.*` operator to multiply the imaginary unit with all the elements in the diagonal matrix produced by `eye(2)`. Finally, note that the command `transpose(B)` or the operator `.'` will transpose the matrix, but not complex conjugate the elements.

Operators for structures and cell arrays

Arithmetic on structure fields and cells array elements is straightforward. First, let us see an example of a structure field operation:

```
octave:89> s = struct("A", [1 2; 3 4], "x", [1; 2]);
```

```
octave:90>s.A*s.x
```

```
ans =
    5
   11
```

and the equivalent cell array operation:

```
octave:91> c = {[1 2; 3 4], [1;2]};
```

```
octave:92> c{1}*c{2}
```

```
ans =
    5
   11
```

Arithmetic operations on entire structures and cell arrays are not defined in Octave.

Solving linear equation systems: left and right division

You may have wondered why division was not included above. We know what it means to divide two scalars, but it makes no sense to talk about division in the context of linear algebra. Nevertheless, Octave defines two different operators, namely, right and left division, which need to be explained in some detail. It is probably easiest to discuss this via a specific example. Consider a system of linear equations:

$$\begin{aligned} 2x_1 + x_2 - 3x_3 &= 1 \\ 4x_1 + 2x_2 - 2x_3 &= 1 \\ -x_1 + x_2/2 - x_3/2 &= 1.5 \end{aligned} \tag{2.6}$$

We can write this in matrix notation as:

$$\mathbf{A}\mathbf{x} = \mathbf{y}, \tag{2.7}$$

where:

$$\mathbf{A} = \begin{bmatrix} 2 & 1 & -3 \\ 4 & 2 & -2 \\ -1 & 1/2 & -1/2 \end{bmatrix}, \ \mathbf{x} = \begin{bmatrix} x_1 \\ x_2 \\ x_3 \end{bmatrix} \text{ and } \mathbf{y} = \begin{bmatrix} 1 \\ 3 \\ 3/2 \end{bmatrix}. \tag{2.8}$$

If the coefficient matrix $\mathbf{A}$ is invertible (in fact it is), we can solve this linear equation system by multiplying both sides of Equation (2.7) with the inverse of $\mathbf{A}$, denoted $\mathbf{A}^{-1}$:

$$\mathbf{x} = \mathbf{A}^{-1}\mathbf{y}. \tag{2.9}$$

In Octave, the command $\text{A}\backslash\text{y}$ is equivalent to $\mathbf{A}^{-1}\mathbf{y}$. Notice the backslash. This is named left division, and you can probably guess why.

The right division (forward slash) command, A/y, is equivalent to $\mathbf{y}\mathbf{A}^{-1}$, which is of course not defined in this case because the vector $\mathbf{y}$ has size 3 x 1 and $\mathbf{A}$ has size 3 x 3; that is, the matrix product cannot be carried out.

Time for action – doing left and right division

1. We need to instantiate the coefficient matrix $\mathbf{A}$ and vector $\mathbf{y}$ first:

    ```
    octave:93> A=[2 1 -3; 4 -2 -2; -1 0.5 -0.5]; y = [1; 3; 1.5];
    ```

2. The solution to the linear equation system, Equation (2.6), is then found directly via the command:

    ```
    octave:94> A\y

    ans =
        -1.6250
        -2.5000
        -2.2500
    ```

    Easy!

What just happened?

It should be clear what happened. In Command 93, we instantiated the matrix A and the vector y that define the linear equation system in Equation (2.6). We then solve this system using the left division operator. Later in *Chapter 6*, we will investigate how the left division operator performs for very large systems.

Let us try the right division operator, even though we know that it will cause problems:

```
octave:95> A/y
```

```
error: operator /: nonconformant arguments (op1 is 3x3, op2 is 3x1)
```

We see the expected error message. The right division operator will, however, work in the following command:

```
octave:96> A/A
```

```
ans =

     1.0000    -0.0000    -0.0000
     0.0000     1.0000    -0.0000
     0.0000     0.0000     1.0000
```

This is the 3 x 3 identity matrix $\mathbf{I}$. This result is easily understood because A/A is equivalent to $\mathbf{AA}^{-1}$. Notice that due to numerical round-off errors and finite precision, the elements in this matrix are not exactly 1 on the diagonal and not exactly 0 for the off-diagonal elements, and Octave therefore displays the elements in floating point format.

What is the result for the command A\A? Try it out to check your answer.

The definitions of the left and right division operators also apply for scalar variables. Recall that the variable a has the value 2:

```
octave:97> 1/a
```

```
ans = 0.5000
```

This is just the fraction 1/2 with a in the denominator. Now, the left division operator:

```
octave:98> 1\a
```

```
ans = 2
```

which is equivalent to the fraction 2/1; that is, a is in the nominator. We can say that a\1 is equivalent to 1/a.

Above we learned that the . operator can be used in connection with other operators. This is also true for the left and right division operators:

```
octave:99> a./A
```

```
ans =

    1.0000     2.0000    -0.6667
    0.5000    -1.0000    -1.0000
   -2.0000     4.0000    -4.0000
```

```
octave:100> a.\A
```

```
ans =

    1.0000     0.5000    -1.5000
    2.0000    -1.0000    -1.0000
   -0.5000     0.2500    -0.2500
```

It is very important to stress that when performing element-wise left and right division with a scalar, you must use the . operator. This is different from addition, subtraction, and multiplication.

For element-wise matrix division, we can use:

```
octave:101> A./A
```

```
ans =

   1   1   1
   1   1   1
   1   1   1
```

Basic arithmetic for complex variables

It is also possible to perform arithmetic operations on complex variables. In fact, we can regard the operations above for real numbers as special cases of more general operations for complex variables.

When adding two complex numbers, we add the real parts and imaginary parts. In Octave, we simply use the + operator:

```
octave:102> z = 1 + 2I; w = 2 -3I;
```

```
octave:103> z + w
```

```
ans = 3 - 1i
```

The same goes for subtraction:

```
octave:104> z - w
```

```
ans = -1 + 5i
```

Multiplication of z and w is simply:

$$zw = (1 + 2i)(2 - 3i) = 2 - 3i + 4i + 6 = 8 + i \qquad (2.10)$$

Let us see if Octave agrees:

```
octave105:> z*w
```

```
ans = 8 + 1i
```

Now, you may recall that when dividing two complex numbers, you multiply the nominator and denominator with the complex conjugate of the denominator. In the case of z/w, we get:

$$\frac{z}{w} = \frac{1 + 2i}{2 - 3i} = \frac{(1 + 2i)(2 + 3i)}{(2 - 3i)(2 + 3i)} = \frac{-4 + 7i}{13} = -\frac{4}{13} + \frac{7}{13}i \qquad (2.11)$$

To perform this division in Octave, we can simply use the left or right division operator:

```
octave:106> z/w
```

```
ans =   -0.30769 + 0.53846i
```

```
octave:107> w\z
```

```
ans = -0.30769 + 0.53846i
```

just as we did for real numbers.

You can also perform addition, subtraction, and multiplication with complex vectors and matrices. You can even solve complex linear equation systems with the left division operator like it was done above for a real equation system.

Summary of arithmetic operators

Let us summarize the operators we have discussed above:

Operator	Example	Description
+	octave:1 > [1 2; 3 4] + [1 0; 0 1] ans = 2 2 3 5	Element-wise addition. Array sizes (dimensions) must match, except for scalar variables. Works for multidimensional arrays.
-	octave:1> [1 2; 3 4] - [1 0; 0 1] ans = 0 2 3 3	Element-wise subtraction. Array sizes (dimensions) must match, except for scalar variables. Works for multidimensional arrays.
*	octave:1> [1 2; 3 4]*[1 0; 0 1] ans = 0 2 34	Matrix multiplication. Number of columns of the left-most matrix must match the number of rows of the right-most matrix, except for scalar variables. Only works for scalars, vectors, and matrices.
/	octave:1> [1 2; 3 4]/[1 0; 0 1] ans = 1 2 3 4	Right division. For the example, it is equivalent to: Only works for scalars, vectors, and matrices. $$\begin{bmatrix} 1 & 0 \\ 0 & 1 \end{bmatrix}\begin{bmatrix} 1 & 2 \\ 3 & 4 \end{bmatrix}^{-1}$$
\	octave:1> [1 2; 3 4]\[1 0; 0 1] ans = -2.0000 1.0000 1.5000 0.5000	Left division. Same as: Only works for scalars, vectors, and matrices. $$\begin{bmatrix} 1 & 2 \\ 3 & 4 \end{bmatrix}^{-1}\begin{bmatrix} 1 & 0 \\ 0 & 1 \end{bmatrix}$$
.	octave:1>[1 2; 3 4].*[1 0; 0 1] ans = 1 0 0 4	Element-wise operator. . + and . - is equivalent to + and -, which are also element-wise operators.
.^	octave:1> [1 2; 3 4].^2 ans = 0 4 9 16	Element-wise power operator. Currently this operator only works for scalars, vectors, and matrices.
' and .'	octave:1> [1 +1*I 2+2*I; 3 4]' ans = 1 - 1i 3 - 0i 2 - 2i 4 - 0i	The complex conjugate transpose operator and the transpose operator. Only works for scalars, vectors, and matrices.

Pop Quiz – understanding simple operations

1. Which of the following operations are valid if **A**, **x**, and **y** are given by Equation (P.2)?

   a) `x + x`   b) `x + y`   c) `x - y'`

   d) `A*x`   e) `x*y`   f) `x*A`

   g) `A\x`   h) `A\y`   i) `x\y`

Have a go hero – doing the dot product

From the vectors **x** and **y** given in Equation (P.2), use Octave to calculate the dot product (also called scalar product) of:

a) **x** and **x**

b) **x** and **y**

Comparison operators and precedence rules

In the previous section, we discussed the basic arithmetic operations. In this section, we will learn how to compare different variables. Octave (like many other programming languages) uses very intuitive operator characters for this. They are:

`x==y`	Evaluates to true if x equals y
`x>y`	Evaluates to true if x is larger than y
`x<y`	Evaluates to true if x is smaller than y
`x>=y`	Evaluates to true if x is greater than or equal to y
`x<=y`	Evaluates to true if x is smaller than or equal to y
`x!=y`	Evaluates to true if x is not equal to y

For Octave's comparison operators, true is equivalent to a non-zero value and false is equivalent to 0. Let us see a few examples—recall the matrix A from Command 93:

```
octave:108> A(2,1) == 1

ans = 1

octave:109>A(2,1) == 2

ans = 0

octave:110> A(2,1) > 0
```

```
ans = 1

octave:111> A(2,1) != 4

ans = 1
```

Instead of using != for "not equal to", you can use ~=.

You may be familiar with these operators from another programming language. However, in Octave you can compare vectors and matrices. To compare the first column in A with another column vector, we use:

```
octave:112> A(:,1) >= [2; 2; 0]

ans =

  1
  1
  0

Octave:113> A > ones(3,3)

ans =

  1  0  0
  1  0  0
  0  0  0
```

that is, the comparison is performed element-wise. This, of course, means that the array dimensions must match except if one of the variables is a scalar.

You can also compare characters using the comparison operators above. However, they cannot be used to compare entire strings. For example:

```
octave:114> "a"=="a"

ans = 1
```

compare the character a with a, and:

```
octave:115> "hello"=="henno"

ans = 1   1   0   0   1
```

compare all character elements in the string hello with the characters in henno (element-wise). However, the command "hello"=="helloo" is not valid, because the two strings do not have the same dimensions. If you wish to compare the two strings, use strcmp (which is an abbreviation for string compare):

```
octave:116>strcmp("hello", "helloo")
```

```
ans = 0
```

meaning false, because the two strings are not the same.

As mentioned above, the result of a comparison operation is either true (value 1) or false (value 0). In computer science, we refer to this as a Boolean type, after the English mathematician George Boole. Note that because Octave is a vectorized programming language, the resulting Boolean can be an array with elements that are both true and false.

 Octave interprets all non-zero values as true.

Precedence rules

You can do many operations in a single command line, and it is important to know how such a command is interpreted in Octave.

Time for action – working with precedence rules

1. Let us see an example:

   ```
   octave:117> A*y + a
   ```

   ```
   ans =
         2.5000
        -3.0000
         1.7500
   ```

   Here, Octave first performs the matrix multiplication between A and y, and then adds a to that result. We say that multiplication has higher precedence than addition.

2. Let us try two other examples:

   ```
   octave:118> A*y.^2
   ```

   ```
   ans =
        4.2500
      -18.5000
        2.3750
   ```

   ```
   octave:119> (A*y).^2
   ```

```
ans =
      0.2500
     25.0000
      0.0625
```

What just happened?

In command 118, because the `.^` operator has higher precedence than `*`, Octave first calculates element-wise power operation `y.^2`, and then performs the matrix multiplication. In command 190, by applying parenthesis, we can perform the matrix multiplication first, and then do the power operation on the resulting vector.

The precedence rules are given below for the operators that we have discussed in this chapter:

When in doubt, you should always use parenthesis to ensure that Octave performs the computations in the order that you want.

Pop Quiz – understanding precedence rules

Let **x** and **y** be given by Equation (P.2). What are the outputs from the following commands? (Note that one of them produces an error!)

a) `2.0./x + y'`   b) `2.0./(x + 2*y')`   c) `2.0/x + y'`

d) `2.0./x' + y`   e) `2.0./(x.^2)' + y`

A few hints

Instead of using the left division operator to solve a linear equation system, you can do it "by hand". Let us try this using the equation system given by Equation (2.6) with the solution given in Equation (2.9). First we need to calculate the inverse of **A** (which exists). This is done via the `inv` function:

```
octave:120>inverse_A = inv(A)

inverse_A =
      0.2500     -0.1250     -1.0000
      0.5000     -0.5000     -1.0000
      0.0000     -0.2500     -1.0000
```

We can now simply perform the matrix multiplication $\mathbf{A}^{-1}\mathbf{y}$ to get the solution:

```
octave:121>inverse_A*y
```

```
ans =
    -1.6250
    -2.5000
    -2.2500
```

This output is similar to the output from Command 94. Now, when Octave performs the left division operation, it does not first invert A and then multiply that result with $\mathbf{y}$. Octave has many different algorithms it can use for this operation, depending on the specific nature of the matrix. The results from these algorithms are usually more precise and much quicker than performing the individual steps. In this particular example, it does not really make a big difference, because the problem is so simple.

 In general, do not break your calculations up into individual steps if Octave already has an in-built operator or functionality that does the same in one single step. It is highly likely that the single operation is faster and more precise.

If we replace the coefficient matrix $\mathbf{A}$ in Equation (2.8) with the following matrix:

$$\mathbf{A} = \begin{bmatrix} 2 & 1 & -3 \\ 4 & -2 & -2 \\ -2 & 1 & 1 \end{bmatrix} \tag{2.12}$$

and try to solve the corresponding linear equation system, Octave will display a warning message:

```
octave:122:> A=[2 1 -3; 4 -2 -2; -2 1 1]; A\y
```

```
warning: dgelsd : rank deficient 3x3 matrix, rank = 2
ans =
     0.3000
    -0.1250
    -0.1750
```

The result in this case is the minimum norm solution to the improperly defined equation system, which we will not discuss here. What is important is the warning message because this tells us that the matrix does not have full rank, that is, the rows (or columns) in the matrix are not linearly independent. This in turn means that no unique solution to the linear equation system exists. If you inspect the matrix, you will quickly see that the third row is just the second row multiplied with minus one half, so these two rows are linearly dependent. You can check the rank of a matrix by:

```
octave:123> rank(A)
```

```
ans = 2
```

This calculation is already done for you in Command 122, and shows up in the warning message. You should, of course, always perform this check if you are not absolutely sure about the rank of a matrix.

Summary

We went through a lot of the basics in this chapter! Specifically, we learned:

- How to instantiate scalar, vector, and matrix variables.
- How to instantiate complex variables.
- How to instantiate a text string.
- How to access and change the values of array elements.
- About structures, cell arrays, and multidimensional arrays.
- How to retrieve important information about the variables.
- How to add and subtract vectors and matrices.
- About matrix multiplication.
- Solving linear equation systems.
- How to compare scalars, vectors, and matrices.
- Some additional helpful functionality.
- Precedence rules.

In the next chapter, we will learn about Octave functions and how to do plotting. We shall make use of many of the things that we have just learned in this chapter.

3

Working with Octave: Functions and Plotting

As promised in Chapter 2, we will now discuss Octave functions in greater detail. The first part of the chapter is devoted to this and will give an introduction to and an overview of some of the most useful functions that Octave provides. In the second part we shall see how to use Octave functions to do two and three dimensional plotting.

Specifically, we will cover:

- ◆ Basic mathematical functions.
- ◆ Miscellaneous helper functions that can initialize variable elements and perform simple analysis of variables.
- ◆ Functions for linear algebra and polynomials.

The second part will take you through the plotting facilities, where you will learn:

- ◆ How to make two- and three-dimensional plots.
- ◆ About multi-plot and multi-graph plotting.
- ◆ How to change the properties of the graph and the figure window.

Octave functions

You can think of an Octave function as a kind of general mathematical function—it takes inputs, does something with them and returns outputs. For example, in Command 20 in *Chapter 2*, we used Octave's `real` function. We gave it the complex scalar input variable z and it returned the real part of z.

Octave functions can in general take multiple inputs (also called arguments or input arguments) and return multiple outputs. The general syntax for a function is:

```
[output 1, output 2, ...] = function name(input 1, input 2, ...)
```

The inputs to and the outputs from a function can be scalars, multidimensional arrays, structures, and so on. Note that the outputs need not to be separated with commas. Since Octave does not operate with type specifiers, the functions must be able to deal with all kind of inputs, either by performing the operations differently (and thereby likely also to return different outputs), or by reporting an error. Sometimes we will use function interface instead of function syntax, but it refers to the same thing.

I prefer to divide Octave functions into three categories:

1. Mathematical functions (for example,exponential and trigonometric functions).

2. Helper functions (for example, the `real` function).

3. Operational functions (for example,the `inv` function from Command 120 in *Chapter 2*).

In Octave, there is no such categorization of course. Hopefully, they are all helper functions in some sense. However, it may help to understand what the differences between them are. It is probably easiest to illustrate how to use Octave functions via the mathematical functions, so let us start with them.

Mathematical functions

Octave provides you with all elementary mathematical functions. Let us go through a few examples.

Time for action – using the cos function

1. In order to calculate cosine of a number, say π, we simply type:

```
octave:1>cos(pi)

ans = -1
```

`pi` is the input argument, `cos` is the Octave function and `-1` is the output from `cos`. When we use a function we often say that we call that function

2. What if we use a vector as input? Well, why not just try. We know how to instantiate a vector:

```
octave:2> x = [0:pi/2:2*pi]

ans =
   0.0000    1.5708    3.1416    4.7124    6.2832
```

Cosine of x is then:

```
octave:3>cos(x)

ans =

   1.0000e+000    6.1230e-017    -1.0000e+000    -1.8369e-016
1.0000e+000
```

that is, Octave calculates the cosine of each element in the vector.

3. In Command 2, we created a row vector, and the result of Command 3 is therefore
    also a row vector. If we use a column vector as input to `cos`:

    ```
    octave:4>cos(x')

    ans =
        1.0000e+000
        6.1230e-017
       -1.0000e+000
       -1.8369e-016
        1.0000e+000
    ```

    it returns a column vector.

What just happened?

In Command 1, we use `pi` as the input argument to the `cos` function. Now, strictly speaking,
`pi` is a function itself. If we call `pi` without any arguments or no parenthesis, it simply
returns the number π.

The output from Command 3 is not exactly zero at $\cos(\pi/2)$ and $\cos(3\pi/2)$ as we might expect.
This is due to the finite numerical precision of a computer calculation. However, from the
result, we see that the values are very close to zero. From Command 3, we see that `cos` returns
a row vector, because the argument was a row vector. In general, if we had called `cos` with an
$n \times m$ matrix (or higher dimensional array), it would simply take the cosine of each element in
the matrix and return the output with that same size. That is, it will work in an element-wise
manner. This is true for most of Octave's mathematical functions and is worth noting.

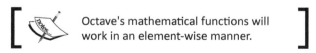

Octave's mathematical functions will
work in an element-wise manner.

Commands 1 and 4 highlight another important point—any operations or function acting on
the input argument(s) will be carried out before the function is called. In Command 1, the
function `pi` is called, and the output from that function is used as input to `cos`. In Command
4, the vector `x` is first transposed, and that result is used as input to the function `cos`. This is
true for all Octave functions.

The table below lists the basic mathematical functions that come with Octave. They are all called in the same manner as `cos`:

Function	Description	Function	Description
sin	Sine	cos	Cosine
tan	Tangent	sec	Secant
cot	Cotangent	csc	Cosecant
log	Logarithm base *e*	log10	Logarithm base 10
exp	The exponential function	sqrt	Square root
power	Power function		

In addition to the table above, all the trigonometric functions have their inverse and hyperbolic cousins defined. For example, the inverse of sine is called `asin` and the inverse hyperbolic of sine is `asinh`.

The following commands yield the same result:

```
octave:5>exp(I*pi)

ans = -1.0000e+000    -    1.2246e-016i

octave:6> power(e,I*pi)

ans = -1.0000e+000    -    1.2246e-016i

octave:7> e.^(I*pi)

ans = -1.0000e+000    -    1.2246e-016i
```

So Octave is also able to handle complex input arguments to mathematical functions!

Polynomials in Octave

Octave has a special way of handling polynomials. As an example, consider the third order polynomial *f* which is a function of *x*

$$f(x) = 2x^3 + 10.1x^2 + 6. \qquad (3.1)$$

We can represent this polynomial via a vector containing the coefficients:

$$\mathbf{c} = [2 \ 10.1 \ 0 \ 6] \tag{3.2}$$

such that the first element is the coefficient for the term with the highest exponent and the last element is the constant term. There is no first order term in the polynomial, which is indicated by the 0 in the coefficient vector **c**. We can now evaluate the function range or value for $x = 0$ by using `polyval`:

```
octave:8> c=[2 10.1 0 6];

octave:9>polyval(c, 0)

ans = 6
```

Also, we can calculate the range using a vector as input, for example, the vector variable `x`, defined in Command 2:

```
octave:10>polyval(c, x)

ans =
  6.0000    38.6723    167.6959 439.5791    900.8324
```

In *Chapter 2*, you learned about operators in Octave, so you could alternatively use:

```
octave:11> 2*x.^3 + 10.1*x.^2 + 6

ans =
  6.0000    38.6723    167.6959 439.5791    900.8324
```

More complicated mathematical functions

Octave provides you with much more than the basic mathematical functions, for example, Bessel functions of different kinds[1]. Since you know about the different arithmetic operators from *Chapter 2*, you can also put together your own mathematical functions using the simple functions as building blocks.

---

[1]*We will not cover these special functions here. Check out the official Octave manual should you be interested in these types of functions.*

Time for action – putting together mathematical functions

1. Let us try to calculate the range of the function:

$$f(x) = e^{-5\sqrt{x}} \sin(2\pi x). \tag{3.3}$$

```
octave:12> x = 0.5;

octave:13> f = exp(-5*sqrt(x))*sin(2*pi*x)

f = 3.5689e-018
```

2. In a more useful vector form:

```
octave:14> x = [0:0.1:1];

octave:15> f = exp(-5*sqrt(x)).*sin(2*pi*x)

f =
  Columns 1  through   7:
0.00000     0.12093    0.10165    0.01650   0.02488   0.00000   -0.01222
  Columns 8  through  11:
-0.01450   -0.01086   -0.00512   -0.00000
```

What just happened?

It should be clear what Commands 12 and 13 do. In Command 15, we must use the element-wise `.*` operator. Had we not done so, Octave would try to perform a matrix multiplication between the vectors given by `exp(-5*sqrt(x))` and `sin(2*pi*x)`, which is not defined, and not what we want either.

We could also have used the element-wise operator in Command 13 when x is a scalar; that is, Command 14 is a generalized version that works for both scalars and vector and matrix arrays.

 Whenever possible, always make generalized versions of your commands such that they work on both array and scalar variables.

The function in Equation (3.3) is a scalar function that maps a real number into a real number. Functions can also map two real numbers into a real number. Equation (1.1) in *Chapter 1* is an example of such a function. Let us try something a bit simpler, namely:

$$f(x, y) = x^2 - y^2 \tag{3.4}$$

and "build" that in Octave's interpreter:

```
octave:16> x = 1; y = sqrt(pi);

octave:17> f = x.^2 - y.^2

f = -2.1416
```

The mathematical functions given in Equations (3.3) and (3.4) are examples of scalar functions. You can, of course, also calculate the range of vector-valued functions. Take, for example, the function:

$$\mathbf{f}(x) = [\cos(x), \sin(x), e^{-x/2}].$$ (3.5)

In Octave we may find the range like this:

```
octave:18> x = pi;

octave:19> f = [cos(x), sin(x), exp(-0.5*x)]

f =
    1    0    4.8105
```

We will return to Equations (3.4) and (3.5) when we learn how to plot graphs of these types of functions.

Helper functions

In *Chapter 2*, we used quite a few helper functions.`ismatrix`, `real`, `eye`, `ones` are some examples. Helper functions work differently from Octave's mathematical functions; for example, it is not meaningful to call `eye` with a non-integer number—try to see what happens if you do.

Rather than embarking on a very long road explaining the entire set of helper functions, we will go through what I think are some of the most important ones, and from these examples, explain the general behaviour.

Generating random numbers

Recall that the `ones` and `zero` functions could help us in creating arrays where all elements had the values 1 or 0, respectively. The function `rand` does the same, except that the elements are uniformly distributed random numbers between 0 and 1 (both excluded). To instantiate a 3 x 5 matrix array with random distributed elements, we can use:

```
octave:20> A = rand(3,5)

A =

        0.72106    0.97880    0.28600    0.92375    0.10514

        0.91879    0.43847    0.30922    0.03529    0.84677

        0.15474    0.43170    0.47812    0.04455    0.04975
```

just as we did with the function `zeros` and `ones`. If `rand` is called without any arguments (same as having no parenthesis at all), it returns a single random number.

Often you will need random numbers from a different distribution. Beside uniformly distributed numbers, Octave can generate:

1. `randn`: normal distribution with 0 mean and variance 1 (from here you can generate normal distributed numbers with arbitrary mean and variance).
2. `randg`: gamma distribution.
3. `rande`: exponential distribution.
4. `randp`: Poisson distribution.

`randn`, `randq`, and `rande` are called with the same arguments as `rand`; that is, the output array dimensions. For `randp`, you will need to specify the mean as the first argument. Type `helprandp` if you have any doubts.

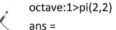

> The `pi` function we used above is also a helper function. It works pretty much like `rand`, for example:
>
> octave:1>pi(2,2)
>
> ans =
>
>   3.1416   3.1416
>
>   3.1416   3.1416
>
> generates a 2 x 2 two-dimensional array with elements having value π.

min and max

Octave provides you with a function that returns the minimum of a one dimensional array. However it can also be called using A above as argument, for example:

```
octave:21> min(A)

ans =

      0.15474      0.43170      0.28600      0.03529      0.04975
```

That is, min calculates the minimum of each column in A. If we apply min to a vector array, for example, using the output we get from Command 21:

```
octave:22> min(ans)

ans = 0.03529
```

Thus, the minimum of the array is given by ans. This is the same as the minimum of A. We could combine Commands 21 and 22 to find the minimum of A directly:

```
octave:23> min(min(A))

ans = 0.03529
```

The max function finds the maximum of an array and works just like min.

 Octave functions that perform vector operations work (as default) in a column-wise manner if the argument is a matrix.

Sorting arrays

Let us see another example of a useful Octave function, namely, sort. This function will sort array elements for you. sort is an example of an Octave function that can be called with different number of input and output arguments, depending on what exactly you want sort to do and what information you wish to retrieve from it[2]. The simplest way to call sort is to give the function a single variable, say the matrix A, as input. Each column in A will then be sorted according to the rule above:

```
octave:24> sort(A)

ans =

      0.15474      0.43170      0.28600      0.03529      0.04975
      0.72106      0.43847      0.30922      0.04455      0.10514
      0.91879      0.97880      0.47812      0.92375      0.84677
```

[2]min *and* max *above are other examples of functions that can be called with a different number of input and output arguments. See the help text for these functions if you are curious.*

Rather than sorting A in ascending order, we can sort the elements in a descending order using the mode input argument `"descend"` (or `'descend'`). You can also sort the array elements row-wise, and you can even ask sort to return an array with the original indices in the new sorted array. Let us see an example of this:

```
octave:25> [S i] = sort(A, 2, "descending")

  S =
     0.97880      0.92375      0.72107      0.28600      0.10514
     0.91879      0.84677      0.43847      0.30922      0.03529
     0.47812      0.43170      0.15474      0.15474      0.04455

  i =
     2    4    1    3    5
     1    5    2    3    4
     3    2    1    5    4
```

The second input argument tells `sort` to sort the elements in A row-wise. If you wish to sort column-wise, you can leave out the second argument or use the value 1.

In total `sort` can be called in 12 different ways—many of which are practically the same. In general `sort` is called as:

```
[S i] = sort(A, dir, opt)
```

If we compare that with the general syntax format, we see that S and i are outputs and A, dir, and opt are input arguments. If `sort` is called with zero or one output argument, it will always return the first in the list, in this case the sorted array. This is true for most Octave functions, but not all as we shall see later. Again, you can see how to call a function by using the `help` command.

find, any, and all

I use `find` quite often and believe it is worth showing you this helper function as well. It is particularly powerful when used together with the different operators we learned about in *Chapter 2*. `find` returns the indices of non-zero elements in an array. For example:

```
octave:26> [i j] = find([0 0; 1 0])

i = 2
j = 1
```

that is, the element in the second row (indicated via i) and the first column (as indicated via j) is a non-zero element. Let us try to use `find` for something useful—what elements in A are less than 0.5?

```
octave:27>  [i, j] = find(A<0.5);
```

Notice that I have stored the output in the variable i and j and suppressed the output to the screen to save space. Now, from *Chapter 2*, we know that the argument to find, A<0.5, returns a matrix with 0 (for false) and 1 (for true). find then simply returns the matrix indices for the elements with value of 1. Let us check if we get what we would expect, for example:

```
octave:28> i(1), j(1)

ans = 3

ans = 1
```

Inspecting the matrix variable A in Command 20, we see that the element in row 3, column 1 is less than 0.5, as found from Command 28. Like sort above, find can be called in different ways. Type help find to see how.

The functions any and all are related to find. The difference is that any returns true if any element in an array is non-zero, and all returns true if all elements are non-zero. The two functions work in a column-wise manner if the argument is a matrix. Let us illustrate this:

```
octave:29> any([0 0; 1 0])

ans =

   1   0
octave:30> all([0 0; 1 0])

ans =

   0   0
```

In Command 29, the input matrix is composed of two columns. The first column has a non-zero element, but the other does not. any therefore returns a 1 and a 0. On the other hand, all returns two zeros, because both columns have at least one zero element.

floor, ceil, round, and fix

It is perhaps easiest to illustrate these four functions by a few simple examples.

Time for action – trying out floor, ceil, round, and fix

1. The floor function:

    ```
    octave:31> floor(1.9)

    ans = 1
    ```

2. The ceil function:
```
octave:32> ceil(1.1)

ans = 2
```

3. The round function:
```
octave:33> round(1.9)

ans = 2
```

4. The fix function:
```
octave:34> fix(pi)

ans = 3
```

What just happened?

From Command 31, we see that `floor` returns the largest integer which is smaller than the input argument, `ceil` the smallest integer that is larger than the input, `round` simply rounds towards to the nearest integer, and `fix` returns the integer part of a real number. With these definitions, we have:

```
octave:35> floor(-1.9)

ans = -2
```

The four functions will work in an element-wise fashion if the input is an array with arbitrary dimensions.

sum and prod

The functions `sum` and `prod` are also very useful. Basically they sum or multiply the elements in an array. Let us see two simple examples:

```
octave:36> sum([1 2; 3 4])

ans =
4   6

octave:37> prod([1 2 3 4])

ans =   24
```

You can also perform accumulated sum and product calculations with `cumsum` and `cumprod`:

```
octave:38>cumsum([1 2; 3 4])

ans =

  1    2
  4    6

octave:39>cumprod([1 2 3 4])

ans = 1    2    6    24
```

Absolute values

Octave has a function called `abs` that can calculate the absolute value. Recall that for a complex number $z = x + iy$ the absolute value is given by $|z| = \sqrt{x^2 + y^2}$ according to Pythagoras' theorem. Let us see a few examples of calculating the absolute value:

```
octave:40> abs(2.3)

ans = 2.3

octave:41> abs(-2.3)

ans = 2.3

octave:42> abs(2 + 2i)

ans = 2.8284

octave:43> abs(-2-2i)

ans = 2.8284
```

`abs` will work in an element-wise manner if the input argument is an array.

Complex input arguments

Except for the `abs` function above, we have not considered how complex numbers are treated in helper functions. Now that we know how to calculate absolute values, we can include a few examples of how functions work when complex numbers are used as input arguments. For example, let us try to find the maximum of a complex array:

```
octave:44>max([1+2i, 2+2i, 2-0.1i])

ans = 2+2i
```

You could imagine that `max` would return the maximum of the real parts and the maximum of the imaginary parts, but it does not. `max` returns the element with the largest absolute value. `min`, of course, returns the element with minimum absolute value.

If `sort` is given an array of complex numbers, it will sort according to the elements absolute value. For example:

```
octave:45> sort([1+2i 2+2i 2-0.1i])

ans =

   2.0000 - 0.1000i    1.0000 + 2.0000i    2.0000 + 2.0000i
```

Try to call other functions with complex input arguments.

Operator functions

Operator functions carry out more complex operations on its arguments. To do this, Octave uses highly optimized algorithms and existing libraries like LAPACK or FFTW. Of course, the helper function `sort` is also based on rather complicated algorithms, but the operation itself (sorting an array) is relatively simple.

Linear algebra

In *Chapter 2*, we learned how to solve linear equation systems using the left division operator. Also, we learned how to calculate the inverse of a matrix. Octave can do much more linear algebra some of which we will discuss in the following.

Time for action – using Octave for advanced linear algebra

1. It is easy to calculate the determinant of a 2 x 2 matrix, but for a 3 x 3 matrix, the calculation becomes tedious, not to mention larger size matrices. Octave has a function `det` that can do this for you:

    ```
    octave:46> A=[2 1 -3; 4 -2 -2; -1 0.5 -0.5];

    octave:47>det(A)

    ans = 8
    ```

    Recall from linear algebra that the determinant is only defined for a square n x n matrix. Octave will issue an error message if you pass a non-square matrix input argument.

2. Let us change A a bit:

    ```
    octave:48> A=[2 1 -3; 4 -2 -2; -2 1 1];

    octave:49>det(A)
    ```

```
ans = 0
```

This result is consistent with the result from *Chapter 2*. A does not have full rank, that is, the determinant is 0.

3. The eigenvalues of an n x n matrix are given by the equation:

$$\det(\mathbf{A} - \lambda\mathbf{I}) = 0. \tag{3.6}$$

To calculate the eigenvalues in Octave, we can use the `eig` function:

```
octave:50> A = [1 2; 3 4];

octave:51>eig(A)

ans =

   -0.3722
    5.3722
```

4. `eig` can also return the eigenvectors. However, given two outputs, the output sequence changes such that the first output is the eigenvectors and the second is the eigenvalues. In Octave, you type:

```
octave:52> [V, L] = eig(A)

V =

   -0.8245    -0.4159
    0.5657    -0.9093

L =

Diagonal Matrix

   -0.3722         0
         0    5.3722
```

The eigenvectors are given by the columns in V, and the eigenvalues are the diagonal elements in L.

What just happened?

We have already discussed Commands 46-51. In Command 52, we include the calculation of the eigenvectors. Notice that the output changes when we call `eig` with two outputs, which is not the usual behavior that we expect from an Octave function. This is to maintain compatibility with MATLAB.

Now, recall that the eigenvector **v** to a corresponding eigenvalue λ is given by the linear equation system:

$$(\mathbf{A} - \lambda\mathbf{I})\mathbf{v} = 0. \tag{3.7}$$

We can write Equation (3.7) as $\mathbf{Bv} = \mathbf{0}$, where $\mathbf{B} = \mathbf{A} - \lambda\mathbf{I}$, that is, the eigenvector, is the null space (or kernel) of the matrix **B**. In Octave, we can calculate the null space directly:

```
octave:53> lambda = L(1, 1);

octave:54> B = A - lambda*eye(2);

octave:55> null(B)

ans =
    0.8245
   -0.5657
```

which is the eigenvector corresponding to the eigenvalue -0.3722 in agreement with the output from Command 52[3]. By the way, what is the rank of **B**? Since you can calculate the null space, you can also calculate the range of matrices. This function is named `orth` and works in the same way as `null`. The following table lists the linear algebra functions that we have covered here and in *Chapter 2*:

Function	Description	Function	Description
det	The determinate	eig	Eigenvectors and eigenvalues
inv/inverse	Matrix inverse	null	Orthonormal null space
orth	Orthonormal range space	rank	Matrix rank

Polynomials

Above, we learned how to represent polynomials in Octave by the polynomial coefficients. Here, we will go through three functions that can help us to find the roots and the coefficients of the polynomial's integral and derivative.

In Command 8, we instantiate an array `c` with elements `[2 10.1 0 6]`, representing the polynomial given in Equation (3.1). To find the roots of this polynomial we use:

---

[3]*If you wish to calculate the eigenvectors, you should of course use* `eig`.

```
octave:56> roots(c)

ans =

   -5.1625   +   0.0000i
    0.0563   +   0.7602i
    0.0563   -   0.7602i
```

that is, the graph crosses the axis once.

The indefinite integral (or antiderivative) of f is given by:

$$\int f(x)dx = \frac{1}{2}x^4 + \frac{10.1}{3}x^3 + 6x \tag{3.8}$$

plus a constant of integration. The derivative is:

$$\frac{df(x)}{dx} = 6x^2 + 20.2x. \tag{3.9}$$

Notice that Equations (3.8) and (3.9) are themselves polynomials which is represented via their coefficient. In Octave, we can easily find the indefinite integral and derivative:

```
octave:57> polyinteg(c)

ans =
    0.5000     3.3667     0.0000     6.0000     0.0000

octave:58> polyderive(c)

ans =
    6.0000    20.2000     0.0000
```

which agree with the calculus above.

Pop Quiz – using simple mathematical functions

1. Let the variable A be given by the command:

    `octave:1> A = rand(2,3);`

2. What are the sizes of the output from the following commands?

    a) `log(A)` b) `log(A')` c) `max(A)`

    d) `sort(A')` e) `sum(A)` f) `cumsum(A)`

3.   Which of the following commands are not valid?

a) `rand(3,3,2)`   b) `polyval([i, 2+i], 3i)`   c) `f=[cos(x), sin(x); x]`

d) `sort(A, 10)`   e) `[I, j] = find(A=0.5)`

Have a go hero – understanding the find function

Let the variable A be instantiated by:

```
octave:1> A = [ 3 3 3; 4 5 1];
```

What is the output from the following command?

```
octave:2> [i,j]=find(A>3); sum(i), sum(j)
```

Two-dimensional plotting

In the second part of this chapter, we will discuss how you can make plots with Octave. Since version 3.0.0, the Octave development team has done a lot to improve the plotting interface in order to obtain larger compatibility with MATLAB. At the same time, the plotting programs have improved significantly, and the plotting facilities have now become quite impressive. Depending on the Octave version you are using, the plotting program may not support all the plotting commands and facilities that we will go through here. Also, the graphical output may be different.

From version 3.4.0, Octave has a built-in native plotting program based on the Fast Light Toolkit[4] (FLTK), but the default plotting program will likely be gnuplot. Therefore, if you have Octave version 3.4.0 or higher installed with the FLTK plotting backend, you can load and change the default plotting toolkit to FLTK by using:

octave:1>graphics_toolkit("fltk")

To change back to gnuplot:

octave:2>graphics_toolkit("gnuplot")

You can see what graphical toolkits are loaded and available with the function `available_graphics_toolkits`.

---

[4]*See* `http://www.fltk.org`

Time for action – making your first plot

Let us try to plot the polynomial, *f*, given in Equation (3.1) in the interval $x \in [-5.5; 1]$:

```
octave:59> x = [-5.5:0.1:1]; f = polyval(c,x);
```

```
octave:60> plot(x, f)
```

You should now see a plot looking somewhat like the one below:

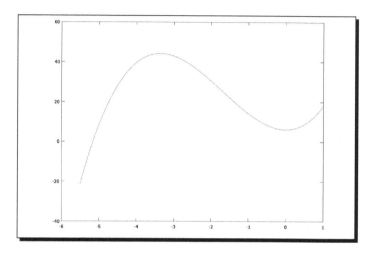

What just happened?

The first input argument to `plot` is the x variable which is used as the *x* axis values. The second is `f` and is used as the *y* axis values. Note that these two variables must have the same length. If they do not, Octave will issue an error. You can also call `plot` with a single input argument. In this case, the input variable is plotted against its indices.

When we plot the graph of *f*, we actually connect the discrete values given by the vector `f` with straight lines. Thus, you need enough points in order for the figure to represent the graph well.

plot and set

There are some things that do not look quite satisfactory in the figure above:

1. The axes are not right, for example, the *x* axis starts from -6, not -5.5.

2. The graph and the window box lines are too thin.

3. The axes are not labelled.

4. The numbers on the axes are too small.

We can fix all that! In fact, there are different ways of doing this, and we will use the most flexible approach.

To do so, we need to:

1. Know more about the function `plot`.
2. Learn about the function `set`.

The general syntax for `plot` is:

```
plot(x, y,fmt, property, value, ...)
```

We have already discussed the two first input arguments. The input argument `fmt` is the plotting format or style. If you leave this out, Octave will use the default blue line. The fourth argument `property`is a property of the graph (for example, the color or linewidth) and `value` is the property value. The dots indicate that you can specify several property and property value pairs.

In general, `set` is called as:

```
set(handle, property, value, ...)
```

where `handle` is a graphic object handle (for example, a handle to an axis), `property` is a property of the graphical object (say range of an axis) and `value` is its value (for example, the interval from -5.5 to 1).

Time for action – changing the figure properties

1. Let us try to change the plot of the graph above. First:

    ```
    octave:61> plot(x, f, "linewidth", 5);
    ```

    This command will create the same plot as above, but here we specify the graph property `linewidth` to have the value 5 rather than 1.

2. To set the correct limits on the axis, we use `set`:

    ```
    octave:62> set(gca, "xlim", [-5.5 1])
    ```

3. We can also use `set` to set the line width of the window box and the font size of the numbers on the axes:

    ```
    octave:63> set(gca, "linewidth", 2)

    octave:64> set(gca, "fontsize", 25)
    ```

4. The axes labels are also set by the `set` function. Here the properties are `"xlabel"` and `"ylabel"`, and the property value is set using the `text` function:

```
octave:65> set(gca, "xlabel", text("string", "x", "fontsize", 25))

octave:66> set(gca, "ylabel", text("string", "f(x)",
"fontsize", 25))
```

5. The figure should now look something like the figure below:

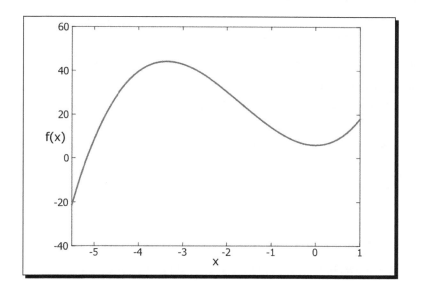

 Many prefer to use single quotation marks around the property label, for example, `'xlim'`. Use whatever you prefer.

What just happened?

In Command 62, the handle input argument gca is actually a function and is an abbreviation for 'get current axis'. The property `"xlim"` stands for x axis limits, which we set to values -5.5 and 1.

You can also set and change the axes labels by using the functions xlabel and ylabel, and you can specify the axes limits with the axis function. However, set is more flexible and once you get used to it, you will find it easy with which to work.

 As you can see from the interface, set can be called with a series of properties and property value pairs. Thus, Commands 62-66 can be merged into a single call to set

```
octave:67> set(gca, "xlim", [-5.5 1], "linewidth", 2, "fontsize", 25,
  "xlabel", text("string", "x", "fontsize", 25), "ylabel",
  text("string", "f(x)", "fontsize", 25))
```

Note: The figures in this text may look different from the screen output you see (especially the font size will likely appear much larger). In general, printed plots look different from the screen plots: what you see is not necessary what you get.

Adding lines and text to your plot

You can also add lines and text to your figure in order to highlight things.For example, you may want to point to the root of the polynomial. To add lines, we use the `line` function:

```
octave:68> line([-5.16 -4], [-2 -20], "linewidth", 2)
```

Here, the line will go from the point (x, y)=(-5.16, -2) to (x, y)=(-4, -20) and have a width of 2. It would also be informative to have a text string stating to what the line actually points. For this we can use the function `text` we saw above:

```
octave:69> text(-3.9, -23, "root", "fontsize", 20);
```

The two numbers (x, y) give the point where the string `"root"` begins. Let us add a bit more information, namely:

```
octave:70> line([0 0], [5 -20], "linewidth", 2)

octave:71> text(-1.0, -22, "local minimum", "fontsize", 20)
```

The figure below shows how the plot looks after adding lines and text:

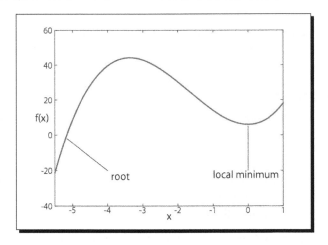

Plot styles and colors

Recall from the function syntax that you can specify to `plot` the format with which the graph should be plotted. For example, to plot Equation (3.1) using circles instead of lines, you can use:

```
octave:72> plot(x, f, "o")
```

The existing graph is deleted just as the axes limits and axes labels can change or disappear. You may find the points too large or too small. The property `markersize` can help you to set the size of the points:

```
octave:73> plot(x,f, "o", "markersize",  4);
```

You can experiment with the marker size value. Other point formats are *, +, x, ., and ^, which can be combined with - to connect the points with a line.

You can also specify to Octave the color you want the graph to be plotted with via the property `color`. Let us re-plot the graph of the polynomial, using points connected with lines in the color red:

```
octave:74> plot(x, f, "o-", "markersize", 4, "linewidth", 2, "color",
"red")
```

```
octave:75> set(gca, "xlim", [-5.5 1], "ylim", [-40 60], "linewidth", 2,
"fontsize", 25, "xlabel", text("string", "x", "fontsize", 25),
"ylabel", text("string", "f(x)", "fontsize", 25))
```

Notice, that because we re-plot the graph, we need to specify the axes properties again, which we do in Command 75. The next figure below shows how the graph looks with this plotting style and color.

Title and legends

The figure can also be fitted with a title and the graph with a legend. The latter is especially relevant when you have several graphs in the same figure. To add a legend stating that the graph is the range of f you use:

```
octave:76> legend("f(x)")
```

and to add a title you can use the `set` function:

```
octave:77> set(gca, "title", text("string",
"My favorite polynomial","fontsize", 30))
```

Notice that `title` is a valid property of the axes object handle, but `legend` is not.

Ticks

You can control the axes tick marks. For example, you may want the numbers -40, -20, ... 60 to be displayed on the y axis. Again, we can use set:

```
octave:78> set(gca, "ytick", [-40:20:60])
```

ytick is the property and the array is the corresponding value. You can also set the *x* axis ticks with the property xtick. It is important to note that the array need not be evenly spaced. You could also use [-40 -30 40 55 60]. Try it out!

Grids

Sometimes it can be helpful to have a grid to guide the eye. To turn on the grid, use:

```
octave:79> grid on
```

To turn the grid off again, simply type:

```
octave:80> grid off
```

The grid will connect the tick marks, so if you have unevenly spaced tick marks, the grid will also be unevenly spaced. The figure below show the final plot after title, legend, ticks and grid have been set.

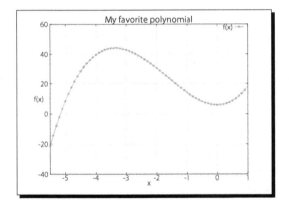

fplot

Many Octave users also use fplot. This function can be used to plot graphs of mathematical functions, hence the prefix f. This is different from plot that plots two data arrays against each other. To plot a sine function in the interval from 0 to 2π with fplot using 50 points, you type:

```
octave:81>fplot("sin", [0 2*pi], 50)
```

 Notice that we need not to specify what to plot on the *x* and *y* axes. fplot figures that out.

Clear the figure window

Just as you can delete or clear variables from the workspace, you can also delete figures. The command:

```
octave:82>clf
```

will do so. Notice that the graphic window remains, but that the content is deleted.

Moving on

Octave enables you to do much more than simply plot a single graph. In this section, you will learn how you can plot multiple graphs in single figure window, how you can have several plotting windows, and how to use subplots.

To show how you can plot multiple graphs in a single window, we plot two polynomials:

$$f_1(x) = 2x^3 + 10.1x^2 + 6 \quad \text{and} \quad f_2(x) = 2x^3 + 10.1x^2 - 10.1x + 6 \qquad (3.10)$$

in the same figure window. Notice that f_1 is the same polynomial as the one given in Equation (3.1).

Time for action – having multiple graphs in the same figure

1. We start by defining the domain and the coefficients representing the polynomial:

```
octave:83> x = [-5.5:0.1:2]; c_1 = [2 10.1 0 6];
c_2 = [2 10.1 -10.1 6];
```

2. We then calculate the ranges of f_1 and f_2:

```
octave:84>  f_1 = polyval(c_1, x); f_2=polyval(c_2, x);
```

3. And plot the graphs:

```
octave:85> plot(x, f_1, "linewidth", 5, x, f_2,
"linewidth", 5, "color", "red")
```

After setting the axes limits, font sizes, and so forth, the figure window looks like the next figure below.

What just happened?

From Command 85, we see that `plot` can plot many graphs in a single call, and that you can even specify the properties and values of each graph.

Alternatively, you can use the command `hold on` to force Octave to not delete the existing graph(s); that is, instead of Command 85, you can use:

```
octave:86> plot(x, f_1, "linewidth", 5);
octave:87> hold on

octave:88> plot(x, f_2, "linewidth", 5, "color", "red")
```

When you want Octave to stop "holding on", you simply type:

```
octave:89> hold off
```

You may wonder how the subscripts are made. Easy! Just use an underscore to indicate that the next character is a subscript. For example, in the figure below, you use:

```
octave:90> text(-3.9, -23, "f_1(x)")
```

If you want more than one character to be a subscript, you can use curly brackets around the characters, for example,`"f_{123}(x)"`. For superscript, you can use ^ (hat) instead of underscore. This feature, however, may not be supported by your plotting toolkit.

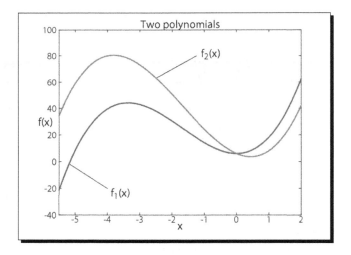

Multiple figure windows

In Octave, you can also work with several figure windows at once. To change to or to create a figure window 2, for example, you type:

```
octave:91> figure(2)
```

The next time you use `plot`, the graph will be shown in window 2. You can go back and work with figure 1 by:

```
octave:92> figure(1)
```

If you have opened many figure windows and have lost track of which figure is the current one, you can use `gcf`:

```
octave:93>gcf
```

```
ans = 1
```

This answer means that the current figure is 1.

Subplots

Rather than opening several figure windows, you can have multiple subplots in the same window. If you want to make subplots, you need to instruct Octave to divide the window into a two-dimensional array of n rows and m columns. For example, to start a figure window with dimensions 2 x 3, that is, with six plots, you use the command:

```
octave:94> subplot(2,3,1)
```

The first two arguments to `subplot` set the window dimensions, and the third tells Octave to plot in the subplot window with index 1. The indices run in a row-wise manner, as illustrated in the figure below. The figure shows an example of a window with six subplots arranged on a 2 by 3 grid where each subplot is plotting something random.

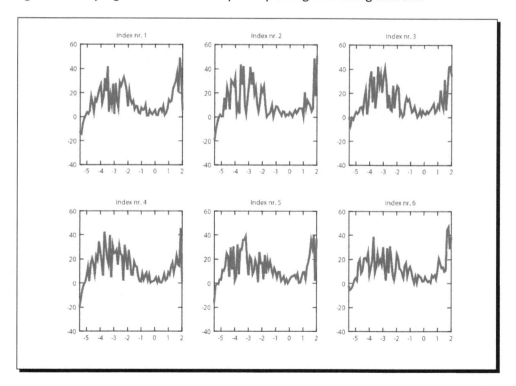

You can now use the `plot`, `set`, `line`, and `text` commands that we have learned earlier in this subplot. To change to subplot 2, you simply type:

```
octave:95> subplot(2,3,2)
```

The subplot functionality becomes particular useful whenever you want to have insets; for example, if you want to zoom in on a particular part of the graph. Let us say you want to plot the graphs of the two functions f_1 and f_2, from Equation (3.10). Instead of plotting them in the same window, we can plot f_2 as an inset.

Time for action – making an inset

1. First we type the command:

   ```
   octave:96> subplot(1,1,1)
   ```

   which will open the main plotting window and allow you to make subplots.

2. Now, to plot the graph of f_1 with line width 5, we use:

   ```
   octave:97>plot(x,f_1, "linewidth", 5)
   ```

3. Set the axis limits to ensure space for the inset:

   ```
   octave:98> set(gca, "xlim", [-6 2.5], "ylim", [-50 70])
   ```

4. When we insert the smaller inset window, we specify the location of the lower-left corner of the inset and the length and height. We do so in fractions of the main plotting window (including the axis ticks). For example:

   ```
   octave:99> axes("position",[0.3 0.2 0.3 0.3])
   ```

5. To plot in the inset, we simply use the basic `plot` function:

   ```
   octave:100> plot(x, f_2, "red", "linewidth", 5)
   ```

What just happened?

In Command 99, the function `axes` is used to control the axes properties. The first argument is the axes property "position", and the second argument is the corresponding value. Unfortunately, you cannot (currently) control this via `set`. Now, the value specifies that the lower-left corner of the inset window is located a fraction 0.3 inside the main window in the x direction and a fraction 0.2 inside the main window in the y direction. The size of the inset is given by the last two elements in the array.

You can now change the axes and text property of the inset as you wish using `set`. The figure below shows the final outcome of our efforts:

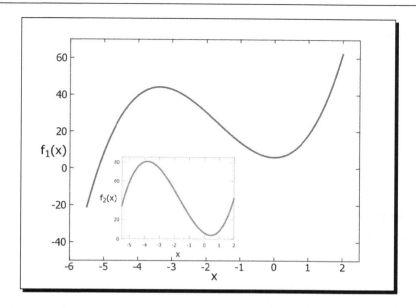

You can add more insets via `axes`. However, you cannot go back to the main window or other insets and make changes. It can therefore take a bit of trial and error before the figure looks just like you want it to.

We end this section by summarizing the different properties and corresponding values discussed here for `plot` and `set`:

`plot`	Property	Property value
	`linewidth`	Numerical value that sets the graph line width (or thickness).
	`makersize`	Size of point styles. A numerical value.
	`color`	Color of graph: `"black"`,`"red"`,`"green"`,`"blue"`,`"magenta"`,`"cyan"`,`"white"`
	`fmt` (not given explicitly)	`"*"`, `"o"`, `"+"`, `"x"`, `"-"`, `"^"` [Note: your plotting toolkit may support more formats].

set	Property	Property value
	`xlim` and `ylim`	x and y range on plot. Numerical array with two elements.
	`fontsize`	Size of tick marks. Numerical value.
	`xlabel` and `ylabel`	The axis labels. String object which can be set via the `text` function.
	`linewidth`	Line width (or thickness) of the figure boundaries. Numerical value.
	`xticks` and `yticks`	Array giving the tick marks.
	`title`	A text string specified using the `text` function.

Saving your plot

You can save (or rather print) your plot to a file via the `print` function. For example:

```
octave:101> print("polynom.png", "-dpng");
```

will print the current window to the file `"polynom.png"` in png (Portable Network Graphics) format. Notice the `-d` before the format specification. This is an abbreviation for "device".

 You can also use print in a non-functional form, for example, Command 101 could be replaced with:

octave:101> print polynom.png –dpng

`print` supports most of the common formats:

eps	Encapsulated PostScript (I recommend this format if your text program or printer supports it).
ps	PostScript.
pdf	Portable Document Format.
jpg/jpeg	Joint Photographic Experts Group image.
gif	Graphics Interchange Format image.
tex	TeX picture (to be included in a TeX document).
pslatex	LaTex picture file for labels and PostScript for the graphics. This enables you to edit the labels later.
png	Portable Network Graphics image.

Type `help print` to see the extensive list of options.

When using the eps and ps format, I prefer to add the `-solid` and `-color` options:

octave:1> print("polynom.eps", "-deps", "-solid", "-color");

This prevents the printed graphs from being shown with dashed or dotted lines and is printed in color.

Pop Quiz – understanding the plotting options

Which of the following properties do not have a correct value associated with it?

a) `"linewidth"` 6   b) `"ylabel"` 34   c) `"fontsize"` Times Roman

d) `"xlim"` `[1:10]`   e) `"xticks"` `[1:10]`   f) `"color"` red

g) `"title""42"`

Have a go hero – making inserts

In this exercise, you will make two plots of the graph of the function given by Equation (3.3). In the main plotting window, the graph is plotted over the interval $x \in [0; 10]$ and in an inset, it is plotted over the interval $x \in [0; 2]$. Follow the guidelines:

1. Give Octave the command: subplot(1,1,1).

2. Instantiate the vector variable `xlarge` with elements in the interval [0;10]. (Make sure that the vector has sufficient elements.)

3. Calculate the range of the function over this interval and plot the graph.

4. Set any property you wish.

5. Instantiate the vector variable `xsmall` with elements in the interval [0;2].

6. Calculate the range of the function over this interval.

7. Use the `axes` function to set the position of the inset at 0.4, 0.4 and with size 0.4 and 0.4.

8. Plot the inset and change any property you wish.

9. Print the figure window to a pdf file named `complex.pdf`.

Compare the printed figure with the screen output.

Three-dimensional plotting

Equations (3.4) and (3.5) define two mathematical functions that are more complicated to visualize and plot compared to the simple polynomials in the previous section. Equation (3.4) is a scalar function that depends on two variables. The graph of such a function can be visualized via a surface plot. Equation (3.5) is a vector valued function and can be plotted as a parametric curve in a three-dimensional space. In this section, we shall see how to do this.

Surface plot

Let us start by making a surface plot of the graph of Equation (3.4) in the interval $x \in [-2; 2]$ and $y \in [-2; 2]$. Since we work with discrete points, we need to evaluate the range of f for all different combinations $(x_1 y_1)$, $(x_2 y_1)$,...$(x_n y_n)$. To do this in an easy way in Octave, we generate two mesh grids such that all combinations can be included when we calculate the graph of f.

Time for action – making a surface plot

1. First we define the domain:

   ```
   octave:102> x = [-2:0.1:2]; y = x;
   ```

2. Then we generate the mesh grids:

   ```
   octave:103> [X Y] = meshgrid(x,y);
   ```

3. We can now calculate the range of f for all combinations of x and y values in accordance with Equation (3.4):

   ```
   octave:104> Z = X.^2 - Y.^2;
   ```

4. To make a surface plot of the graph we use:

   ```
   octave:105> surface(X,Y, Z)
   ```

   The result is shown below:

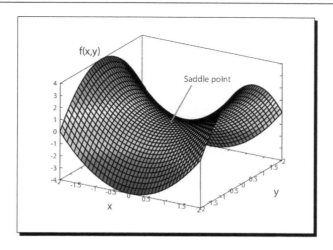

What just happened?

In Command 103, X is simply a matrix, where the rows are copies of x, and Y is a matrix where the columns are copies of the elements in y. From X and Y, we can then calculate the range as done in Command 104. We see that Z is a matrix. Also, notice that surface uses the mesh grids and the resulting Z matrix as inputs.

You can, of course, change the different properties—just like we did for two-dimensional plotting. For example:

```
octave:106> surface(X,Y,Z, "linwidth", 4)
```

```
octave:107> set(gca, "linewidth", 2, "fontsize", 20, "xlim", [-2 2])
```

```
octave:108> set(gca, "xlabel", text("string", "x", "fontsize", 30)
```

```
octave:109> set(gca, "ylabel", text("string", "y", "fontsize", 30)
```

You can also add text strings and lines to your three-dimensional plot:

```
octave:110> text(-3.2, 1, 3, "f(x,y)", "fontsize", 30)
```

```
octave:111> line([0 0], [0 1], [0 2], "linewidth", 5, "color", "red")
```

```
octave:112> text(-0.5, 1.5, 1.8, "Saddle point", "fontsize", 25)
```

Notice that you need to specify three coordinate points to text and line because we work in a three dimensional space. The result is shown above in the previous figure.

view and colormap

You can change the position of the viewer looking at the plot. This is done by the `view` function. The arguments to `view` are the azimuth and elevation angles φ and θ. See the illustration below:

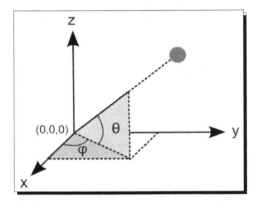

To set the view to $(\varphi, \theta)=(35,30)$, use:

```
octave:113> view(35,30)
```

The result is shown in the surface plot above.

You can change the surface color using `colormap`. Commands 114 and 115 show a few examples of this and with different views:

```
octave:114>colormap("gray"); view(-35, 30);
```

```
octave:115>colormap("summer"); view(0,0);
```

The results are shown below:

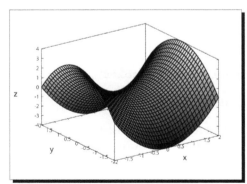
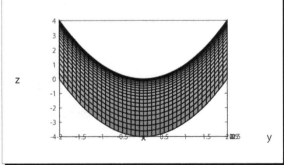

Valid color maps are:

jet (default)	summer	copper
hsv	spring	gray
hot	autumn	bone
cool	winter	pink

You can also use the function `mesh`. This works just like `surface`, except that it does not fill out the mesh grid with a color. Try it out!

Contour plots

It can be difficult to see the fine details in a surface plot. Here contour plots may help. In Octave, you can use one of three functions to do contour plots: `contour`, `contourf`, and `contour3`. They are called like `surface`, for example, `contourf(X,Y,Z)` and `contour3(X,Y,Z)`. You can specify to the functions how many contour levels you want (fourth argument). The default is 10. Also, you can control the properties. Let us see two examples:

```
octave:116>contourf(X,Y,Z, 20);
```

```
octave:117> contour3(X,Y,Z, "linewidth", 6);
```

The results from Commands 116 and 117 are shown below:

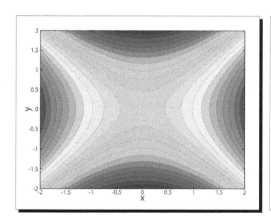 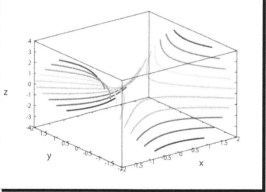

Three-dimensional parametric plots

Finally, let us plot the graph of the function given by Equation (3.5). As mentioned above, this is a parameterized curve in space.

Time for action – plotting parametric curves

1. First, we need to instantiate the variable x, for example:

```
octave:118> x = linspace(0, 10*pi)';
```

2. Then, we calculate the range of *f*:

```
octave:119> f = [cos(x), sin(x), exp(-0.5*x)];
```

3. Just check that we got the right size:

```
octave:120> size(f)

ans =
100    3
```

4. We can now plot the curve using plot3:

```
octave:121> plot3(f(:,1), f(:,2), f(:,3), "linewidth", 4)
```

5. To set the right properties, we can use:

```
octave:122> set(gca, "linewidth", 2, "fontsize", 20);

octave:123> set(gca, "xlabel", text("string", "x","fontsize", 30);

octave:124> set(gca, "ylabel", text("string", "y","fontsize", 30);

octave:125> set(gca, "zlabel", text("string", "z","fontsize", 30);

octave:126> set(gca, "zlim", [0 1.2])

octave:127> text(0.9, -0.25, 0.9, "t=0", "fontsize", 30)

octave:128> view(20,30)
```

Phew! The final figure is shown below:

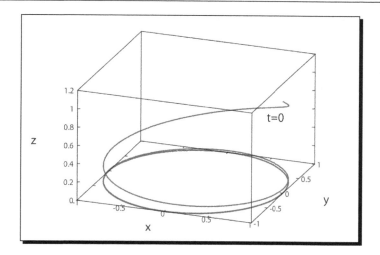

What just happened?

In Command 119, we calculated the range of the interval—notice the transpose operator in Command 118! In Command 120, we checked the size of the variable f and in Command 121, we used plot3 to plot the curve. After that, we just changed the figure properties in order to make it a bit nicer.

Have a go hero – revisiting peaks

Recall Equation (1.1) in *Chapter 1*. Use meshgrid and surface to reproduce the figure that the command peaks creates.

Summary

We learned a lot in this chapter about Octave functions and plotting.

Specifically, we covered:

- ◆ Octave functions in general.
- ◆ Mathematical functions including how polynomials are represented in Octave.
- ◆ Helper functions.
- ◆ Operator functions.
- ◆ How to calculate the range of more complicated mathematical functions.
- ◆ Two dimensional plotting.
- ◆ How to plot several graphs in the same figure window, subplots, and how to navigate between multiple figure windows.

- ◆ Three-dimensional plotting including contour plots
- ◆ How to change the figure and axis properties

In the next chapter, we will see how scripts can be used to execute a sequence of commands so that you do not need to retype the same commands over and over.

4

Rationalizing: Octave Scripts

Often you will need to execute a sequence of commands. Instead of typing these commands directly into Octave's command prompt, you can write them in a text file and then execute that file from the prompt. This enables you to make any necessary changes later and then execute (or run) the file again without having to go through the tedious labour of rewriting every single command. A file composed of a single command or a sequence of commands is referred to as a script file or just a script. In this chapter, you will learn how to write both simple scripts and scripts that include more complicated program flows.

Sometimes it is useful to save your work, that is, to save the variables that contain the main results of your efforts. This chapter will also go through how you can do this in Octave, and show how you can load the variables back into Octave's workspace.

To summarize, in this chapter you will learn:

- ◆ What a script is and how to execute it.
- ◆ How to control the execution of commands in a script using the `if` and `switch` statements.
- ◆ To use `for`, `while`, and `do` statements.
- ◆ Control exception handling.
- ◆ How to save and load your work.
- ◆ About printing text to the screen and how to retrieve inputs from the user.

Writing and executing your first script

We will start with something very simple. In *Chapter 3*, we discussed how to retrieve the minimum value of an array (Commands 20-23). Let us try to do the same thing, but this time using a script.

Time for action – making your first script

1. Start the Octave interactive environment and open the editor:

```
octave:1> edit
```

2. Write the following commands in the editor, but leave out the hash marks (#) and the code line numbers to the right. They are used only for reference:

```
Code Listing 4.1
A = rand(3,5);                                          #1
                                                        #2
min(min(A))                                             #3
```

Downloading the example code

You can download the example code files for all Packt books you have purchased from your account at http://www.PacktPub.com. If you purchased this book elsewhere, you can visit http://www.PacktPub.com/support and register to have the files e-mailed directly to you.

3. Save the file as `script41.m` (notice the extension `.m`) under the current directory or anywhere in the Octave search path directory.

4. Now executing the commands in the script file is done by simply typing:

```
octave:2> script41

ans = 0.1201
```

What just happened?

In Command 1, we opened the editor and we then wrote two Octave commands. When we ask Octave to execute the text file in Command 2, it will execute each command in the file.

Since we did not add a semicolon at the end of line 3 in Code Listing 4.1, the command returns the result in `ans` which is then displayed.

The file extension `.m` is needed for compatibility with MATLAB. However, you do not actually need it in order to execute the script. To ensure that the script is executed no matter what the extension is, you can use `source("file name")`, where `file name` is replaced with the actual name of the file.

Scripts may not begin with the keyword `function` since this makes Octave interpret the file as a function file rather than a script. We will come back to the `function` keyword and its meaning in the next chapter.

Improving your script: input and disp

It is possible to interact with the user. This can be done by using the `input` and `disp` functions. `input` is in general called using:

```
a = input(prompt string, "s")
```

where `prompt string` is a text string and `"s"` is an optional argument that must be included if the input is a string. Following are a few examples using the Octave command prompt as testing ground:

```
octave:3> a = input("Enter a number: ");

Enter a number: 42

octave:4 > a

a = 42

octave:5> s = input("Enter a string: " );

Enter a string: Hello World

error: 'Hello' undefined near line 4 column 1

octave:6> s = input("Enter a string: " , "s");

Enter a string: Hello World

octave:7> ischar(s)

ans = 1
```

Notice that `ischar` returns true (1) if the argument is a character or character array. In Command 5, Octave issues an error because it tries to assign s the value of a variable named `Hello`. In order to specify that s should be assigned the string `Hello World`, we need to include the optional argument `"s"` in the `input` function as shown in Command 6.

`input` can only assign a value to a single variable, and it is not particularly useful to fill large cell arrays or structures. `input` does, however, accept array inputs, for example:

`octave:8> A = input("Enter matrix elements: ")`

`[1 2; 3 4]`

```
A =
   1   2
   3   4
```

You can print text and variable values to the screen using `disp`:

`octave:9> disp("a has the value"), disp(a)`

`a has the value`

`42`

Notice that when given a variable as input, `disp` works as if you had typed the variable name without a trailing semicolon. `disp` can also display structures and cell arrays.

We can use `input` and `disp` to interact with the user of the script.

Time for action – interacting with the user

1. Open a new file and write the following commands in the editor:

```
Code Listing 4.2
nr = input("Enter the number of rows in the matrix: ");     #1
nc = input("Enter the number of columns in the matrix: ");  #2
                                                            #3
A = rand(nr,nc);                                            #4
                                                            #5
minA = min(min(A));                                         #6
                                                            #7
disp("The minimum of A is");                                #8
disp(minA);                                                 #9
```

Save it as `script42.m`.

2. Executing Code Listing 4.2, we get:

```
octave:10>script42

Enter the number of rows in the matrix: 12

Enter the number of columns in the matrix: 20

The minimum of A is

0.00511
```

What just happened?

Code Listing 4.2 allows the user to specify the size of the array (lines 1 and 2). Just like Code Listing 4.1, the script then finds the minimum of the array. The result is printed using the `disp` function.

Flush please

On some systems, the text that you want to print to the screen may be buffered. Basically, this means that the text can sit in a queue and wait to be displayed and can potentially be an annoying problem. To be sure to avoid this, you can flush the buffer before you prompt the user for input. This is done via the command `fflush(stdout)`, where `stdout` is the output buffer (or stream). For example, to ensure that the stdout stream is flushed before `input` is called in Command 3, we use:

```
octave:11> fflush(stdout);

octave:12> a = input("Enter a number: ");

Enter a number: 42
```

Comments

When your script becomes larger and more complicated, it is useful to have comments explaining what the commands do. This is particularly useful if you or any other person will use or make changes to the script later. Any line beginning with a hash mark # or percentage sign % will be ignored by the interpreter, for example:

```
octave:13> a

a = 42

octave:14> # a

octave:15> % a
```

From the above commands, you can see that if you omit the hash mark or percentage characters, Octave prints the value of a (which is 42 as seen by the output from Command 13). Starting the line with # or % simply makes Octave ignore that line.

Let us add a few comments to Code Listing 4.2 above and flush the stdout stream:

```
Code Listing 4.3
# flush the output stream                                       #1
fflush(stdout);                                                 #2
                                                                #3
# Get the number of rows and columns from the user             #4
nr = input("Enter the number of rows in the matrix: ");        #5
nc = input("Enter the number of columns in the matrix: ");     #6
                                                                #7
# Instantiate A and assign the elements random numbers         #8
A = rand(nr,nc);                                                #9
                                                                #10
# Evaluate the minimum value                                    #11
minA = min(min(A));                                             #12
                                                                #13
# Print the result to the screen                                #14
disp("The minimum of A is");                                    #15
disp(minA);                                                     #16
```

I use hash mark when writing comments, but this is not compatible with MATLAB, which uses the percentage sign.

If you want to be able to execute your scripts in MATLAB, use the % character when you write comments.

Very long commands

Sometimes you need to write a very long command. For example, we saw in *Chapter 3* that the function set can be called with many arguments. To break a command into several lines, you can use three full stops (periods) . . . or back slash \. For example, line 5 in Code Listing 4.3 can be broken into two lines by:

```
nr = input("Enter the number of rows ...

        in the matrix: ");
```

or:

```
nr = input("Enter the number of rows \

          in the matrix: ");
```

The backslash is traditionally used in Unix type systems to indicate that the line continues. The three full stops are used for compatibility with MATLAB.

 If you want to be able to execute your scripts in MATLAB use . . . to indicate that the command line continues.

Workspace

Whenever you execute an Octave script from the Octave command prompt, the variable instantiated in the script is stored in the current workspace and is accessible after the script has finished executing. Let us illustrate this with an example:

```
octave:16> clear

octave:17> who

octave:18> script41

ans = 0.62299

octave:19> who

Variables in the current scope:

A ans
```

It is important to keep track of what variables you have instantiated, including variables instantiated in the scripts. Assume that we have happily forgotten that A was instantiated through Command 18 and we now type the following command:

```
octave:20> A(:,1) = [0:10]

error: A(I,J,...) = X: dimension mismatch.
```

Now Octave complains about the dimension mismatch because we cannot change the length of one of the columns in A. Had A not been instantiated previously, this command would be perfectly valid. To avoid this (as well as other problems), I often call `clear` at the beginning of the script. This will clear all variables you have instatiated, so be careful when doing this!

For GNU/Linux and MacOS X users

Under GNU/Linux and MacOS X, you can call an Octave script directly from the shell, so you do not need to start Octave's interactive environment first. To do this we simply need to:

1. Find out where Octave is installed. Typically the executable will be at:`/usr/bin/octave`.

2. Add the following line at the very start of your script file, say `script43.m`:

   `#! /usr/bin/octave -qf`

3. Save the file and exit Octave.

4. Make sure that you are in the directory where the file is saved. At the shell prompt, write:

   `$ chmod u+x script43.m`

   to allow the file to be executed.

5. Now type:

   `$./script43.m`

   You should see the script being executed, just as it would be from the Octave prompt.

Pop Quiz – understanding disp and input

Which of the following commands will issue an error or warning?

a) `disp(32)`   b) `disp(3,2)`   c) `s=input("Enter textstring: ");`
d) `disp("Min.ofA is:",min(A))`   e) `fflush`

Have a go hero – using scripts for plotting

In *Chapter 3*, we plotted a parameterized curve in three dimensions using `plot3`. Use `plot3` inside a script to plot the graph of the following vector valued function:

$$\mathbf{f}(x) = [\cos(x), x, \sqrt{5x}] \tag{P.1}$$

for $x \in [0; 8\pi]$. Make changes to the axes label font size, text, and the line width by editing the script. When you are satisfied with the figure, print it to a file in any format you find appropriate.

Statements

In the previous section, we learned how to write a very simple script and we saw that a script is just a sequence of commands. In this section, you will learn how to use statements in order to control the behaviour of a script. This enables you to code scripts that can perform different and much more complicated tasks.

Prime numbers

We will discuss the different type of statements: if, for, while, and so on by evaluating whether a number is a prime number or not. As you know, a prime number (or just a prime) x is a natural positive number that has exactly two divisors—1 and itself. Adivisor y is a natural positive number larger than 1 such that the division x/y has no remainder. From the definition of a prime, we may write a simple program flow chart as shown below. Notice that if 2 is a divisor, then we need not check for any other even number. The algorithm is of course extremely naïve and there are much more efficient ways of evaluating whether a number is a prime number or not.

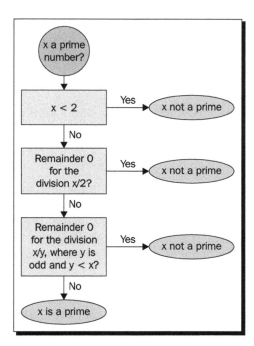

Decision making – the if statement

From the program flow chart, it is seen that we can decide if a number is not a prime by evaluating whether the number is smaller than 2 or if the remainder of the division $x/2$ is zero. To do so in Octave, you can use the `if` and `elseif` statements. In general the syntax is:

```
if condition 1
   do something (body)
elseif condition 2
   do something else (body)
...
else
   do something if no conditions are met (body)
endif
```

If `condition 1` is true (nonzero), the `if` statement body is executed. If `condition 1` is false and `condition 2` is true, the `elseif` body is executed. The `elseif` and `else` statements are optional. Let us illustrate the usage by a small code snippet that checks if the two first conditions in the flow chart are met:

```
if ( x<2 )
   disp("x not a prime");
elseif ( rem(x,2)==0 )
   disp("x not a prime");
else
   disp("x could be a prime number");
endif
```

The `rem` function returns the remainder of $x/2$. It is important to underline that if the first `if` statement body is executed, meaning that if the comparison operation $x < 2$ evaluates to true, the `elseif` and `else` statements are not evaluated. The Octave interpreter simply jumps to the line after the `endif` statement. Likewise, if `rem(x,2)==0` is true, the `else` statement is not executed. This happens only if both the conditions to `if` and `elseif` are false.

You can have statements in Octave's command prompt as well. It is always a good idea to do simple tests here. To actually see what the code snippet above does, we use:

```
octave:21> x=9;

octave:22> if ( x<2 )

>disp("x not a prime");
```

```
>elseif ( rem(x,2)==0 )

>disp("x not a prime");

>else

>disp("x could be a prime number");

>endif

x could be a prime number
```

but it is not. If you have made a coding error or typo anywhere, Octave will tell you so.

 If the condition is an array, the `if` and `elseif` statement body is only executed if all elements in the array are true.

Interlude: Boolean operators

In the code snippet above, we wrote two lines that were identical. Every line of code is error-prone and repeating code should be avoided if possible unless there is a particular reason not to. Octave provides you with a set of so-called Boolean operators (the third type of operator that you will learn in this book). They enable you to include several comparisons within a single statement such that you can avoid repeating code.

Octave's Boolean operators are divided into element-wise and short-circuit operators.

Element-wise Boolean operators

There are three element-wise Boolean operators, namely, `&`, `|`, and `!`. Perhaps it is easiest to discuss how they are used through a couple of examples from the Octave prompt:

```
octave:23> A=eye(2); B=[1 2;3 4];

octave:24> A==eye(2) & B==eye(2)

ans =
   1   0
   0   0
```

Command 23 is trivial. In Command 24, we use the & operator between two Booleans given via the comparison operators A==eye(2) (left Boolean) and B==eye(2) (right Boolean). Recall from *Chapter 2* that the comparison operators == evaluates to Boolean types. Now, the left Boolean is a 2 x 2 matrix where all the elements are true because == compares element-wise and evaluates to true for all matrix elements. For the same reason, the right Boolean gives a 2 x 2 matrix where all the elements have value false except for the element at row 1 column 1. The & operator then simply evaluates if the elements in the left Boolean and the right Boolean are both true. If so, the result of the Boolean operation is true. This is illustrated in the below figure. Note if both values are false, the & operator evaluates to false:

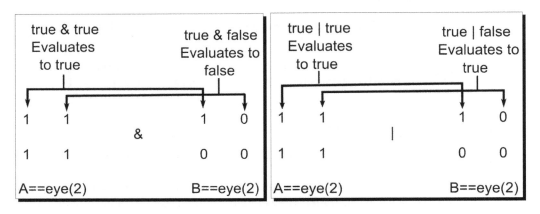

Unlike the & operator, the | operator evaluates to true if the left Boolean is true or if the right Boolean is true. For example:

```
octave:25> A==eye(2) | B=eye(2)

ans =

   1   1
   1   1
```

since A is simply equal to eye(2).

The Boolean operator ! negates. This means that if a Boolean a is true, !a is false. For example, since A is the 2 x 2 identity matrix, it can be thought of as a Boolean, where the diagonal components have values true and off-diagonal components have value false. The negation of A is:

```
octave:26> !A

ans =

   0   1
   1   0
```

Boolean operators have lower precedence than comparison operators.

Short-circuit Boolean operators

The & and | operators go through the Booleans element-wise, meaning that the operator evaluates the Boolean value for all pairs in the variables. Sometimes you may just want to know if, say A is equal to `eye(2)` and if B is equal to `eye(2)`, without caring about the individual elements. For this purpose you can use short-circuit Boolean operator &&

```
octave:27> A==eye(2) && B==eye(2)

ans = 0
```

This tells you that this is not the case. Likewise we can use the the short-circuit operator || to check if A or B is equal to `eye(2)`:

```
octave:28> A==eye(2) || B==eye(2)

ans = 1
```

This is because when A was instantiated, it was set to `eye(2)`.

The table below summarizes the output from the Boolean operators &, &&, | and ||:

Operators	Boolean 1	Boolean 2	Result
& and &&	true	true	true
	true	false	false
	false	false	false
| and ||	true	true	true
	true	false	true
	false	false	false

The Boolean operators are commutative; such that true& false is equivalent to false & true.

Using Boolean operators with an if statement

Instead of using the `if` and `elseif` statement construction in the previous code snippet, we can now apply both conditions to the same `if` statement:

```
if ( x<2 | rem(x,2)==0 )
  disp("x is not a prime");
else
  disp("x could be a prime");
endif
```

If x is, for example, 2, then the comparison operation x<2 evaluates to false and rem(x,2)==0 evaluates to true, so the | Boolean operator evaluates to true according to the table and the condition in the if statement is met. On the other hand, if x is 9, then the comparison operationsx<2 and rem(x,2)==0 evaluate to false and the if statement body is not executed. In this example, you could also use the short-circuit Boolean operator || because x is a simple scalar.

Nested statements

Like other programming languages, you can have if statement constructions within an if, elseif, or else statement. For example:

```
if ( x<2 | rem(x,2)==0 )
  disp("x is not a prime");
else
  if ( x>3 & rem(x,3)==0 )
    disp("x not a prime");
  else
    disp("x could be a prime");
  endif
endif
```

The switch statement

Some programmers prefer to use the switch statement construction over if statements. This is often possible and can help to significantly improve the readability of the code. The general syntax is:

```
switch option
case option
  do something (body)
case option
  do something else (body)
...
otherwise
  do something default (body)
endswitch
```

The use of the switch statement can be illustrated by rewriting the previous code snippet:

```
switch ( x<2 | rem(x,2)== 0 )
  case 1
    disp("x not a prime");
```

```
   otherwise
      disp("x could be a prime");
   endswitch
```

It should be clear what the program flow is.

Loops

From the program flow chart shown above, it can be seen that we need to calculate the remainder of the division x/y for all values of y that are smaller than x, so if x is large, we need to call rem many times. In Octave, we can do so using the for, while, or do statements.

The for statement

The syntax is simple:

```
for condition
   do something (body)
endfor
```

The for statement and the corresponding endforconstruct a so-called for-loop. A for-loop is executed as long as condition is true. Let us see a code snippet:

```
for y=3:x-1
   if ( rem(x, y)==0 )
      disp("x not a prime");
   endif
endfor
```

The first time Octave executes the for loop, y is set to 3 before the rest of the loop is executed. The second time, y is set to 4, and so on. We say that y is incremented with 1. When y equals x, the condition is not met because y runs from 3 to and including $x-1$, as specified in line 1 and the loop stops executing.

From our definition of prime numbers, we know that we need not calculate the remainder of all the even numbers. We can skip the even numbers by letting y have the values 3, 5, 7, and so on. This is done by starting at $y=3$ and then incrementing y by 2, which is done by replacing line 1 in the code snippet with the following:

```
for y=3:2:x-1
```

In this way, we carry out only half the computations.

Also, in the code snippet above, the remainder is calculated for all y<x, even though we know that if it equals 0 for just one single y, x is not a prime. It would therefore be convenient to break out of the loop whenever this condition is met—not only do we decrease the number of computations, but we also get rid of a text string repeatedly telling us that x is not a prime. To this end, Octave has a break command (or keyword) which will make Octave to break out of the loop, but continue executing any code after the loop. The updated version of the code is:

```
for y=3:2:x-1
   if ( rem(x,y)==0 )
      disp("x is not a prime");
      break;
   endif
endfor
```

Instead of breaking out of a loop if some condition is met, you may want the loop to continue. You can tell Octave to continue looping via the continue keyword. In a moment, you will also see that this keyword should be used with some care.

The while and do statements

As an alternative to for loops, you can use while and do statements. The syntax for the while construction is:

```
while condition
   do something (body)
endwhile
```

The reimplementation of the code snippet above is straight forward:

```
y=3;
while y < x
   if ( rem(x,y)==0 )
      disp("x is not a prime");
      break;
   endif
   y = y + 2;
endwhile
```

In line 1, we initialise the value of y to 3 before we enter the while loop. Code lines 3-6 check if x is not a prime, and in line 7, y is incremented with 2.

Note that break can also be used to break out of a while loop.

Instead of ending the statement bodies with `endif`, `endfor`, and so forth, you can simply use `end`. This is compatible with MATLAB's syntax.

We could perhaps be tempted to use the `continue` keyword instead, for example:

```
(Leads to an infinite loop)

y=3;
while y<x
   if ( rem(x,y)!=0 )
      continue;
   else
      disp("x is not a prime");
   endif
   y = y + 2;
endwhile
```

However, this leads to an infinite loop because `continue` will make the interpreter skip all the commands inside the loop body including the line `y = y + 2`, meaning that `y` is never incremented and the comparison operation `y<x` is always true.

You can force Octave to execute a loop once and then continue that loop if a certain condition is met. The syntax is:

```
do

   something (body)

until condition
```

Again, the code snippet can be changed to illustrate this construction:

```
y=3;
do
   if ( rem(x,y)==0 )
      disp("x is not a prime");
      break;
   endif
   y = y + 2;
until y>=x
```

Note that we have to use the comparison `y>=x` (and not `y<x`) here.

Incremental operators

In the previous three code snippets, the variable y is incremented. Octave supports the C style incremental and decremental operators (which is the last operation type in this book). For example, to increment a variable y with 1, we can use `y += 1` or `y++` which are both equivalent to $y = y+1$. In general you can increment y by any number, x, using `y += x`. To decrement, we simply use `y--` or in general `y-= x`.

Since Octave is a vectorized programming language, the incremental operators also work on multidimensional arrays, incrementing element-wise.

Strictly speaking, the incremental operation y++ will return the old value of y before incrementing it. For example:

```
octave:29> y=0; y++

ans = 0

octave: 30> y

ans = 1
```

Therefore, be aware of any side effects when you use Boolean operators. Take for example the two commands:

```
octave:31> x=0; y=0; a=(x++ & y++)

ans  =  0
```

and

```
octave:32> x=0; y=0; a=(y++ & x++)

ans  =  0
```

After the Command 31 $x=1$ and $y=0$, but after the Command 32 $y=1$ and $x=0$. This is because the incremental operation $x++$ increment x with one but returns the old value 0. This means that the left Boolean is false, hence the Boolean `x++ &y++` is false no matter what `y++` evaluates to according to the table above. `y++` is therefore not evaluated. The same argument holds for Command 32.

Nested loops

Like the `if` statement, you can have nested loops. For example, if you wish to sum up all elements in a matrix variable `A` with `nr` rows and `nc` columns, you can use the code snippet:

```
sum=0;
for n=1:nr
  for m=1:nc
    sum += A(n,m);
  endfor
endfor
```

I strongly recommend that you use the function sum (*Chapter 3*) to compute the sum of an array because this function executes much quicker than the nested loop construction above.

 If you use nested loops, break will break out of the inner-most loop.

Putting it all together

In the previous sections, we learned how to control program flow using different statements. In this section, we will put the code snippets together and make a script that follows the programming flow chart for computing whether a number is a prime or not. In the last part of this section, we will expand the code and make the necessary changes to the script such that it can calculate an entire sequence of primes.

The approach that we will use here (and there are quite a few different ones) is to assume that the number x entered by the user is a prime. This is done by setting a Boolean variable is_x_prime to true. The script then checks this assumption using the if and for statements discussed above and if it is found that x is not a prime, the script will set is_x_prime to false and break out of the for-loop. At the end, the script then writes whether x is a prime or not depending on the value of is_x_prime:

Code Listing 4.4

```
## Script that evaluates whether a number is a prime or not   #1
                                                               #2
# Retrieve input                                              #3
fflush(stdout);                                               #4
x = input("Enter a number: " );                               #5
                                                               #6
# Assume x is a prime                                         #7
is_x_prime = 1;                                               #8
                                                               #8
# Go through the steps in the programming flow chart          #10
# Based on the code snippets in the text                      #11
if ( x!=2 & (x<2 | rem(x,2)==0) )                             #12
  is_x_prime = 0;                                             #13
else                                                          #14
  for y=3:2:x-1                                               #15
```

```
    if ( rem(x,y)==0 )                                    #16
      is_x_prime = 0;                                     #17
      break;                                              #18
    endif                                                 #19
  endfor                                                  #20
endif                                                     #21
                                                          #22
if ( is_x_prime )                                         #23
  disp("x is a prime");                                   #24
else                                                      #25
  disp("x is not a prime");                               #26
endif                                                     #27
```

Line 12 needs some explanation. If we had used the code snippet from above:

```
x<2 | rem(x,2)==0
```

directly, the number 2 would have been evaluated as not being a prime. By using the & Boolean operator, we exclude this special case. Had we not included the parenthesis, Octave would have evaluated the line from left to right, or equivalently as:

```
(x!=2 & x<2) | rem(x,2)==0
```

which evaluates to false | true, which in turn gives true according to the above Boolean table. If the condition is true, the body of the if statement is executed telling you that 2 is not a prime. The parenthesis force Octave to first evaluate (x<2 | rem(x,2)==0) giving true and since false & true yields false, the if statement body is not executed.

Let us test the script. Save the file as script44.m, for example, and execute it at the Octave prompt:

```
octave:33> script44

Enter a number: 2

x is a prime

octave:34> script44

Enter a number: 109221

x is not a prime

octave:35> script44

Enter a number: 109211

x is a prime
```

I bet you did not know that! As mentioned earlier, Octave has a true arsenal of helpful functionalities, so it also has its own built-in function, `isprime`, that can tell you if a number is a prime or not. Check if your script agrees with Octave's function and notice the difference in execution speed for large input values.

If you want to calculate a whole sequence of primes, then it is not practical to use the script from Code Listing 4.4. However, we can easily modify it to meet our needs. The strategy is the same, but instead of prompting the user for a specific number, she will have to enter the number of primes she wants to retrieve starting from 2. The primes are stored in the array `prime_sequence`:

Code Listing 4.5

```
## Script that calculates a sequence of primes          #1
                                                        #2
# Clear the prime array                                 #3
clear prime_sequence;                                   #4
                                                        #5
# Retrieve user input                                   #6
fflush(stdout);                                         #7
nprimes = input("Enter number of primes (>0): ");       #8
                                                        #9
# Initializing x to 2 - gets rid of a comparison        #10
# operation inside the loop                             #11
x = 2;                                                  #12
                                                        #13
# Initialize counter to 1 since 2 is a prime            #14
prime_counter = 1;                                      #15
prime_sequence(prime_counter) = x;                      #16
                                                        #17
while prime_counter<nprimes                             #18
  # Assume x is a prime number                          #19
  is_x_prime = 1;                                       #20
                                                        #21
  # if the remainder of x/2 or x/y for y<x is zero then #22
  #x is not a prime.                                    #23
  if ( rem(x,2)==0 )                                    #24
    is_x_prime = 0;                                     #25
  else                                                  #26
    for y=3:2:x-1                                       #27
      if ( rem(x,y)==0 )                                #28
        is_x_prime = 0;                                 #29
        break;                                          #30
      endif                                             #31
    endfor                                              #32
```

```
    endif                                                         #33
                                                                  #34
    # if is_x_prime is true (1) then save the value of            #35
    # x in an array                                               #36
    if ( is_x_prime )                                             #37
      prime_counter++;                                            #38
      prime_sequence(prime_counter) = x;                          #39
    endif                                                         #40
                                                                  #41
    x++;                                                          #42
  endwhile                                                        #43
```

It should be clear how the program flows. However, two points should be made:

◆ Since we need not allocate memory in advance, the length of the array `prime_sequence` increases as the script finds more and more prime numbers (line 39).

◆ Also, we can clear `prime_sequence` in line 4 even if it is not instantiated, which is the situation the first time we execute the script.

Now, save the script as `script45.m` and execute it:

```
octave:36> script45

Enter number of primes (>0): 10

octave:37> prime_sequence

prime_sequence

   2    3    5    7    11    13    17    19    23    29
```

Try to increase the number of primes in the sequence, say enter 20, 100, and 1000. Notice how long it takes to compute the primes as you increase the length of the sequence. According to the World Wide Web, the largest prime computed is today (August 2010) $2^{243112609}-1$, so you probably do not want enter the competition using Code Listing 4.5! Computing the first 1000 prime numbers using Code Listing 4.5 took my computer 213.64 seconds. Octave's own function `primes` could do the same in 0.02 seconds—a speedup of around a 10^6 %[1].

Exception handling

In the situation where an error occurs in a script, Octave will print an error message and normally (that is, hopefully) return to the command prompt. The values of the variables will then be whatever they were assigned before the error occurred.

---

[1]Note that the input to `primes` *is not the number of primes you want to find!*

With the `try` and `unwind_protect` statements, you can force Octave to execute commands in a script even after an error has occurred. The general syntaxes are:

```
try
    something (body)
catch
    cleanup if an error has occurred (body)
end_try_catch
```

and

```
unwind_protect
    do something (body)
unwind_protect_cleanup
    cleanup whether an error has occurred or not (body)
end_unwind_protect
```

As you can see, the difference between the two constructions is that the `try-catch` only executes the body after `catch` if the body in `try` produces an error, whereas the `unwind_protect-unwind_protect_cleanup` construction always executes the cleanup part. If an error occurs outside the construction, the cleanup part will of course not be executed.

In Code Listing 4.4, we store the user input in a variable x. Assume that you use the script as a part of a larger project where x stores a value of something important that you wish to keep. Of course, you could rename x in `script44.m` to something different, but you can also use the `unwind_project_cleanup` statement as seen in the following code snippet:

```
# Stores the original value of x
original_x = x;
unwind_project
    fflush(stdout)
    x = input("Enter a number: " );
    ..# As in Code Listing 4.4
unwind_protect_cleanup
    disp("Recovering the original value of x");
    x = original_x;
end_unwind_protect
```

After executing the script, x will always be assigned the original value even if an error occurs in the body of the `unwind_project`. For example, if we deliberately make an error by giving a string input rather than a number, then the following error message will occur:

```
octave:38>x.a = 1.0; x.b = "Hello World";

octave:39> x

x=

{

a   =  1

b   = Hello World

}

octave:40>script46

Enter a number (>0): Hello World

error: evaluating assignment near line...

Recovering the original value of x

octave:41> x

x=

{

a   =  1

b   = Hello World

}
```

In this particular example, x is never assigned a new value because `input` fails, but you can see, the interpreter enters the body of the `unwind_protect_cleanup` statement.

Pop Quiz – understanding statements and Boolean operators

1. Which of the following Boolean operations return true?

   a) true | false   b) true & false   c) true && false
   d) false & false   e) (true | false) & false   f) true | (false & false)
   g) 1 | 0

2. What text is printed to the screen if the following code snippet is executed?

```
for n=1:3
  for m=1:2:5
    printf("%d %d", n, m);
      if ( m==2 )
        break;
      endif
    endfor
endfor
```

3. What is wrong with the following code (find at least three mistakes)?

```
for n=1:10
  m=1;
  while m<=10
    printf("n is %d, m is %d \n", m, n);
  endfor
endwhile
```

4. What is wrong with the following code (find at least three mistakes)?

```
s=input("Enter a text string: ");

if ( s=="Hi" )
  disp("You entered Hi");
elseif
  disp("You did not enter Hi");
end
```

Added flexibility – C style input and output functions

The function disp is easy to use. However, it has limitations. For example, we can display only a single variable with disp and it always prints a newline character after displaying the variable value

Octave has implemented most of the very flexible input and output functionality that you may know from C. If not, do not worry, we will go through the most important one here, namely the printf function. Functions that can write and read to and from files, such as fprintf, fgets, and fscanf, are also supported in Octave: if you want to know more about these functions, I strongly recommend you to look in the Octave manual.

printf

`printf` is an acronym for print formatted text. The general syntax is:

`printf(template, ...)`

Here, template is a text string and can also include text format specifiers and/or escape sequences. The `...` indicates optional arguments. For example:

```
octave:42>for n=1:5

>printf("n is %d\n", n);

>endfor

n is 1

n is 2

n is 3

n is 4

n is 5
```

Here the template includes a text `n is`, a format specifier `%d`, and the escape sequence `\n`. `%d` instructs `printf` to print the value of n as an integer and the sequence `\n` means new line. Since we specify a format, there must be an argument with a value to print. This is given by the value of `n`. The commonly used format specifiers and escape sequences are listed in the below table:

Format specifiers		Escape sequence	
%d	Integer format	\n	Newline
%f	Floating point format	\t	Horizontal tab
%e or %E	Scientific floating point format	\b	Backspace
%c	Character format	\r	Carriage return
%s	String format		

Try to change the format specifier and escape sequence characters. For example:

```
octave:43> for n=1:5

>printf("n is %f \t", n);

>endfor

n is 1.0000   n is 2.0000   n is 3.0000   n is 4.0000   n is 5.0000
```

When we calculated the first 1000 primes, it took some time and it would be nice to somehow know how far in the computation the script has come. The below code listing shows an example of how we can extend Code Listing 4.5 such that the script prints a message whenever it finds a prime:

```
While prime_counter<nprimes
...
  if ( is_x_prime )
    prime_counter++;
    prime_sequence(prime_counter) = x;
    printf("\r");
    printf("Found prime: %d - %d to go  ", \
       x, nprimes-prime_counter);
    fflush(stdout);
  endif

    x++;
endwhile
printf("\n");
```

The following points should be made: in the first call to printf we just print an escape character, \r, which means that the next output will be printed at the beginning of the line. In the second call to printf, we perform a computation inside the optional argument list. This is perfectly legal since, as we know, these operations are performed before calling the function[2]. Finally, we must flush stdout in order to ensure that the template is actually printed to the screen when we call printf. Try to comment out the fflush(stdout) command and see how the script behaves. You may not see any difference!

Pop Quiz – printing with printf

What is printed to the screen if the following commands are executed?

a) printf("Hello World\r");

b) printf("Hello World\b \n");

c) printf("Hello World\b \t\n");

d) printf("%d\n", 2);

e) printf("%f\n", 2);

f) printf("%e\n", 2);

---

[2]*As discussed above, incremental operators have side effects, so they should always be used with care.*

Saving your work

If you use `script45.m` to compute a very long sequence of primes, it would probably be a good idea to save the variable `prime_sequence` to avoid calculating the sequence again. Saving variables in Octave is easy. Simply use:

```
octave:44> save primes.mat prime_sequence
```

to save `prime_sequence` in a file called `primes.mat`. If you want to save more than one variable, you just write all the variable names after the file name. The general syntax is:

```
save -option1 -option2 filename variable1 variable2 ...
```

where `-option1 -option2` specifies the file format, `filename` is the name of the file (for example, `primes.mat` in Command 44) and `variable1 variable2 ...` is the list of variables that you wish to save. You can use wildcards to save all variables with a specific pattern, for example, if `variable1` is given as `primes*`, all variables with prefix `primes` will be saved. If you do not specify any variables, all variables in the current workspace are saved.

 In Command 44, I have used the extension `.mat`, but you can use any filename you wish with or without the file extension.

From your editor, try to open the file `primes.mat`. You will see something like this:

```
# Created by Octave 3.2.4, Sun Aug 29 12:30:20 2010 ...
# name: prime_sequence
# type: matrix
# rows: 1
# columns: 1385
 2 3 5 7 11 13 17 19 23 29 31 37 41 43 47 53 59 61 67 71 73 79 83 89
...
```

Here you can see that Octave has added five lines beginning with a hash mark, #. This is referred to as the heading. Here various information is stored, like who created the file (in the case Octave, it could also be a username) and the name of the variable. If you load the file into Octave's workspace, the interpreter will go through the heading and create a variable called `prime_sequence` (overwriting any existing one) with the rows, columns, and values listed. Of course, the heading and therefore the file cannot be read by other programs unless they are specially designed to do so. If you save more than one variable, a header will be written for each one.

You can tell Octave to change the output format such that it can be read by other programs. This is specified via the options listed below.

Option	Description
-text	Saves the variables in readable text format with information about the variables (names, dimensions, and so on.) Also, Octave prints a small file header about who created the file and when. This option is set as default.
-ascii	Saves the variables in ASCII format. This format will not include variable information. This is not recommended if you save more than one variable and wish to load them into Octave at a later stage. This is useful when data is read by other programs.
-binary	Saves the variables in Octave's own binary format. This could speed up things.
-hdf5	Portable binary format.
-vx or –Vx	Saves the variables in MATLAB format. Currently, x can have values 4, 6, or 7 and indicates the MATLAB version number.
-zip or -z	Compressed output format (for saving hard disk space). This option can be used together with any format option above.

For example, to save `primes_sequence` in simple ascii format, use:

```
octave:45> save -ascii primes.dat prime_sequence
```

Take a look at the output file. You can, of course, type `help save` to see all the available options.

Loading your work

Let us see how one can load the variable(s) stored in a file. First, we clear the workspace to be sure that we actually load the variable `prime_sequence` stored in the file `primes.mat`:

```
octave:46> clear; whos

octave:47> load primes.mat

octave:48> whos

Variables in the current scope:

Attr     Name                 size           Bytes    Class

====     ====                 ====           =====    =====

prime_sequence               1x1385         11080    double
```

Notice that Octave treats the numbers as doubles, since we have not explicitly told it otherwise.

The general syntax for `load` is:

```
load -option1 -option2 filename
```

where the options are the same as above for the `save` command. For example, to load the data stored in the ascii file `primes.dat`, we can use:

octave:49> load -ascii primes.dat

octave:50> whos

Variables in the current scope:

Attr	Name	size	Bytes	Class
====	====	====	=====	=====
	prime_sequence	1x1385	11080	double
	primes	1x1385	11080	double

Notice that when loading an ascii file like we did in Command 49, Octave will create a variable called `primes` that contains the prime sequence. It is infortunate that we chose to load data into a variable called `prime in this example`, since this stops you from using the built-in function of the same name.

In general, if the file does not contain a heading, Octave will create a variable having the name of the data file, excluding the extension, overwriting any existing variable or function with that name.

Functional forms

To avoid the problem of overwriting existing variables and function names, you can use the functional form of `load`. For example, to load data stored in an ASCII file named `primes.dat` into a variable, say `prime_sequence` you can use:

octave:51>prime_sequence = load("primes.dat", "ascii");

This will also work if you have saved the data in other formats, if and only if the data file contains a single simple variable and not a structure or cell array. I therefore recommend that you use the default text format when you save and load your data files, unless there is a specific reason not to.

`save` also has a corresponding functional form, for example, Command 40 could be replaced with:

octave:40> save("prime.mat", "prime_sequence");

Have a go hero – investigating the prime gab

In this exercise, we will analyse the prime sequence a bit. The so-called prime gap g_n is defined as the difference between a prime p_n and the next one p_{n+1}, that is:

$$g_n = p_{n+1} - p_n \tag{P.2}$$

1. Use `script45.m` to calculate the first 1000 primes.
2. Save the prime sequence in a file named `primes_1000.mat`.
3. Write a script that loads the prime sequence and calculates the prime gap using a for loop.
4. Plot the first 100 prime gaps.
5. Optional: Instead of using a for-loop you can use Octave's `diff` function. Check out `diff`'s help text and replace the for-loop with `diff`.

Summary

In this chapter, we have learned how to:

- Write a simple script and execute it.
- Use the control statements `if` and `switch`.
- Use `for`, `while`, and `do` statements.
- Perform exception handling with the `unwind_protect` and `try` statements.
- Put everything together in order to write a script with complicated program flow.
- Save and load our work using the `save` and `load` commands.
- Use the `printf` function.

In the next chapter you will use the statements learned here when you code your own Octave functions.

Extensions: Write Your Own Octave Functions

In this chapter, you will learn how to write your own Octave functions. This will not only enable you to utilize more of Octave's built-in functionality, it also makes it possible to extend Octave to do pretty much anything you want it to in a highly reusable and modular manner.

After reading this chapter, you will be able to:

- ◆ Write your own Octave functions.
- ◆ Check and validate user inputs to the functions.
- ◆ Write function help text.
- ◆ Define mathematical functions that can be used by Octave to solve different numerical problems.
- ◆ Perform simple debugging of your functions.
- ◆ Vectorize your code.

Your first Octave function

In general, the syntax for a function is:

```
function [output1, output2, ...] = functionname(input1,input2,...)
   do something (body)
endfunction
```

where `output1`, `output2`, ... are the output variables generated by the function and `input1`, `input2`, ... are inputs to the function and are also referred to as input arguments. The function has a name specified by `functioname`. The commas separating the outputs are optional. Both output and input arguments are optional and can be scalars, matrices, cell arrays, text strings, and so forth.

Let us first discuss a simple example. Our first function will perform a simple task; it will evaluate the minimum and maximum values of a vector array. We design the function such that the user enters an array and the function then returns the minimum and maximum values. Recall that the maximum and minimum values of an array can be obtained through the Octave functions `max` and `min`.

Time for action – programming the minmax function

1. Open your text editor and write the following code

```
Code Listing 5.1
function [minx, maxx] = minmax(x)                          #1
                                                           #2
  maxx = max(x);                                           #3
  minx = min(x);                                           #4
                                                           #5
endfunction                                                #6
```

2. Save the code as `minmax.m` under the current directory or anywhere in the Octave search path.

3. To execute the function type the following commands at the Octave command prompt:

```
octave:1> a = rand(1, 5)

a =

   0.573584    0.588720    0.112184    0.052960    0.555401

octave:2> [mina, maxa] = minmax(a)

mina = 0.052960

maxa = 0.588720
```

as we would expect.

What just happened?

From line 1 in Code Listing 5.1, we see that the function name is `minmax`, the function takes the input `x`, and returns two outputs `minx` and `maxx`. It should be clear what code lines 3 and 4 do. The `endfunction` keyword ends the function body. We will adopt the C term "function definition" to refer to the function code, so Code Listing 5.1 is the function definition of `minmax`.

 Instead of `endfunction`, you can use `end` for compatibility with MATLAB.

In Command 1, we instantiated a random vector array, `a`, with 5 elements. We then used `a` as input to the function in Command 2. It is important to understand that when we do this, Octave copies the values stored in `a` into the array `x` which is instantiated inside the function (line 1 in Code Listing 5.1). Octave then performs the commands given in lines 3 and 4 in the code listing. When Octave returns from the function to the command prompt, it copies the values stored in the variables `minx` and `maxx` to `mina` and `maxa`, respectively. See the diagram below. In this way, Octave instantiates local copies of the inputs and outputs. We say that Octave functions follow a "call-by-value" strategy.

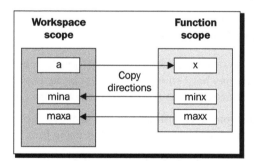

Another very important point is that the variables instantiated inside the function body (for example `maxx` and `minx`) are not a part of the workspace. In general, the variables instantiated inside the function scope are hidden from the calling scope. Let us check that:

```
octave:3> who

Variables in the current scope:

a    maxa    mina
```

These variables are instantiated in Commands 1 and 2 and are a part of the workspace scope. The variables instantiated inside the function `minmax` are not visible. In fact, after we return from the function, we have lost any chance to retrieve the values from the function scope.

In *Chapter 2*, we learned about the function `setfield`; see Command 40. When we called this function, we had to use the structure variable `s` as both input and output. We can now understand why; setting the structure field inside the function scope will not affect the structure field's value in the workspace scope. We therefore have to copy the structure back to the workspace after setting the field inside `setfield`.

The filename must be the same as the function name, for example, `minmax`, and must have the extension `.m`. In the case where the function name and the filename do not match, Octave may try to execute the function defined in the file, but it will issue a warning.

 A function filename must be the same as the function name that it defines and have the postfix `.m`. A function file must start with the `function` keyword.

Scripts versus functions

For this particular simple example, you may as well have used a script. However, there are at least three reasons to make functions rather than scripts:

1. If you try to solve a complex problem, your script often becomes very large and the program flow becomes hard to follow. Here it can be useful to break the script up into one or more functions that are called from a script composed of just a few lines.

2. In large scripts you may accidentally use the same variable names for different things. This is error prone and can be avoided using functions.

3. Your functions may be reused to solve other problems, so you need not copy parts of one script into another. Not only is this more work, it is also error prone to copy code from script to script.

Defining functions at the command prompt

You can define functions directly from the command prompt. For example:

```
octave:4> function [minx, maxx] = minmax(x)

>minx = min(x);

>maxx = max(x);

>endfunction
```

The same function scope rules apply, meaning that `minx` and `maxx` are still not a part of the workspace even though the function is defined via the command prompt. Unless you are testing a function or you only need a small one time helper function, I recommend that you define functions through a function file because it is then easily edited and recycled later. A function defined from the prompt is, of course, deleted when you exit Octave.

Writing a function help text

It is always useful to have help text (or documentation) describing the usage and purpose of a function. For example, if you type `help plot`, Octave will print a help text describing the purpose and usage of `plot`.

It is straightforward to write help text. Octave interprets the first comment section in a function file as the help text, that is, the first lines that begin with a hash mark, `#`, or percentage sign, `%`. In the code listing below, it is shown how such help text can be created for the `minmax` function:

```
Code Listing 5.2
#                                                         #1
# Usage:                                                  #2
#   [minx, maxx] = minmax(x)                              #3
#                                                         #4
# Returns the minimum and maximum values of a vector      #5
# array x                                                 #6
#                                                         #7
                                                          #8
function [minx, maxx] = minmax(x)                         #9
                                                          #10
# Using the Octave build-in max and min functions        #11
  maxx = max(x);                                          #12
  minx = min(x);                                          #13
                                                          #14
endfunction                                               #15
```

This will produce the help text:

```
octave:5> help minmax

usage:

[minx, maxx] = minmax(x)

Returns the minimum and maximum values of a vector

array x
```

Note that in line 11, we have made a comment line which is not printed as a help text. Octave only uses the first continuous comment section as a help text. This means that if we leave out the help text in lines 1-7, the comment line is printed as help. It also means that you can put the help text anywhere in the function file as long as it is placed before any comments.

To save space, I will write no or very limited help texts, but you can add as much as you wish including version number, license, copyrights, authors, and much more. Depending on your settings (see *Chapter 1*), the editor may write a default heading with this information when you open a new file.

Checking the function call

Octave functions should be able to handle many different user inputs. For example, what if the user enters a string or a matrix array as input to minimax? Or what if she assigns the output to three variables instead of two? Let us see what happens when we do that:

```
octave:6> [mina maxa] = minmax("Hello World")

error: max: wrong type argument 'string'

error:...

octave:7> [mina maxa] = minmax([1 2; 3 4])

mina =

   1      2

maxa =

   1      4

octave:8> [a b c] = minmax([1 2 3 4])

mina = 1

maxa = 4

error: element number 3 undefined in return list
```

In Command 6, minmax is called with a string input argument. This string is passed to max (line 12 in Code Listing 5.2), which then issues an error. It would be desirable to catch this error before calling max, because the user could easily be confused if she gets an error message from max and not from minmax, which is the function she called.

In Command 7, `minmax` is called with a matrix input. Even though the function is not intended to be able to handle matrix arrays, the function returns the minimum and maximum values of each column in the matrix. This is of course due to the fact that `max` and `min` work in a column-wise manner as discussed in *Chapter 3*. Nevertheless, since `minmax` was originally designed to work on vector arrays only, we need to handle matrix input somehow.

Finally, we receive a generic error message if we call `minmax` with three or more output variables. We should present an informative error message to the user if the function is not called with the correct number of input and output arguments.

The usage, warning, and error functions

In Octave, you can print usage and warning messages to the user through the functions of the same name: `usage` and `warning`. In their simplest form, they print a text message to the user with the prefix `usage:` and `warning:` The difference between `usage` and `warning` is that `usage` forces the interpreter to exit the function after printing the usage message, but `warning` will continue to execute the commands in the function body after the message has been printed.

We can easily check if the input to `minmax` is a matrix array or a character array and apply `usage` and `warning` to print appropriate messages to the user:

```
Code Listing 5.3
function [minx, maxx] = minmax(x)                              #1
                                                               #2
  [nr nc] = size(x);                                           #3
  if ( nr>1 &nc>1 )                                            #4
    warning("Input to minmax is a matrix array: \              #5
    output will be vectors");                                  #6
  elseif ( ischar(x) )                                         #7
    usage("Input to minmax cannot be a character array");      #8
  endif                                                        #9
                                                               #10
  maxx = max(x);                                               #11
  minx = min(x);                                               #12
                                                               #13
endfunction                                                    #14
```

In line 3, we use the built-in function `size` to obtain the number of rows and columns in the input variable. If both are larger than 1, the variable is a matrix array. Now, since the function actually works with matrices, we will just warn the user that the output will be vector arrays rather than scalars.

You should only use `warning` if the function will execute properly after the message.

If the input is a character array, the message `usage: Input cannot be a character array` is displayed (line 8) using `usage` and the function stops executing.

Instead of `usage` you can use `error`, which prints an error message with prefix `error:` and then breaks out of the function. Line 8 in Code Listing 5.3 can, for example, be replaced with:

```
error("Input to minmax cannot be a character");
```

`error` is usually used when an unexpected error occurs somewhere in the function, whereas `usage` is used when checking user input.

It is always a good idea to write the name of the function that prints the message. You can have a script with many function calls where only one of them fails. If you do not write the name of that function in the error message, it can be tedious to go through every single call.

nargin and nargout

In Command 8, `minmax` was called with three output arguments, which led to an error message stating that the third output in the return list was undefined. Whenever an Octave function is called, the variables `nargin` and `nargout` are automatically assigned the number of inputs and number of outputs the function was called with. Let us see an example:

```
octave:9> function fun()

>printf("Number of inputs: %d  Number of outputs: %d \n", \

>nargin, nargout);

>endfor

octave:10> fun(2,3,4)

Number of inputs: 3 Number of outputs: 0

octave:11>  [a,b,c]=fun()

Number of inputs: 0 Number of outputs: 3

error: value on right hand side of assignment is undefined
```

Octave will print an error message in Command 11 because it cannot assign any values to the variables in the return list. Think of `nargin` as "Number of ARGuments IN" and `nargout` as "Number of ARGuments OUT".

We can now deal with the error produced in Command 8:

Code Listing 5.4

```
function [minx, maxx] = minmax(x)                                #1
                                                                 #2
  if ( nargin!=1 )                                               #3
    usage("Number of inputs to minmax must be 1");               #4
  elseif ( nargout>2 )                                           #5
    usage("Number of outputs from minmax cannot exceed 2");      #6
  endif                                                          #7
                                                                 #8
  [nr nc] = size(x);                                             #9
  if ( nr>1 &nc>1 )                                              #10
    warning("Input to minmax is a matrix array:\                 #11
    output will be vectors");                                    #12
  elseif ( ischar(x) )                                           #13
    usage("Input to minmax cannot be a character array");        #14
  endif                                                          #15
                                                                 #16
  maxx = max(x);                                                 #17
  minx = min(x);                                                 #18
                                                                 #19
endfunction                                                      #20
```

In line 6, we only print a usage message if `nargout` is larger than 2. In this way, the user is also allowed to call `minmax` with just 1 or no output and thereby only retrieve the minimum of the vector array. We also check in line 3 if the number of inputs is correct before checking whether the input has the right size and is of the right type. If we had not done this and called `minmax` without any inputs, the call to `size` would be invalid, and Octave prints a generic error message that can be hard to trace back.

With these improvements, let us now retype Commands 6-8:

```
octave:10> [mina maxa] = minmax("Hello World")

usage: Input to minmax cannot be a character array

error:...

octave:11> [mina maxa] = minmax([1 2; 3 4])

warning: Input to minmax is a matrix: outputs will be vector arrays

mina =

   1      2
```

```
maxa =

   3       4

octave:12> [a b c] = minmax([1 2 3 4])

usage: Number of outputs to minmax cannot exceed 2

error:...
```

In Commands 10 and 12, you see a usage message (that you wrote) and an error message printing where the error happened. Sometimes you may get a quite long series of error messages, because the function that you called, called a second function that called a third function where some error occurred. When this happens, the error messages may trace backwards, printing a lot of information to the screen. Usually you can figure out what happened by studying the first and last error messages.

 When tracing errors, it is a good idea to begin by checking the first and last error messages.

In Code Listing 5.4, the main part of the function body is dealing with checking whether the function call was done correctly—and we did not catch all possible mistakes! It may seem a bit tedious to perform these checks, but it can be useful if another person will make use of your code.

Pop Quiz – understanding functions

1   Which of the following function definitions are erroneous?

a)
```
a = fun(x)
  a = sin(x);
endfunction
```

b)
```
function a = fun(x y z)
  a = x + y + z;
endfunction
```

c)
```
function fun()
  printf("Hello World\n");
end
```

d)
```
# my sine function
function a = fun(x)
  # Usage: a = fun(x)
  a = sin(x);
endfunction
```

e)
```
function [a, b] = fun(x)
  a = sin(x);
endfunction
```

f)
```
function a = fun(x, y)
  b = sqrt(x);
  c = sqrt(y)*b;
end
```

2.   What are the variables `nargin` and `nargout`?

Convert the script in Code Listing 4.15 to a function. Let the function name be `myprimes`.

Writing and applying user-supplied functions

In *Chapter 3*, we saw how to "build" mathematical functions directly via the Octave command prompt. Here we will do the same thing, but we will do it properly this time and use Octave functions.

Consider the following vector valued function which we will call the Sel'kov function (an explanation follows later):

$$\mathbf{f}(x,y) = [f_1(x,y), f_2(x,y)] = [-x + 0.1y + x^2y, b - 0.1y - x^2y]. \tag{5.1}$$

b is some positive real number that we can vary as we like. We can write Equation (5.1) in a slightly different way by letting $(x,y)=(x_1,x_2)=\mathbf{x}$:

$$\mathbf{f}(\mathbf{x}) = [f_1(x_1,x_2), f_2(x_1,y_2)] = [-x_1 + 0.1x_2 + x_1^2x_2, b - 0.1x_2 - x_1^2x_2]. \tag{5.2}$$

When we write an Octave function for Equation (5.2), we can specify the value of b in at least three different ways:

1. We can simply set the value of b inside the function (inside the function scope)
2. We can let b be input to the function
3. We can let b be a *global* variable such that its value is accessible from both the workspace and inside the function scope

The first option is a bad choice, because we then have to change the value of b inside inside the function every time we need to change it. As we shall see later, option 2 is not a good choice either because it will prevent us from performing numerical analysis of the function. So we here we will use the third option. To specify a variable as global, we use the `global` qualifier:

```
Code Listing 5.5
function f = selkov(x)                              #1
  global global_b;                                  #2
                                                    #3
  f(1) = -x(1) + 0.1*x(2) + x(1).^2*x(2);           #4
  f(2) = global_b - 0.1*x(2) - x(1).^2*x(2);        #5
                                                    #6
endfunction                                         #7
```

I use the prefix `global_` to underline the fact that the variable is global, but it is not mandatory. In Code Listing 5.5, `global_b` has no value and we need to set this before we call `selkov`. For example, from the Octave command prompt:

```
octave:13> global global_b = 12;

octave:14>selkov([0 0])

ans =

   0    12

octave:15>global_b = 23;

octave:16>selkov([0 0])

ans

   0    23
```

 Note that the function in Code Listing 5.5 should check how the user calls it. For example, the input x must be a vector array with length 2.

We can check if `global_b` is a global variable via `isglobal`:

```
octave:17>isglobal("global_b")

ans = 1
```

A variable can also be specified as persistent. This means that the value of the function variable is not change between calls to the function. The following commands illustrate this:

```
octave:18> function fun()

>persistent a = 0;

>disp(a); a++;

>endfunction

octave:19> fun(), fun(), fun()

0

1

2
```

Notice that we assigned a the value zero. a will only have this value the first time that `fun` is called.Had we not used the persistent specifier, a would be zero in every function call. Persistent variables can be very handy if you need to increment a variable after each function call. They are not accessible from the workspace.

Using fsolve

You may wonder when a global variable can be useful: we could just pass the parameter b as an input to the function. Suppose we wish to solve (numerically!) the nonlinear equation system:

$$\mathbf{f}(\mathbf{x}) = \mathbf{0}, \tag{5.3}$$

where **f** is given in Equation (5.2). From *Chapter 2*, we know how to do this if **f** is a linear function, but not if it is nonlinear as in the Sel'kov function. To find one solution near a certain point (or an initial guess), we can use Octave's built-in function `fsolve`. In its simplest form, the syntax for this function is:

```
x=fsolve(fun, xguess, option)
```

where `fun` is a user-supplied function that can have the syntax:

```
f = fun(x),
```

`xguess` is the starting guess of the solution to Equation (5.3) and `option` is a structure containing optional input arguments. In the input argument list of `fun`, you cannot specify any parameter list, only the free varying variable x, so here the global variable `global_b` comes in handy.

The user-supplied function `fun` can have another syntax which we will discuss later. Let us first try with the simple form.

As an example, we first specify an initial guess and set the parameter *b* using the command:

```
octave:20>global_b = 0.25; guess = [1 1];
```

We then find one solution to the corresponding nonlinear equation system:

```
octave:21>fsolve("selkov", guess)

ans =

   0.25000    1.53846
```

Changing b, we get:

```
octave:22>global_b = 0.6;

octave:23>fsolve("selkov", guess)

ans =

   0.60000    1.30435
```

Nonlinear equations can have many solutions. In the best case, `fsolve` finds one—which one depends on the initial guess.

Of course, you can not be sure that `fsolve` will find a solution to any arbitrary initial guess. How "good" the guess must be to ensure that `fsolve` converges to a solution depends on the function.

Providing the Jacobian

To improve the convergence, you can provide the Jacobian matrix to `fsolve`, such that this matrix is returned as a second output from the user-supplied function. For the Sel'kov function, the Jacobian reads:

$$\mathbf{J} = \begin{bmatrix} \dfrac{\partial f_1}{\partial x_1} & \dfrac{\partial f_1}{\partial x_2} \\ \dfrac{\partial f_2}{\partial x_1} & \dfrac{\partial f_2}{\partial x_2} \end{bmatrix} = \begin{bmatrix} -1 + 2x_1 x_2 & 0.1 + x_1^2 \\ -2x_1 x_2 & -0.1 - x_1^2 \end{bmatrix}, \tag{5.4}$$

where f_1 and f_2 is given via Equation (5.2) above. The revised function that includes the Jacobian is then written as:

```
Code Listing 5.6
function [f, J]= selkovjac(x)                              #1
   global global_b;                                        #2
                                                           #3
   f(1) = -x(1) + x(2) + x(1).^2*x(2);                     #4
   f(2) = global_b - x(2) - x(1).^2*x(2);                  #5
                                                           #6
   J(1,1) = -1 + 2*x(1)*x(2);                              #7
   J(1,2) = 0.1 + x(1)^2;                                  #8
   J(2,1) = -2*x(1)*x(2);                                  #9
   J(2,2) = -J(1,2);                                       #10
endfunction                                                #11
```

We need to specify to `fsolve` that the user-supplied function now returns the Jacobian. We can do this via the optional structure input argument to `fsolve`, which can be created through Octave's optimization structure building function `optimset`:

```
octave:24> opt = optimset("Jacobian", "on")

opt =

{

Jacobian = on

}
```

Check if `opt` really is a structure via `isstruct`. We now call `fsolve` with the optional structure argument , making a random starting guess of the solution:

```
octave:25>fsolve("selkovjac", [0.1 -2], opt)

ans =

    0.60000      1.30435
```

which gives the same solution to Equation (5.3) as Command 23 even with a very different initial guess.

Using Isode – dynamical analysis of the Sel'kov model

The Sel'kov function is actually a model for a particular part of glycolysis. It is the metabolic pathway that produces adenosine tri-phosphate (ATP) from sugar and adenosine di-phosphate (ADP). In fact, the variable x_1 and x_2 represent the concentrations of the molecules fructose-6-phosphat (F6P) and ADP in this pathway[1]. The dynamics of the Sel'kov model for the glycolysis is given via:

$$\frac{dx_1}{dt} = -x_1 + 0.1x_2 + x_1^2 x_2$$

$$\frac{dx_2}{dt} = b - 0.1x_2 - x_1^2 x_2$$

(5.5)

---

[1]*For the interested reader, I recommend the text book "Mathematical Biology: I. An Introduction, 3rd edition", J.D. Murray, Springer-Verlag(2002).*

We can write this in a vector form:

$$\frac{d\mathbf{x}}{dt} = \mathbf{f}(\mathbf{x}), \qquad (5.6)$$

where $\mathbf{f}(\mathbf{x})$ is given in Equation (5.2). Equation (5.6) is a system of autonomous coupled ordinary differential equations. The term autonomous refers to the fact that the right-hand side does not explicitly depend on time. If we wish to know how x_1 and x_2 evolve (that is, how the concentrations of the molecules vary with time), we need to solve the differential equation system given some initial conditions.

Octave has a powerful function that can solve ordinary differential equation system numerically. This is referred to as a numerical solution to Equation (5.6). The syntax is in its simplest form:

```
x = lsode(fun, xinit, t)
```

where `fun` is a user-supplied function describing the right-hand side of Equation (5.6), `xinit` is the initial condition, and `t` is a vector array specifying the times at which the solution to the differential equation system is printed[2]. The user-supplied function has the following syntax:

```
f = fun(x,t)
```

The second argument is optional and only makes sense if the differential equation system is non-autonomous.

Time for action – using lsode for numerical integration

1. Since we have an autonomous system, we can simply use the function given in Code Listing 5.5 as input to `lsode`. First, we specify the time vector array to contain 200 elements equally spaced from 0 to 50 as well as the initial condition:

```
octave:26>global_b = 1; t = linspace(0,50,200); init = [0.4 0.2];
```

2. Next we call `lsode` to obtain a numerical solution to the Sel'kov model:

```
octave:27> x = lsode("selkov", init, t);
```

3. Now, the output variable x contains the solutions to x_1 and x_2 in a column-wise manner, meaning column one is the solution for x_1 and column two for x_2. We can then plot the columns versus the time vector array, for example:

---

[2]*See* `http://www.netlib.org/alliant/ode/prog/lsode.f` *for details.*

```
octave:28> plot(t, x(:,1), "-r", "linewidth", 5, t, x(:,2), "-b",
    "linewidth", 5);
```

4. The result (or something close to it, depending on your plotting program) is shown in the left-hand side window in the figure below.

If we repeat Commands 26-28, where we set the variable `global_b` to 0.6, the result is very interesting. See the right-hand side window:

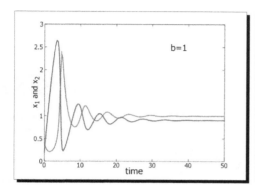 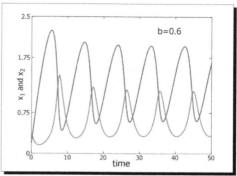

What just happened?

In Command 26, we define the value of b through the global variable `global_b`. We also specify the times at which `lsode` should print out the solution to the differential equation system and what the initial condition is. In Command 27, we then solve the Sel'kov model using `lsode` and the solution is plotted as x_1 and x_2 versus time. Notice that the differential equation system has two independent variables and we plot both.

The two chemical compounds go from relaxing to a steady state where they do not change with respect to time to a continuous oscillatory behavior. You should check this statement by increasing the time span. This behavior is due to the fact the system undergoes a Hopf-bifurcation which means that the dynamical behavior changes qualitatively.

Inline functions

In Octave, you can define inline functions. An inline function can be quite useful when you want to define simple functions. For example:

```
octave:29> f = inline("x + exp(-x)")

f =

f(x) = x + exp(x)

octave:30> f(0)

ans = 1
```

It is not possible to do much validation and error checking in inline functions and I will not use this function type in the book.

Pop Quiz – implementing mathematical functions as Octave functions

Implement the following mathematical functions as Octave functions:

    a) $f(x) = x + \sin(x)$ **b)** $f(t) = [\sin(t), t^2, \cos(t)]$

    c) $f(x, y, z) = x + y/z, z > 0$ **d)** $f(t) = \exp(-iwt)$

Have a go hero – bifurcation in the Sel'kov model

As mentioned in the text, the Sel'kov model changes qualitative behaviour when b is varied. This is called a bifurcation. Mathematically, a bifurcation occurs when the real part of at least one of the eigenvalues of the corresponding linear system changes sign. Therefore, we can locate the bifurcation point by studying the eigenvalues of the Jacobian as a function of b. In this exercise, we shall use `selkovjac`, `fsolve`, and `eig` to locate one bifurcation point. In order to do so, we go through the following steps:

1. Set `global_b` to 0.35.
2. Find the solution to Equation (5.3) for this value of `global_b` using `fsolve`. This solution is referred to as a fixed point.
3. Find the Jacobian for this point using `selkovjac`.
4. Use `eig` to calculate the eigenvalues of the Jacobian.
5. Is the real part of the eigenvalues positive or negative?
6. If the real part has changed sign, you have found the bifurcation point. If not, increment `global_b` with 0.01 and go back to *step 2*.

Hint: write a script that performs a loop through item 2-5.

More advanced function programming: Monte Carlo integration

Many scientific problems involve computations of integrals. If f is a scalar function of one variable and integratable, we can write the integral as:

$$I = \int_a^b f(x)dx = F(b) - F(a), \tag{5.7}$$

where $F(x)$ is the anti-derivative of f. Calculating the integral of most functions analytically can be a daunting and often impossible task, which is why we turn to the numerical alternative.

There are different ways to compute the integral numerically. Here we will write a function that uses the Monte Carlo method. Later we discuss the other integration methods that come with Octave. Now, assume that f is positive in the interval $x \in [a;b]$ and has a maximum M here. We can then form a rectangle with area given by $(b - a) \times M$. This is illustrated in the figure below. Here random points lie inside the rectangle with area $(b - a) \times M$, where $b = 2$, $a = 0.5$ and $M = 0.4356$. The blue curve represents the graph of a function f which integral we seek to compute.

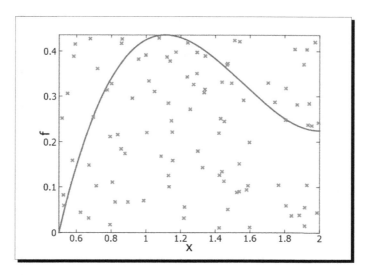

If we randomly set points (or shoot darts) inside the rectangle, the fraction of points/darts located under the graph of f is the same as the ratio between the area under f and the area of the entire rectangle. This means that we can approximate the integral to:

$$I \approx \frac{N_{under}}{N_{total}} \, (b - a) \, M, \tag{5.8}$$

where N_{under} is the number of random points located under the graph and N_{total} is the total number of random points set in the entire rectangle.

This idea is relatively easy to implement in a program flow chart as done in the figure below. Note that the inequalities should include equalities as well, for example $a \leq x \leq b$, rather than $a < x < b$. However, since we use Ocatve's `rand` function, the end-points are not included in the interval.

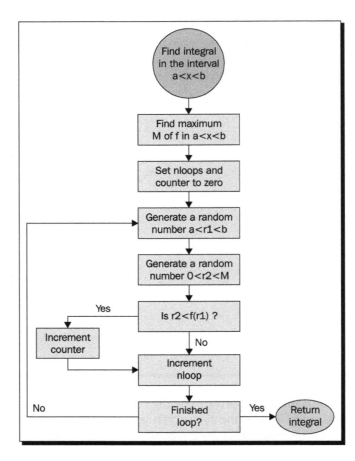

From the flow chart, we see that we need to generate random numbers. To this end, we can use Octave's `rand` function that picks out a random number between 0 and 1 from a uniform distribution.

The program flow chart suggests the following syntax for the function which we will call `mcintgr`:

```
I = mcintgr(fun, a, b, mcloops)
```

where `I` is the computed value of the integral, `fun` is the user-supplied function, `a`and`b` are the limits, and `mcloops` is the number of Monte Carlo loops we wish to perform. Before programming the integrator, we need to address a few things.

The feval function

When we write an Octave function that calls a user-supplied function, we must call the latter using Octave's `feval` function. The reason for this is that Octave functions work via the call-by-value strategy as discussed above. This means that when you pass a function, it is the function name (a string) and not a function object that is copied into the executing function.

The syntax for `feval` is:

```
[output1, output2, ...] = feval(function name, input1, input2, ...)
```

where `output1, output2,...` are outputs from the function with name `function name` that takes `input1, input2, ...` as inputs. `feval` can also be called from the command prompt , so let us illustrate its usage here by using `feval` to call `minmax`:

```
octave:31> [mina maxa] = feval("minmax", rand(10,1))

mina = 0.02174

maxa = 0.72132
```

Here `feval` calls `minmax` with one argument, namely, a random vector. The output from `minmax` is then returned to the user through `feval`.

You need not use `feval` from the command prompt or in your scripts, only when you call a user-supplied function inside the scope of a function.

You can also let the function accept so-called function handles as input arguments rather than the function name, but here we will stick to the more traditional way of calling user-supplied functions. If you want to know about function handles, check out the Octave manual.

Validating the user-supplied function

There are two potential problems we should address. Firstly, what if the user passes a function that does not exist? This problem can be dealt with using `exist`. This function takes as input a string and returns a non-zero value if there exists a variable, function, file, or directory by that name. The exact return value specifies what the string is associated with. Unfortunately, under the current version (Octave 3.2.4), `exist` does not distinguish between variable names and user-supplied functions in Windows, so in order to keep compatibility, we will only check if `exist` returns a non-zero value or not.

Secondly, we should check if the function returns a scalar and if this return value is positive, since our algorithm only computes the integral for functions that are positive in the interval from a to b. Fortunately, we can check this by functions we have learned already, namely, `min` and `length`.

We are now ready to program the Monte Carlo integrator. Once again to limit the space, I have omitted the help text:

Code Listing 5.7

```
function I = mcintgr(fun, a, b, mcloops)          #1
                                                   #2
  # Check input args                               #3
  if ( nargin != 4 | nargout> 1 )                  #4
    usage("mcintgr is called with 4 inputs and 1 output");   #5
  endif                                            #6
                                                   #7
  # Check if user supplied function exists         #8
  if !exist(fun)                                   #9
    usage("mcintgr: Sure about the function name?");   #10
  elseif ( length(feval(fun,a)) != 1 )             #11
    usage("Function passed to mcintgr must be a scalar\   #12
      function");                                  #13
  endif                                            #14
                                                   #15
  # Find maximum value of f                        #16
  x = linspace(a,b);                               #17
  y = feval(fun,x);                                #18
                                                   #19
  # Check if f is positive                         #20
  if ( min(y) < 0 )                                #21
    usage("mcintgr: the function must be positive in \   #22
    the interval");                                #23
  endif                                            #24
                                                   #25
  # Set max of m                                   #26
  maxy = max(y);                                   #27
                                                   #28
  # Calculate the interval                         #29
  l = b - a;                                       #30
                                                   #31
  # Initialize the counters                        #32
  counter = 0;                                     #33
  nloops = 0;                                      #34
                                                   #35
  # Main mc loop                                   #36
  while ( nloops<= mcloops )                       #37
    r1 = a + l*rand;                               #38
    r2 = maxy*rand;                                #39
                                                   #40
    fr1 = feval(fun,r1);                           #41
```

```
        if ( r2<fr1 )                          #42
           counter++;                           #43
        endif                                   #44
                                                #45
        nloops++;                               #46
     endwhile                                   #47
                                                #48
     # The integral                            #49
     I = counter/mcloops*maxy*l;               #50
                                                #51
  endfunction                                   #52
```

As with `minmax`, the main part of the function code deals with checking the inputs: there are many more things we could check, for example, if b is smaller than a, and if they are scalars. The actual Monte Carlo loop consists of only 9 lines of code.

Three points should be made. The `if` statement in lines 21-24 checks if the function is positive in the interval specified via the variables a and b. This is done using 100 evenly spaced points in the interval (line 17 and 18). If the function varies rapidly or if the interval is large, this check may not suffice. We have used the symbol I as the integral. This is also used as the symbol for the imaginary unit. Is this a problem? Not really, since I is only used inside the function scope and will not affect the workspace variables. Finally, since the numerical method is based on random numbers, the value of the integral will be different from one function call to the next even if we try to evaluate the same integral. It is therefore a good idea to present the result as a statistical mean with an uncertainty associated. In *Chapter 7* we will see how this is done in Octave.

It is time to test the function. It is a good idea to test things using a problem where you already know the result. For example, the integral of sine in the interval $[0; \pi]$ is:

$$I = \int_0^\pi \sin(x)dx = -\cos(\pi) + \cos(0) = 2. \tag{5.9}$$

Using `mcintgr` with 100 Monte Carlo loops, we get:

`octave:32>mcintgr("sin", 0, pi, 100)`

`ans = 1.9790`

With 10000 Monte Carlo loops:

`octave:33>mcintgr("sin", 0, pi, 10000)`

`ans = 2.0063`

As expected, this is a better approximation for the integral. We can also define our own function in a file or directly from the command prompt and then use the Monte Carlo integrator to compute the integral:

```
octave:34> function y = fun(x); y = x.^(4/3).*log(x)./cosh(x.^2 + x);
endfunction
```

```
octave:35>mcintgr("fun", 1, 3, 10000)
```

```
0.029267
```

This one is hard to do by hand!

We must also check the user interface, whether the usage messages are printed as we intended. First, let us enter an invalid function name:

```
octave:36>mcintgr("notvalid function", 0, 1, 1000)
```

```
usage: mcintgr: Sure about the function name?
```

```
error:...
```

To see if we have checked correctly for a scalar function, we first define a vector valued function, for example:

```
octave:37> function y=fun(x); y(1) = sin(x); y(2)=1; endfor
```

```
octave:38> fun(pi)
```

```
ans =
```

```
   1.2246e-16    1.0000e+000
```

Let us use this function when calling `mcintgr`:

```
octave:39>mcintgr("fun", 0, pi, 10000)
```

```
usage: Function passed to mcintgr must be a scalar function
```

```
error:...
```

Finally, if we pass a function that has negative values in the interval we integrate over:

```
octave:40>mcintgr("sin", 0, 2*pi, 10000)
```

```
usage: mcintgr: the function must be positive in the interval
```

```
error: ...
```

Things work as expected.

Using quad and trapz for numerical integration

Octave has a built-in function `quad` that can perform the same task as `mcintgr`. The function is named after the algorithm it is based on, namely, quadrature, which is basically just a weighted sum of the function values[3]. In a simple form, `quad` can be called as:

```
octave:41> quad("sin", 0, pi)

ans = 2
```

where `"sin"` is Octave's sine function and `0` and `pi` are the lower and upper limits. As you see, `quad` is very precise and perhaps you also noted that it executes very quickly. Use `help quad` to see all possible usages of `quad`.

Sometimes you may not have a well-defined mathematical function, but a series of points from a data file. In this situation you can use `trapz`, which integrates a data set using the trapezoidal rule. This algorithm is not as accurate as quadrature. To illustrate `trapz`, let us first generate a data set from a sine function and then use the data as input to `trapz`:

```
octave:42> x= linspace(0,pi); y = sin(x);

octave:43>trapz(x, y)

ans = 1.9998
```

Using 100 data points, `trapz` is slightly more inaccurate as compared to `quad`, but you can increase the number of points to obtain a better result.

A final note: you may wonder why anyone would want to use the Monte Carlo method. It is apparently slow and inaccurate compared to other methods. We have only treated simple functions that depend on a single variable and here the Monte Carlo method is relatively slow and not the method of choice. In the case of functions that depend on several variables, we end up with multiple integrals and this method may be advantageous compared to the quadrature and trapezoidal schemes, especially in higher dimensions.

Vectorized programming

The Monte Carlo loop in Code Listing 5.7 is programmed like we would do it if we used C or another low-level programming language. This is really not how we should do it in Octave! As you know, Octave is a vectorized language and is specially designed to perform operations on arrays. For example, if we want to find the element-wise sum of two vectors we would use:

```
c = a + b;
```

[3]You can read more in "Numerical Recipes: The Art of Scientific Computing, 3rd Edition", Press et al., Cambridge University Press (2007).

and not:

```
for n=1:length(a)
  c(n) = a(n) + b(n);
endfor
```

There are at least three reasons why you want to use the first option in Octave:

1. The code executes much faster. In *Chapter 8*, we shall see how we measure executing speeds and study how much faster vectorization really is.

2. The number of code lines that you have to write is reduced significantly, reducing the potential coding errors.

3. Any dimension mismatch can easily be picked out by the Octave interpreter and a meaningful error message is printed.

Let us see how we can vectorize mcintgr.m.

The Monte Carlo loop consists of generating a series of random numbers and then comparing those random numbers with the function value. Instead of doing this inside a loop, we can generate all the random numbers at once, find the corresponding function values and then compare the entire arrays.

Time for action – vectorizing the Monte Carlo integrator

Using the method above, the vectorized version of mcintgr is:

Code Listing 5.8
```
function I = mcintgrv(fun, a, b, mcloops)          #1
                                                   #2
  # Find maximum value of f                        #3
  x = linspace(a,b);                               #4
  f = feval(fun,x);                                #5
  maxf = max(f);                                   #6
                                                   #7
  # Generating random arrays                       #8
  r1 = rand(mcloops,1);                            #9
  r2 = rand(mcloops,1);                            #10
                                                   #11
  # Get random x and y values                      #12
  l = b - a;                                       #13
  x = a + l.*r1;                                   #14
  y = maxf.*r2;                                    #15
  fx = feval(fun, x);                              #16
                                                   #17
```

```
    # Counts the number of points that lie under the graph    #18
    counter = length(find(y<fx));                              #19
                                                               #20
    # The integral                                             #21
    I = counter/mcloops*maxf*l;                                #22
                                                               #23
  endfunction                                                  #24
```

What just happened?

The vectorized function is called with the exact same inputs and outputs as `mcintgr`. The code should be straightforward to understand, perhaps except line 19. Here we first perform a comparison between the value of the function and the random points. This comparison operation results in a Boolean array which is passed to `find`, that returns the indices of all true elements in the array. By retrieving the number of indices using `length`, we can then simply count the number of points that lie under the graph of the function.

On my machine, the vectorized version of the Monte Carlo integrator executes around 300 times faster than the "conventional" method. Using vectorized programming, you can also avoid many loops that perform trivial tasks and clutter the code. In fact, once you get used to it, vectorized code is much easier to read and coding errors easier to spot. Therefore, always think about the possibility of vectorizing your code.

Scripts should also be vectorized whenever possible

Simple debugging

In earlier versions of Octave, you had to add `printf` or `disp` function calls whenever you were tracking down bugs in your code. This is quite annoying and you find yourself "polluting" your code with statements and function calls just to track down a silly typo. Octave now comes with a simple, but very useful debugger. A debugger is basically a tool that lets you monitor, and to a certain extent control, the variables inside a function. These are usually hidden from the workspace, that is, the user cannot easily track down what and where things went wrong without the debugger.

Code Listing 5.9 shows a modified version of Code Listing 5.8. Only one line has been changed and the function will now produce nonsense. For example:

```
octave:44>mcintgrdb("sin", 0, pi, 1000)

ans = -0
```

This we know is not right.

```
Code Listing 5.9
function I = mcintgrdb(fun, a, b, mcloops)          #1
                                                     #2
   x = linspace(a,b);                                #3
   f = feval(fun,x);                                 #4
   maxf = max(f);                                    #5
                                                     #6
   r1 = rand(mcloops,1);                             #7
   r2 = rand(mcloops,1);                             #8
                                                     #9
   l = a - b;                                        #10
   x = a + l.*r1;                                    #11
   y = maxf.*r2;                                     #12
   fx = feval(fun, x);                               #13
                                                     #14
   counter = length(find(y<fx));                     #15
                                                     #16
   I = counter/mcloops*maxf*l;                       #17
                                                     #18
endfunction                                          #19
```

Let us not try to find the coding error by simply comparing the two functions line-by-line. Let us instead use the debugger.

First, we need to instruct the debugger to stop somewhere in the code. When we have done so, we can monitor the values of each variable as we step through the code. We have no clue yet as to what went wrong, so we should just start our monitoring from the beginning. With dbstop, we can achieve this:

```
octave:45>dbstop("mcintgrdb", 1)

ans = 3
```

The first input to dbstop is the function name and the second is the line where we want Octave's interpreter to stop. This is also referred to as a break point. Now, in line 1 we have no commands, just the function name and input and output variable declarations. dbstop is smart enough to recognize this and will stop at line 3, where the first command is. This information is given to you via the output, ans=3.

dbstop will not call the function for you, so we need to do this:

```
octave:46>mcintgrdb("sin", 0, pi, 1000)

mcintgrdb: line 3, column 4
```

```
keyboard: stopped …
```

```
3: x=linspace(a,b)
```

As you can see, Octave stops executing the function `mcintgrdb` at line 3 as we expected. Once we have entered the debugging mode, you will see the debug prompt

```
debug>
```

This prompt works like the usual Octave prompt, but you can now access the variables that are in the function scope:

```
debug> b
```

```
b = 3.1416
```

which means that the variable b was assigned the value of π as intended. You can even give commands and assign values to variables. For example:

```
debug> c = sin(b)
```

```
ans = 1.2246e-16
```

This will instantiate a new variable c with a value close to zero.

Let us step through the code. Moving one line down to line 4 we use:

```
debug>dbnext
```

```
mcintgrdb: line 4, column 4
```

```
keyboard: stopped …
```

```
4: f=feval(fun, x)
```

We are now at line 4. In this manner, we can go through the code line by line carefully checking that the variables have the values that we expect them to have. If you are absolutely certain that a part of your code is bug-free, you do not have to step through every single line, but simply skip the next, say 6 lines, using:

```
debug>dbnext 6
```

```
mcintgrdb: line 11, column 4
```

```
keyboard: stopped …
```

```
11: x = a + l.*rl;
```

We know that the variable x should be a random array with elements in the interval from 0 to π. We can check this:

```
debug> min(x)

ans = -3.1391
```

so something has gone wrong here. x is given by a, 1, and r1, and we can check the values of these variables:

```
debug> a

ans = 0

debug> l

l = -3.1416
```

This is not right because 1 should be a (positive) length. Line 10, is of course,where the error is—it should be l=b-a.

To leave the debugging mode you type:

```
debug>dbquit
```

and you are back at the Octave prompt (and can no longer access variables inside the function scope). If we call mcintgrdb, we will go back into debug mode, because we have not cleared or deleted the break point. To do so, we call dbclear:

```
octave:47>dbclear("mcintgrdb")
```

You can set multiple break points with dbstop and jump directly to the next break point via the dbcont command instead of stepping through the code as we did above. If there are no more break points, the function simply executes normally and exits the debug mode after it finishes.

> Debugging mode cannot be used for built-in functions like sin or length. You can, however, debug scripts.

Multiple function file

Above we have defined one function in one function file. The function file had to have the same name as the function plus the added postfix .m. There is a way to have multiple functions defined in one file. This can be quite useful if you want to reduce the number of function files. The trick is to let Octave treat the file as a script file, that is, to avoid using the keyword function at the beginning of the file. In principle you can use anything you want[4], but I prefer something harmless like 1;.

---

[4]*well, except* function.

For example, we can write the following function definitions in any file, say `funcollect.m`:

```
Code Listing 5.10
1;                                                          #1
                                                            #2
function fun1()                                             #3
                                                            #4
  printf("Hello from fun1\n");                              #5
                                                            #6
endfunction                                                 #7
                                                            #8
function fun2()                                             #9
                                                            #10
  printf("Hello from fun2\n");                              #11
                                                            #12
endfunction                                                 #13
                                                            #14
function printall()                                         #15
                                                            #16
  printf("Hello from everyone:\n");                         #17
  fun1();                                                   #18
  fun2();                                                   #19
                                                            #20
endfunction                                                 #21
```

and then execute the file from the Octave prompt as if it was a script:

octave:49>funcollect

The functions defined in `funcollect.m` can now be called:

octave:50> fun1()

Hello from fun1

octave:51>printall()

Hello from everyone:

Hello from fun1

Hello from fun2

Since Octave treats the file as a script file, you can have plotting commands and so forth anywhere inside the file. However, you must first define the functions before you use them in the script part or in any other functions.

Pop Quiz – understanding vectorization

Vectorize the following code snippets:

a)
```
for n=1:rows(A)
    b(n) = A(n,1) + 1.0;
endfor
```

b)
```
s=0;
for n=1:length(a)
    if ( a(n) > 1.0 ) s += a(n);
endfor
```

c)
```
m=1;
for n=1:2:length(a)
    b(m) = a(n);
    m++;
endfor
```

d)
```
for n=2:length(a)
    c(n-1) = 0.5*(a(n) - a(n-1));
endfor
```

Have a go hero – using the debugger

The listing below shows a new version of `mcintgrb`. Unfortunately, there is still a bug. Copy the code into an editor and save it under the current directory. Then use the debugger to track down the bug:

Code Listing 5.11
```
function I = mcintgrdb(fun, a, b, mcloops)        #1
                                                  #2
    x = linspace(a,b);                            #3
    f = feval(fun,x);                             #4
    maxf = max(f);                                #5
                                                  #6
    r1 = rand(mcloops,1);                         #7
    r2 = rand(mcloops,1);                         #8
                                                  #9
    l = a - b;                                    #10
    x = a + l.*r1;                                #11
    y = maxf.*r2;                                 #12
    fx = feval(fun, x);                           #13
                                                  #14
    counter = length(find(y>fx));                 #15
                                                  #16
    I = counter/mcloops*maxf*l;                   #17
                                                  #18
endfunction                                       #19
```

Summary

In this chapter, you learned:

- ◆ To write your own Octave function.
- ◆ To check for user input and write warning and usage messages if needed.
- ◆ How to write a help text .
- ◆ How to define Octave functions that can be used by Octave to solve different numerical problems.
- ◆ About inline functions.
- ◆ To write your own functions that take user-supplied functions as input.
- ◆ More about the importance of vectorization.
- ◆ How to perform simple debugging of your function.

You are now ready to move on to the second part of the book and use your skills to write your own Octave package.

6

Making Your Own Package: A Poisson Equation Solver

In Chapter 1. we learned where to find and how to install Octave packages. Packages are basically a collection of functions (and possibly scripts) that are related to some particular scientific field or programming area. For example, the finance package has functionality that can help you to solve different financial problems and multi-core is a package that provides support for multi-core CPUs.

In this chapter, you will learn how to make your own Octave package. The package will be able to solve the one and two-dimensional Poisson equation. The reason to choose this classical example is that the mathematics is relatively simple, the programming part is not too complicated, and more importantly, the package can be used to solve a range of interesting problems encountered in engineering, fluid dynamics, electrostatics, biological population dynamics, and much more.

This chapter is divided into three parts. In part one, the application of the Poisson equation is discussed in relation to heat conduction problems. If you are familiar with the Poisson equation, you can skip this part of the chapter. Part two is concerned with the algorithm that we will use to solve the Poisson equation, and in part three we implement the solver and build the package.

After reading this chapter, you will know:

- ◆ How to build an Octave package.
- ◆ About the one and two-dimensional Poisson equation subjected to Dirichlet boundary conditions.

- ◆ The finite difference scheme.
- ◆ How to use sparse matrices in Octave.
- ◆ How to solve the Poisson equation numerically using Octave.

The main purpose of this chapter is to illustrate how you can build an Octave package and therefore we shall not go into many details with the finite differencing scheme, the applications, and so on. There are an impressive amount of introductory and advanced textbooks that deal with all these issues in great detail. For the interested reader, I recommend:

1. *"Computational Fluid Dynamics – the basics with applications", J. Anderson Jr., McGraw-Hill (1995).*
2. *"Numerical Recipes: The Art of Scientific Computing, 3rd Edition", Press et al., Cambridge University Press (2007).*
3. *"Computational Methods for Fluid Dynamics", J. H. Ferziger and M. Peric, Springer-Verlag (1999)*
4. *"Partial Differential Equations for Scientists and Engineers", S. J. Farlow, Dover Publications (1993).*

The Poisson equation – two examples of heat conduction

We all have an intuitive idea about heat and temperature, so the easiest way to illustrate the Poisson equation is probably through the heat conduction equation.

One-dimensional heat conduction

Consider a gold rod of length L suspended between two wires both having some temperature T_0 that we will specify later. The rod is covered by a heater that transfers heat into the rod at some rate Q given in units of Watts per volume (W m^{-3}). See the figure below:

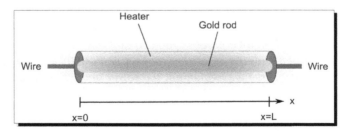

This means that we have heat flowing into the rod at every point along its axial direction, the x direction, and heat flowing out at the ends. One obvious question is: what is the temperature inside the gold rod? Before we answer this question, we must specify that we are only interested in the final temperature, not what happens when we switch the heater on and off. This is called the steady state temperature profile.

[The Poisson equation is used to describe steady state situations.]

To answer the question, we first need to write up the relevant heat conduction equation. If we let the gold rod's axial direction be in the x direction as shown in the figure, and if we assume that the temperature does not vary in any other directions (or in time), this equation reads:

$$\frac{\partial^2 T(x)}{\partial x^2} = -\frac{Q}{K}, \tag{6.1}$$

where $T(x)$ is the temperature profile and k is the thermal conductance. For gold, k is around 319 Watts per Kelvin per meter (W K^{-1} m^{-1}) at room temperature. The right-hand side is sometimes denoted the source (or production) term for obvious reasons and often we shall call the x variable a spatial coordinate.

Now, Equation (6.1) is a differential equation and is an example of a one-dimensional Poisson equation. To solve the differential equation, we must specify the boundary conditions—here they are simply given by the temperature of wires (heat sinks) at the ends of the rod, namely:

$$T(0) = T_0 \quad \text{and} \quad T(L) = T_0. \tag{6.2}$$

It is, in fact, possible to solve Equation (6.1) subjected to the boundary conditions, Equation (6.2), by direct integration. This gives:

$$T(x) = \frac{Q}{2K} x(L - x) + T_0 \tag{6.3}$$

that is, the temperature profile is a parabola with a maximum at $x = L/2$. Equation (6.3) is thus the solution to the Poisson equation above. You can easily check if this statement is true by simply differentiating Equation (6.3) twice with respect to x.

The Poisson equation is an example of an elliptic partial differential equation and is also referred to as a boundary value problem.

Two-dimensional heat conduction

The one-dimensional problem of heat conduction can be extended to two dimensions. For example, a plate (of some given material) may be connected to a hot wire at some point as shown in the figure below. The plate is sandwiched between isolating material such that heat can only flow to and from the plate through the sides. If the plate is sufficiently "flat" as illustrated in the figure, we can safely assume that the temperature does not vary with the plate height.

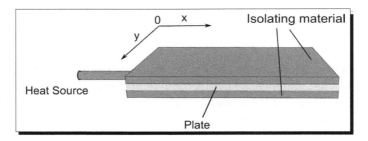

In this situation there is no source term because everything happens on the boundaries. The heat conduction equation reads:

$$\frac{\partial^2 T(x, y)}{\partial x^2} + \frac{\partial^2 T(x, y)}{\partial y^2} = 0. \tag{6.4}$$

We can compare this equation with Equation (6.1) and we see that there is an additional second order derivative term on the left hand side. This is simply due to the fact that we now consider a two dimensional problem, that is, heat is conducted in both the x and y directions. Equation (6.4) is a special type of Poisson equation because the source term is zero and is often called a Laplace equation.

Since the plate has four sides, we need to specify the boundary conditions on each one of them in order to complete our mathematical description of the problem. The boundary condition at $T(0, y)$ is in principle given by some step function since the heat flow given by the wire is discontinuous. However, we will approximate it with a continuous function, say a sine function, giving:

$$T(0, y) = A \sin(\pi y / L_y) + T_0, \quad T(L_x, y) + T_0, \quad T(x, 0) = T_0 \quad \text{and} \quad T(x, L_y) = T_0, \tag{6.5}$$

where A indicates the maximum temperature difference between the heat source, that is, the hot wire, and the surrounding medium which has temperature T_0. L_x and L_y are the length of the plate in the x and y directions, respectively.

It is actually also possible to obtain an analytical solution to this boundary value problem, that is, to find the temperature in the plate at every point (x, y). However, this is quite cumbersome especially if we had not made the assumption about the boundary condition. If we had included a complex source term, the problem may not be solvable by any known analytical method, which is why the numerical solutions become useful.

The Poisson equation

From the two examples above, we see that we can write the Poisson equation for some variable ϕ (the temperature for example) as:

$$\frac{\partial^2 \phi(x)}{\partial x^2} = f(x) \tag{6.6}$$

in one dimension, or:

$$\frac{\partial^2 \phi(x, y)}{\partial x^2} + \frac{\partial^2 \phi(x, y)}{\partial y^2} = f(x, y) \tag{6.7}$$

in two dimensions. In short notation, we write this:

$$\nabla^2 \phi = f, \tag{6.8}$$

where ∇^2 is the Laplace operator. We emphasize that ϕ is a function of one or two variables by using $\phi(x)$ and $\phi(x, y)$, respectively. Note that we assume that ϕ is twice differentiable with respect to the spatial coordinates x and y and that the source term f in general is a function of these coordinates as well.

The Dirichlet boundary condition

In the examples above, we have only dealt with problems where the variable has certain specified values at the system boundaries. This type of boundary condition is called the Dirichlet boundary condition (or boundary condition of the first type). One can also have other types of boundary conditions; however we shall limit ourselves to the simple Dirichlet type.

It is the partial differential equation given by Equation (6.8) subjected to the Dirichlet boundary condition that we seek to solve numerically using Octave.

Pop Quiz – identifying the Poisson equation

Which of the following equations are Poisson equations?

a) $\dfrac{\partial \phi}{\partial x} + \dfrac{\partial \phi}{\partial y} = 0$

b) $\dfrac{\partial^2 \phi}{\partial x^2} = -\dfrac{\partial^2 \phi}{\partial y^2} + C$

c) $\dfrac{d^2 u}{dx^2} = -\dfrac{\rho F}{2\eta}$

d) $\dfrac{\partial f}{\partial t} = -C \dfrac{\partial^2 u}{\partial x^2}$

e) $\dfrac{\partial^2 \phi}{\partial x^2} + \dfrac{\partial^2 \phi}{\partial y^2} = 0$

f) $\dfrac{\partial^2 z}{\partial x^2} - \sin(x) + \dfrac{\partial^2 z}{\partial y^2} + C = 0$

Finite differencing

The first step in our numerical implementation of the solver is to discretize the spatial coordinates into grid points (or nodes). The one-dimensional case is shown in the figure below, where the x coordinate is discretized into N_{grid} grid points:

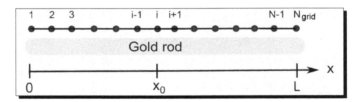

If the distance between the grid points Δx is constant, it can easily be seen that it is given by $L/(N_{grid} - 1)$. With this arrangement, the second order derivative of ϕ at $x = x_0$ can then be approximated by an algebraic equation:

$$\frac{\partial^2 \phi(x)}{\partial x^2}\bigg|_{x=x_0} \approx \frac{\phi_{i-1} - 2\phi_i + \phi_{i+1}}{\Delta x^2} \quad \text{for small } \Delta x, \tag{6.9}$$

where i is then the grid point located at x_0. This approximation is said to be of second order accuracy and is considered to be a good approximation for sufficiently small Δx, or equivalently, for a large number of grid points. Equation (6.9) is called the finite difference approximation to the second order derivative $\partial^2 \phi / \partial x^2$. It comes from the basic definition of the derivative of a function, so no magic here. See the references listed in the beginning of this chapter, if you are curious.

If we substitute Equation (6.9) into Equation (6.6), the discretized one-dimensional Poisson equation reads:

$$\frac{\phi_{i-1} - 2\phi_i + \phi_{i+1}}{\Delta x^2} = f_i, \quad 1 < i < N_{grid}. \tag{6.10}$$

Since we only treat Dirichlet boundary conditions here, we let $\phi_1 = \phi(0)$ and $\phi_{Ngrid} = \phi(L)$. In the example of the gold rod, we then simply set the end grid points to the same temperature as the two metal wires, T_0.

With only little effort, we can extend the one-dimensional case to two dimensions. We have two spatial directions and the domain must then be discretized with respect to both coordinates, as shown in the figure below:

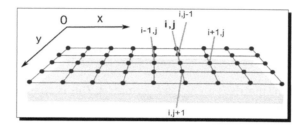

Following the same idea as for the one dimensional case, the left-hand side of Equation (6.7) can be approximated to:

$$\frac{\partial^2 \phi(x,y)}{\partial x^2} + \frac{\partial^2 \phi(x,y)}{\partial y^2} \approx \frac{\phi_{i-1,j} - 2\phi_{i,j} + \phi_{i-1,j}}{\Delta x^2} + \frac{\phi_{i,j-1} - 2\phi_{i,j} + \phi_{i,j+1}}{\Delta y^2}, \qquad (6.11)$$

that is, the discretized two-dimensional Poisson equation is:

$$\frac{\phi_{i-1,j} - 2\phi_{i,j} + \phi_{i-1,j}}{\Delta x^2} + \frac{\phi_{i,j-1} - 2\phi_{i,j} + \phi_{i,j+1}}{\Delta y^2} = f_{i,j}, \quad 1 < i,j < N_{grid} \qquad (6.12)$$

if the number of grid points are the same in the x and y directions. Our numerical solver will use Equations (6.10) and (6.12) to solve the one and two-dimensional Poisson equation.

From finite difference to a linear equation system

By applying the finite difference approximation, we have transformed the partial differential equations into algebraic equations. This is a crucial point. If we inspect Equation (6.10) carefully, we realize that we simply have a system of linear equations:

$$\begin{aligned}
\phi_1 &= \phi(0) \\
\phi_1 &= 2\phi_2 + \phi_3 = f_2 \Delta x^2 \\
\phi_2 &= 2\phi_3 + \phi_4 = f_3 \Delta x^2 \\
&\cdots \\
\phi_{Ngrid-2} &- 2\phi_{Ngrid-1} + \phi_{Ngrid} = f_{Ngrid-1} \Delta x^2 \\
\phi_{Ngrid} &= \phi(L)
\end{aligned} \qquad (6.13)$$

such that the value of ϕ at each grid point is the unknown that we seek to find. In matrix notation, we can write this as (of course, you should check that this is correct):

$$
\begin{bmatrix}
1 & 0 & 0 & & & & \\
1 & -2 & 1 & \cdots & & 0 & \\
0 & 1 & -2 & & & & \\
\vdots & & & \ddots & & \vdots & \\
& & & -2 & 1 & 0 & \\
0 & & \cdots & 1 & -2 & 1 & \\
& & & 0 & 0 & 1 &
\end{bmatrix}
\begin{bmatrix}
\phi_1 \\
\phi_2 \\
\phi_3 \\
\vdots \\
\vdots \\
\phi_{N\,grid-1} \\
\phi_{N\,grid}
\end{bmatrix}
=
\begin{bmatrix}
\phi(0) \\
f_2 \Delta x^2 \\
f_3 \Delta x^2 \\
\vdots \\
\vdots \\
f_{N\,grid-1} \Delta x^2 \\
\phi(L)
\end{bmatrix}
\tag{6.14}
$$

Notice that the coefficient matrix is an $N_{grid} \times N_{grid}$ matrix. This is an important result since we know from *Chapter2* how to solve such linear equation systems using Octave.

Equation (6.14) is perhaps a bit surprising the first time you see it. Solving something as complicated as a partial differential equation suddenly reduces to the task of solving a linear equation system. As mentioned above, this is simply due to the finite difference approximation where the derivative is reduced to a simple algebraic equation system.

We can use the same basic strategy for the two-dimensional equation. In order to be able to write the problem in a proper matrix form, it is convenient to rearrange the grid points into a one-dimensional array (a vector) rather than using the two-dimensional array depicted in the figure. Thus, if a grid point has indices (i, j) on the two-dimensional grid, the corresponding one-dimensional vector index is given as:

$$
n = (j - 1)N_{grid} + i,
\tag{6.15}
$$

where N_{grid} is the number of grid points in the x direction. For simplicity, from now on, we shall only consider two-dimensional grids with size $N_{grid} \times N_{grid}$, that is, with the same number of grid points in x and y directions. Furthermore, if we let the grid point spacing be the same in both these directions, that is, $\Delta x^2 = \Delta y^2 = \Delta^2$, Equation (6.12) can now finally be rewritten as:

$$
\phi_{n-1} + \phi_{n+1} + \phi_{n-N\,grid} + \phi_{n+N\,grid} - 4\phi_n = f_n \Delta^2.
\tag{6.16}
$$

From this equation, we can write up the coefficient matrix for the two-dimensional Poisson problem (some boundary points for $i = 1$ and $i = N_{grid}$ are not shown):

$$
\begin{bmatrix}
1 & 0 & & & & & & & \\
0 & 1 & & & \cdots & & & 0 & \\
 & & \ddots & & & & & & \\
 & & 1 & & 1 & -4 & 1 & & \\
 & & 1 \cdots & 0 & 1 & -4 & \cdots 1 & & \\
 & & & 0 & 0 & 1 & & 1 & \\
 & & & & & \ddots & & & \\
 & 0 & & & \cdots & & 1 & 0 & \\
 & & & & & & 0 & 1 &
\end{bmatrix}
\tag{6.17}
$$

This matrix has dimensions $N_{grid}^2 \times N_{grid}^2$, so that if the initial two-dimensional grid had dimensions 100 x 100, Equation (6.17) represents the coefficient matrix for a system of 10,000 linear equations with 10,000 unknowns!

The coefficient matrices, Equations (6.14) and (6.17), include the boundary points and can be left out without losing any information. However, I prefer to keep them here for convenience.

Interlude: Sparse matrices

One thing that you may have noticed from the coefficient matrices is that the vast majority of the matrix elements are zeros. For example, for a two-dimensional problem with $N_{grid} = 100$ the coefficient matrix has 100 million elements, but only 48416 of the elements will be non-zero (and out of these, only 0.8% will be boundary points). Such matrices are called sparse matrices. If we store all the elements in the matrix (zeros and non-zeros), we will need 800MB, which is not the way we want to go. Fortunately, we can tell Octave that a matrix is sparse and Octave will only use memory for the non-zero elements.

Time for action – instantiating a sparse matrix

1. In Octave, we can define a matrix to be sparse using the `sparse` function. The simplest way to instantiate a sparse matrix with, say 5 rows and 6 columns, is:

```
octave:1 > A=sparse(5,6)

A=

  Compressed Column Sparse (rows=5, cols=6, nnz=0, [0%])
```

2. To assign non-zero values to elements in the matrix, you simply use normal assignments, for example:

```
octave:2> A(1,2) = 42; A(3,:)=3;

octave:3> A

A =
```

```
Compressed Column Sparse (rows=5, cols=6, nnz=7, [23%])

  (3,1) ->1

  (1,2) -> 42

  (3,2) -> 1

  (3,3) -> 1

  (3,4) -> 1

  (3,5) -> 1

  (3,6) -> 1
```

3. It is possible to extract the full matrix (and include all the zeros) from sparse matrix by using the `full` function:

```
octave:4> B=full(A)

B =

    0   42    0    0    0    0

    0    0    0    0    0    0

    3    3    3    3    3    3

    0    0    0    0    0    0

    0    0    0    0    0    0
```

What just happened?

The message returned in Command 1 tells us that Octave interprets the variable as a sparse matrix with 5 rows and 6 columns. The `nnz` variable indicates the number of non-zero elements in the matrix. Here none of the elements has been initialized, so `nnz` equals 0. After Command 2, we see that we have 7 non-zero elements corresponding to 23 % of all matrix elements. Note that the elements in a sparse matrix are printed in a different manner than what we are used to. The parentheses indicate the row and the column indices of all non-zero elements and are printed column-wise.

You can perform operations on a sparse matrix, just as you do on normal matrix arrays, and sparse matrices can also have complex elements.

 The current version of Octave (version 3.2.4) only supports sparse two-dimensional arrays. Higher dimensional sparse arrays may be supported in future versions.

This way of creating a sparse matrix is not very efficient because every time we assign a value to the array, Octave has to reallocate memory (and therefore communicate with the operating system). This significantly increases the execution time if you fill in many elements. If you know the number of non-zero elements in the matrix, you can use an alternative way to create the sparse matrix. In the *Have a go hero* exercise later in this chapter, you will see how to do this. In order not to get lost in details here, we will use the simple method described above since this suffices for our purpose.

Memory usage

You can see how much memory Octave uses for the variables A (Commands 1-2) and B (Command 4) with whos. A takes up 112 bytes, whereas B uses 240 bytes (corresponding to 30 doubles of 8 bytes each). You might expect A to use 56 bytes and not 112. The reason for the additional memory usage is that Octave needs to keep track (and therefore use memory storage) of where the non-zero elements are located. Therefore, only instantiate a matrix as sparse if it has sufficiently many zeros.

We are now ready to implement the Poisson solver.

Implementation and package functions

Above, it was shown that we need to solve the equation:

$$\mathbf{A\varphi = b}, \qquad\qquad (6.18)$$

where $\mathbf{A}$ is the coefficient matrix, given in Equations (6.14) and (6.17), φ is the vector that we are trying to find and represents, for example, the temperature at the grid points. The vector $\mathbf{b}$ has elements given by the source term and grid distance for interior grid point, as well as the boundary conditions for boundary points. We may write this as:

$$\text{interior points: } b_n = f_n \Delta^2,$$
$$\text{boundary points: } b_n = \phi_n, \, n = 1, N_{grid} \qquad (6.19)$$

To solve the Poisson equation, we basically need to:

1. Specify the source term and the boundary values.
2. Generate the coefficient matrix.
3. Solve the linear equation system.

In addition, we need to convert between the vector and matrix arrays for the two-dimensional case.

Since **b** is given by the problem, we only need to create the coefficient matrix. We will choose here to program one Octave function that generates the matrix for the one-dimensional Poisson equation and another function that generates the matrix for the two-dimensional case.

The coefficient matrix for one dimension

The function `cmat_1d` generates the coefficient matrix for Equation (6.14) and is given below in Code Listing 6.1:

```
Code Listing 6.1
#                                                          #1
# Usage:                                                   #2
#       A = cmat_1d(ngrids)                                #3
#                                                          #4
# Coefficient matrix for the one-dimensional              #5
# Poisson equation.                                        #6
# The return matrix is a sparse type.                      #7
#                                                          #8
                                                           #9
function A = cmat_1d(ngrids)                               #10
                                                           #11
  if ( nargin!=1 | nargout>1 )                             #12
    usage("Invalid call");                                 #13
  elseif ( ngrids< 1 )                                     #14
    usage("Input argument not valid");                     #15
  endif                                                    #16
                                                           #17
  A = sparse(ngrids, ngrids);                              #18
                                                           #19
  A(1,1)=A(ngrids,ngrids)=1;                               #20
                                                           #21
  for n=2:ngrids-1                                         #22
    A(n,[n-1 n n+1])= [1 -2 1];                            #23
  endfor                                                   #24
                                                           #25
endfunction                                                #26
```

From Code Listing 6.1, we see that the user calls the function with one single argument, the number of grid points. Lines 1-16 deal with documentation and function call validation. In line 18, we instantiate the output as a sparse matrix with dimensions N_{grid} x N_{grid}. The boundary points (first and last grid points) are set in line 20.

From the coefficient matrix, we see that each row has three elements with values 1, -2, 1. If the row represents an interior grid point, we assign these three values to the correct matrix elements inside the `for` loop (lines 22-24) with a single vectorized command in order to avoid a nested loop.

Once again, I stress that this way of declaring a sparse matrix is not appropriate for very large matrices, because we have to reallocate memory every time we assign a value to the matrix. In the exercise at the end of the chapter, you will be asked to instantiate the matrix in a different manner and implement this into an optimized version of `cmat_1d`.

This is all the coding we need to do in order to solve the one dimensional Poisson equation.

The coefficient matrix for two dimensions

The coefficient matrix for the two-dimensional Poisson problem is a bit more complicated to program because of the boundary points, but it follows the same basic idea as Code Listing 6.1 and the interface is the same. I will omit the documentation section and the function call checks in the code:

```
Code Listing 6.2
function A = cmat_2d(ngrids)                              #1
                                                          #2
  ngrids2 = ngrids^2;                                     #3
  A = sparse(ngrids2, ngrids2);                           #4
                                                          #5
  for n=1:ngrids2                                         #6
                                                          #7
    if ( n<ngrids | n>ngrids2-ngrids |                   #8
      rem(n-1,ngrids)==0 | rem(n, ngrids)==0 )            #9
      A(n,n) = 1;                                         #10
    else                                                  #11
      c_indices = [n-ngrids, n-1, n, n+1, n+ngrids];      #12
      A(n, c_indices) = [1 1 -4 1 1];                     #13
    endif                                                 #14
  endfor                                                  #15
                                                          #16
endfunction                                               #17
```

Here the boundary points are extracted in code lines 8-9. The first and second statements pick out the upper and lower boundary points where $i = 1$ and $i = N_{grid}$ and the third and fourth statement pick out the boundary points on the 'side' of the domain, where $j = 1$ and $j = N_{grid}$. See the figure above. It should be clear what lines 12-13 do. `c_indices` is just an auxiliary array.

The conversion function

Recall that whenever we are dealing with two-dimensional domains, we rearrange the two-dimensional grid points into a one-dimensional array using Equation (6.15). The motivation for this rearrangement was that we can formulate the problem as a linear equation system. From the user's point of view, it would be intuitive to visualize the solution in two dimensions rather than in one dimension (it is a two-dimensional problem after all). Also, it is much easier for the user to provide the source term and boundary conditions through the two-dimensional array rather than setting up the vector **b** herself. The package should therefore provide the user with some functionality that can do the transformation between the one and two-dimensional arrays. Code Listing 6.3 shows one such function that can perform the transformation both ways, that is, from a two-dimensional array to a one-dimensional array and vice versa according to Equation (6.15):

```
Code Listing 6.3
# Usage:                                                          #1
#    b = vecmat_convert(a)                                        #2
#                                                                 #3
# If a is a vector returns corresponding matrix.If a is a matrix  #4
# returns corresponding vector according to n=(i-1)*Ngrids + j    #5
#                                                                 #6
# Notices                                                         #7
#   1) the matrix must be square                                  #8
#   2) if a is vector sqrt(length(a)) must be a whole number      #9
#   3) and that if vecmat_convert returns a vector it             #10
#      is a column vector                                         #11
#                                                                 #12
                                                                  #13
function  b = vecmat_convert(a)                                   #14
                                                                  #15
  type = isvector(a);                                             #16
  switch type                                                     #17
                                                                  #18
  case 0                                                          #19
                                                                  #20
    if ( !issquare(a) )                                           #21
      usage("Input not a square matrix");                         #22
    endif                                                         #23
                                                                  #24
    ngrids = rows(a);                                             #25
    for i=1:ngrids                                                #26
      for j=1:ngrids                                              #27
        n=(i-1)*ngrids + j;                                       #28
        b(n)=a(i,j);                                              #29
      endfor                                                      #30
```

```
      endfor                                              #31
    b = b';                                               #32
                                                          #33
  case 1                                                  #34
                                                          #35
    ngrids = sqrt(length(a));                             #36
    if ( ngrids != floor(ngrids) )                        #37
      usage("sqrt(length(a)) must be a whole number");    #38
    endif                                                 #39
                                                          #40
    for i=1:ngrids                                        #41
      for j=1:ngrids                                      #42
        n=(i-1)*ngrids + j;                               #43
        b(i,j) = a(n);                                    #44
      endfor                                              #45
    endfor                                                #46
                                                          #47
  otherwise                                               #48
    error("Something is wrong with the input variable");  #49
  endswitch                                               #50
                                                          #51
  endfunction                                             #52
```

The code should be straightforward. One thing to notice however, is that in line 29, we fill up the return vector which will be a row vector. In line 32, we transpose the vector such that the function returns the vector as a column vector.

Testing the functions

Before we begin to solve interesting physics problems, we must check that the three functions work as intended.

The coefficient matrices

In cmat_1d and cmat_2d, the coefficient matrices for one and two-dimensional systems are generated. We could check the output from each function manually by printing the elements one-by-one, but this is a tedious task and you are likely to miss some of the mistakes (well, I know I am). We should instead make a graphical representation of the matrices. To this end, the imagesc function comes in handy.

Basically, the `imagesc` function displays matrix elements with a colour depending on their values. If we choose a gray colour map, black elements indicate the minimum value in the matrix and white indicates maximum values. All the other elements are then toned gray depending on their value—the higher value the lighter the gray. This is ideal for our purpose since our matrices follow a certain pattern and contain only three different values, -2, 0, and 1 for the one-dimensional Poisson problem and -4, 0, and 1 for the two-dimensional problem.

Let us go ahead and try it out.

Time for action – using imagesc

1. Let us first consider a one dimensional problem with 20 grid points. The coefficient matrix is generated by calling `cmat_1d`:

   ```
   octave:5> A=cmat_1d(20);
   ```

2. To set the gray colour map, use (also see *Chapter 3*):

   ```
   octave:6> colormap("gray");
   ```

3. To make a scaled image of the matrix, we use:

   ```
   octave:7> imagesc(full(A))
   ```

   The result is shown in the left-hand side figure below.

What just happened?

Notice that in Command 7, we use the full matrix of A because `imagesc` does not currently support sparse matrices. It is easy to see that matrix elements indeed follow the matrix given by Equation (6.14).

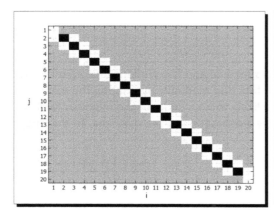 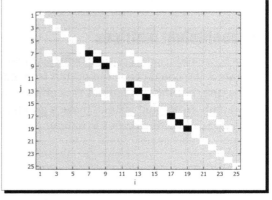

For the two-dimensional problem, we can do the same. The result is shown in the right figure for a domain discretized into a 5 x 5 grid. For this grid size, we have 16 boundary points which are given by ones (white) on the matrix diagonal and only 9 interior points given by -4 (black)—see Equation (6.17). The so-called "fringes" on each side of the diagonal represent the finite differencing between the different rows in the two-dimensional grid. By the way, why are the zero elements in the right figure brighter than in the left figure?

[Instead of imagesc, you can use the spy function. This will show all non-zero elements in the matrix array, but it does not indicate the values.]

The figure also illustrates the sparseness of the problem. For the one-dimensional case, only 14 % of the matrix elements are non-zero and for the two-dimensional problem, it is only 9.8 %. As mentioned above, for larger arrays this is even more extreme!

Comparison with analytical solution

In the example of the gold rod, we could actually find the analytical solution given in Equation (6.3). We should always check against analytical solutions when possible!

Time for action – comparing with analytical solution

1. First we type in the physical constants given by the problem. Let us use $Q = 10$ kiloWatts per meter cubed (kW m^{-3}), $k = 319$ Watts per Kelvin per meter (W K^{-1} m^{-1}), $L = 0.5$ meter and $T_0 = 273$ Kelvin:

   ```
   octave:8> Q=10000; k = 319; L=0.5; T_0=273;
   ```

2. We then need to specify the number of grid points (including the boundary grid points):

   ```
   octave:9>N_grids = 20;
   ```

   This gives a grid spacing of $\Delta = \dfrac{L}{N_{grid}-1}$:

   ```
   octave:10> delta = L/(N_grid-1);
   ```

3. From this, we can set the source term and boundary values:

   ```
   octave:11> b = -Q/k*delta^2*ones(N_grids,1);
   octave:12> b(1)=b(N_grids)=T_0;
   ```

4. Next, we need the coefficient matrix which we obtain from cmat_1d:

   ```
   octave:13> A=cmat_1d(ngrids);
   ```

5. We have now specified everything that we need in order to calculate the temperature profile: the vector b and the matrix A. The temperature profile is then found by solving the linear equation system. In Octave, we use the left division operator:

```
octave;14> T=A\b;
```

That's it!

What just happened?

The commands were explained above, but we should of course display the result somehow. We know how we can do this from *Chapter 3*:

```
octave:15> x=linspace(0,L,ngrids); plot(x,T);
```

The result is shown in the figure below, where the numerical solution is given by the red squares and the analytical solution, Equation (6.3), is plotted with a blue line.

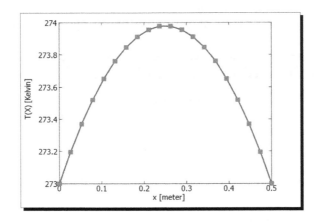

We see a perfect agreement which indicates that our implementation is correct.

Two dimensions

We formulated a two-dimensional heat problem in Equations (6.4) and (6.5). Since the source term is zero, this is an example of a Laplace equation, a special case of the Poisson equation. Let us find a numerical solution to this using our functions.

Time for action – solving a two-dimensional Laplace equation

1. We start by specifying the temperature at the edges of the plate, the number of grid points, and the spatial coordinate (recall that the package only supports square domains such that $y = x$):

```
octave:16> T_0 = 300; N_grids = 50; L = 0.1; x = linspace(0, L,
  N_grids);
```

2. The source term is zero:

```
octave:17> B = zeros(N_grids, N_grids);
```

3. The boundary conditions can be specified as:

```
octave:18> B(:,1) = sin(pi*x/L) + T0; B(1,:) = T0; (N_grids,:)=T0;
  B(:,N_grids)=T0;
```

4. To convert B into the appropriate vector format, we use the vecmat_convert function(Code Listing 6.3):

```
octave:19> b = vecmat_convert(B);
```

5. The coefficient matrix is generated via the command:

```
Octave:20> A = cmat_2d(N_grids);
```

6. The solution is therefore:

```
octave:21> t = A\b;
```

7. Now t is a vector and contains the numerical solution to the problem. This is not really what we want to end up with since the problem is two-dimensional. We call vecmat_convert again to convert the vector into a matrix:

```
octave:22> T = vecmat_convert(t);
```

8. We can visualize the solution through the following command:

```
octave:23> [X Y] = meshgrid(x,x); surf(X,Y,T); view(50,30);
```

9. The output is shown in the figure below:

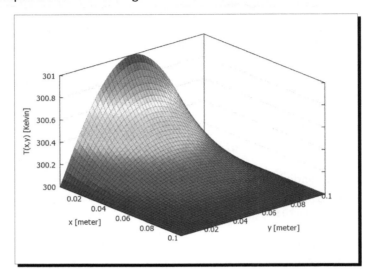

What just happened?

Again, the commands were explained above. Did you notice how fast Octave was able to solve the equation system in Command 21? On my workstation, it took around 0.09 seconds—and we are dealing with 2500 equations and unknowns! Surprisingly perhaps, it is generating the coefficient matrix that takes up most of the time (around 0.3 seconds).

Octave chooses the fastest method to solve the linear equation system. This choice depends on the coefficient matrix. In our case it is a weak diagonally dominant matrix, because the sum of the off-diagonal elements in the matrix is equal to the absolute value of the diagonal element for each row.

 If you study the Poisson equation on the same grid, but for different boundary conditions and source terms, you need only generate the coefficient matrix once.

I will leave it up to you to compare the result with the analytical solution.

More examples

Once we start feeling comfortable with the functions, we can find the solution to more complicated problems, for example, the two dimensional Laplace equation:

$$\nabla^2 \phi = 0 \qquad (6.20)$$

subjected to boundary conditions:

$$\phi\,(x,\,0) = \phi(x,\,L) = \sin\,(\pi\,x\,/\,L), \quad \phi\,(0,\,y) = \phi\,(L,\,y) = \sin\,(\pi y\,/\,L)\,. \qquad (6.21)$$

Something even more exotic, the Poisson equation:

$$\nabla^2 \phi\,(x,\,y) = f\,(x,\,y)\,, \qquad (6.22)$$

with boundary conditions:

$$\phi\,(x,\,0) = \phi(x,\,L) = 0, \quad \phi\,(0,\,y) = \phi\,(L,\,y) = 0, \qquad (6.23)$$

where the source term f is given by randomly positioned spikes with some amplitude, say 3. Solutions to these two problems are shown in the figure below using a grid size 80 x 80:

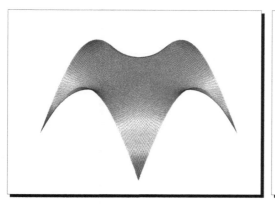 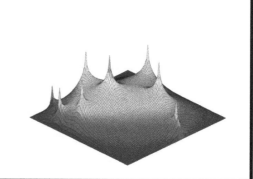

Wrapping everything into one function

We can easily wrap everything into a single function. This function then simply takes the source term and the boundary values as input. If the input is a vector, we have a one dimensional Poisson equation, otherwise, if it is a matrix, we a have two- dimensional Poisson equation. The number of grid points will also be specified via the source input array.

In Command 11, we multiply the interior source term with Δ^2 in accordance with Equation (6.19). It would be a nice feature if the function can take care of this as well. We can let an optional second argument be the domain length (again, recall that we only support square domains). If this argument is given to the function, the interior source term will be multiplied with Δ^2.

A programming flow chart of a wrapping function as shown below, and the corresponding function `pois_fd` is given in Code Listing 6.4. To save some space, validation of the inputs and outputs are omitted.

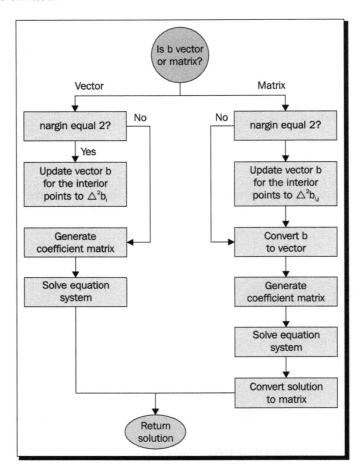

Code Listing 6.4

```
#                                                                    #1
# Usage:                                                             #2
#   phi = pois_fd(b, L)                                              #3
#                                                                    #4
# Solves the one and two dimensional Poisson equation using          #5
# finite difference.                                                 #6
#                                                                    #7
# b can be a vector (one dimension) or matrix (two dimensions)       #8
# and specifies the source term and boundary conditions.            #9
#                                                                    #10
```

```
# L is the length of the simulation domain and is optional.     #11
# If provided the source term is updated to b=delta^2*b.        #12
#                                                                #13
                                                                 #14
function phi = pois_fd(b, L)                                     #15
                                                                 #16
  type = isvector(b);                                            #17
                                                                 #18
  switch type                                                    #19
  case 0                                                         #20
    if ( !issquare(b) )                                          #21
      usage("Input matrix must be square");                      #22
    endif                                                        #23
                                                                 #24
    ngrids = rows(b);                                            #25
    if ( nargin==2 )                                             #26
      delta = L/(ngrids-1);                                      #27
      b(2:ngrids-1, 2:ngrids-1) = ...                            #28
      delta^2*b(2:ngrids-1, 2:ngrids-1);                         #29
    endif                                                        #30
                                                                 #31
    b = feval("vecmat_convert",b);                               #32
    A = feval("cmat_2d", ngrids);                                #33
    phi = A\b;                                                   #34
    phi = feval("vecmat_convert", phi);                          #35
                                                                 #36
  case 1                                                         #37
    ngrids = length(b);                                          #38
    if ( nargin==2 )                                             #39
      delta = L/(ngrids-1);                                      #40
      b(2:ngrids-1) = delta^2*b(2:ngrids-1);                     #41
    endif                                                        #42
                                                                 #43
    A = feval("cmat_1d", ngrids);                                #44
    phi = A\b;                                                   #45
                                                                 #46
  otherwise                                                      #47
    error("Something is wrong with the input argument");         #48
  endswitch                                                      #49
                                                                 #50
endfunction                                                      #51
```

Whenever we call `cmat_1d`, `cmat_2d`, or `vecmat_convert`, we use the `feval` function. You can also call the functions directly.

Let us reuse the problem of the temperature profile in the gold rod to make an example of how to use this function:

```
octave:24> b=-10000/319*ones(20,1); b(1)=b(20)=273;
octave:25> T = pois_fd(b, 0.5);
```

which produces the same values of T as seen above.

Note that `pois_fd` will have to generate the coefficient matrix every time it is called. This means that it may not be a good choice to use this function if you have to study the Poisson equation on the same grid dimensions, but for different boundary conditions and source terms.

Have a go hero – optimizing the usage of the sparse function

To optimize the `cmat_1d` and `cmat_2d`, we must instantiate the sparse array differently. The sparse function also supports the following syntax:

```
A= sparse(i, j, values, n, m);
```

where I and j are the row and column indices for the non-zero elements, `values` is an array with the element values, and n and m give the size of the matrix.

For example, to instantiate the sparse matrix from Commands 1 and 2, we could use:

```
octave:34> A = sparse([1 3 3 3 3 3 3], [2 1 2 3 4 5 6],\
[42 3 3 3 3 3 3], 5, 6);
```

In this way, Octave knows the number of non-zero elements and can allocate the needed memory using one single communication with the operating system.

Of course, you can use auxiliary arrays to hold the indices and values:

```
octave:35>r_indices = [1 3 3 3 3 3 3]; c_indices = [2 1 2 3 4  5 6];
values = [42 3 3 3 3 3 3];
octave:36> A = sparse(r_indices, c_indices, values, 5,6);
```

From this information, optimize `cmat_1d` such that it contains no loops and no need for memory reallocation at all. Check your implementation with `imagesc` (or `spy`).

Try to estimate the speed-up you gained from this optimization using 10000 grid points. (On my machine the speed-up is around 110.)

The pois-solv package

We can now gather the four functions `cmat_1d`, `cmat_2d`, `vecmat_convert`, and `pois_fd` into an Octave package. There are a few advantages of packing the functions together rather than just copying the individual m-files:

- The files are archived into single standard file format.
- You can install the package easily with the `pkg` command, load and unload the functions, and not be concerned with where the functions are located (that is, if they are in the Octave search path).
- With the package, you can add any relevant information about the functionality.
- You can upload the package to Octave-Forge.

There are a few things we need to do in order to package the functions properly.

Organizing files into the package directory

First you will need a package directory—we will call this directory `poissolv`[1], but you can call it whatever you want. Inside the package directory, we have the following files and directory:

1. The DESCRIPTION file: this text file contains a description of the package, for example, the version number and author. This file is mandatory.

2. The COPYING file: contains the license under which the package is released. We shall use GNU General Public License version 3 or later. This file is also mandatory. Note that this license will affect any application using the package. See the full license agreement (link is given below).

3. The INDEX file: a text file that lists the package functions in different categories. The INDEX file is optional.

4. The `inst` directory: a directory containing all the package m-files. It is not mandatory, but the `inst` directory must be included if the package consists of any m-files, which it usually will.

Let us see examples of the files one-by-one.

---

[1]*Not to be confused with the package name **pois-solv***

The DESCRIPTION file

An example of the `DESCRIPTION` file is shown below:

```
# DESCRIPTION file for the pois-solv package        #1
Name: pois-solv                                     #2
Version: 0.1.0                                      #3
Date: 6-12-2010                                     #4
Title: pois-solv                                    #5
Author: Jesper Hansen, nomail@somedomain.org        #6
Maintainer: Jesper Hansen                           #7
Description: Solver for the one and                 #8
  two-dimensional Poisson equation                  #9
using finite differencing.                          #10
License: GPL version 3 or later                     #11
```

Line 1 begins with a hash mark and is a comment line—just like comment lines in scripts and functions. In lines 2-11, we list the package name, version number, date, and so forth. Each of these lines begins with a keyword, for example, `Version`. The keywords are recognized by the packaging program and many of them must be included in the `DESCRIPTION` file. The ones listed above are the mandatory ones. You can also provide a link to a web page if additional information can be found there using the keyword `Url`.

A new line plus a space (lines 8-10) is interpreted by the package manager as a line continuation.

The COPYING file

The user must be informed about the package license. Is it legal to make copies of the package and give it to your friends? Can you modify the code and distribute that? All this information is provided in the license agreement in the COPYING file.

As mentioned above, we shall use GNU General Public License version 3 or later versions. From the web page, `http://www.gnu.org/licenses/gpl.html`, you can read more about this license and download a text file with a generic license agreement that needs only little editing for most purposes. In a modified and very short form (again to save some space), the pois-solv package license reads:

```
The pois-solv package is free software: you can redistribute    #1
it and/or modify it under the terms of the GNU General          #2
Public License as published by the Free Software Foundation,    #3
either version 3 ofthe License, or any later version.           #4
                                                                #5
pois-solv is distributed in the hope that it will be useful,    #6
but WITHOUT ANY WARRANTY; without even the implied warranty     #7
of MERCHANTABILITY or FITNESS FOR A PARTICULAR PURPOSE. See     #8
<http://www.gnu.org/licenses/> for more information.            #9
```

Usually you would also include a license agreement in each m-file.

The INDEX file

The package contains three basic functions, namely, `cmat_1d`, `cmat_2d`, and `vecmat_convert`, as well as the wrapper function `pois_fd`. We can specify this to the packaging program with the `INDEX` file:

```
# Index file for pois-solv                          #1
                                                    #2
toolbox >>pois-solv                                 #3
Basic functions                                     #4
 cmat_1d.m cmat_2d.m vecmat_convert.m               #5
Wrapper function                                    #6
pois_fd.m                                           #7
```

Line 2 is mandatory and specifies the package name to the package manager.

Building the package

I assume that we have saved all thepackage files (m-files and `INDEX`, `COPYING`, and `DESCRIPTION` files) in the same directory. To build the package, we go through the following steps:

1. Make the package directory:

   ```
   octave:26> mkdir"poissolv"
   ```

   > Note: On Windows systems, you may need to provide the full path, for example, the above command should be
   >
   > **octave:27>mkdir"C:/Document and Settings/GNU Octave/poissolv"**

2. Make the inst subdirectory:

   ```
   octave:28> mkdir"poissolv/inst";
   ```

   Again, you may need to provide the full path on Windows.

3. Copy the files `DESCRIPTION`, `COPYING`, and `INDEX` to the package directory, for example:

   ```
   octave:29> copyfile("DESCRIPTION", "poissolv");
   ```

4. Copy the m files into the `inst` sub directory:

   ```
   octave:30> copyfile("cmat_1d.m", "poissolv/inst/");
   ```

   and so forth for `cmat_2d.m`, `vecmat_convert.m` and `pois_fd.m`.

5. Archive and compress the package directory:

    ```
    octave:31> tar("pois-solv.tar", "poissolv");
    octave:32> gzip("pois-solv.tar");
    ```

6. Finally, build the Octave package:

    ```
    octave:33> pkg build ./ pois-solv.tar.gz
    ```

We used the package manager command `pkg` in *Chapter 1*, when we discussed how to install Octave packages—it can also be used to build them. Command 31 will produce a file called `pois-solv-0.1.0.tar.gz` which is your Octave package.

 You can, of course, do steps 1-5 in a terminal under GNU/Linux or via Explorer in Windows. Windows may not have the programs tar and gzip installed, but it comes with the Octave Windows distribution.

You should now try to install your package. How to do this was explained in *Chapter 1*. Also, use the package manager to get a description of the package.

Here, we have only gone through the very basics of how to build packages. There are many other features that can be helpful when you want to do something more sophisticated. For example, a package can be dependent on certain versions of other packages, or have C++ or Fortran code associated with it, which may need to be compiled. Consult the Octave manual if you want to do more advanced package building.

Limitations and possible extensions to the package

There is of course room for improvement and extensions to the package, for example:

1. `cmat_1d` and `cmat_2d` are not optimized in that they instantiate the sparse arrays in a way that forces Octave to reallocate memory. The functions are therefore slow for very large grid sizes. In the exercise above, it was shown how this can be fixed.

2. We use Octave's built-in linear equation solver. While fast, we could possibly reduce the execution time by using a different method. For example, a so-called relaxation method may be relevant for large system sizes.

3. We could improve the accuracy by using higher order finite difference schemes.

4. By implementing coordinate transformation methods, the package can support different geometries.

5. We have completely ignored the three-dimensional Poisson equation. A natural extension of the package would be including a solver for this problem.

6. We could implement other types of boundary conditions.

7. Make implementations of more advanced and precise numerical techniques like finite elements.

You probably have some things to add to the list yourself. If we wish to improve the package, we should first think about where to start. For example, if the time spent on solving the linear equation system is much smaller than it is for generating the coefficient matrix, we should first try to optimize `cmat_1d` and `cmat_2d` before we move on and implement a new linear equation solver. We saw that this was actually the case: Octave's linear equation solver spends 0.09 seconds on solving an equation system of 2500 unknowns (it is very unlikely that we can do better than that even if we tried to use a specialized algorithm), whereas our current implementation of the `cmat_2d` took 0.3 seconds.

If we increase the grid size, this difference becomes even more pronounced: for a two dimensional problem with size $N_{grid} \times N_{grid} = 200 \times 200$, we have 40 thousand linear equations that need to be solved. Octave's solver is capable of doing this in around 1.1 second on my PC, but it takes 149 seconds to generate the coefficient matrix. This means that we can gain a lot from focusing on ways to optimize `cmat_2d` (and `cmat_1d`), especially if we need to solve large systems.

Summary

The main purpose of this chapter was to introduce you to making your own Octave package. Specifically, we learned about:

♦   The one and two-dimensional Poisson equation.

♦   The finite difference scheme for second order derivatives.

♦   How sparse matrices can be used in Octave.

♦   The `imagesc` function.

♦   Wrapper functions.

♦   The `DESCRIPTION`, `COPYING`, and `INDEX` package files.

♦   The Octave package manager `pkg`, and how to use this to build your own Octave package.

There is much more to know about Octave packages, but hopefully you can use this chapter as a starting point when you build your first package.

7

More Examples: Data Analysis

Octave is an ideal tool to perform many different types of data analysis. The data can be generated by other programs or be collected from a database and then loaded into Octave's workspace. The data analysis tools in Octave are based on a truly impressive arsenal of different functions. We will only discuss a few of them here, namely, how to perform the simplest statistical analysis, function fitting, and Fourier (or spectral) analysis using the fast Fourier transform.

In brief terms, upon reading this chapter, you will learn:

- ◆ More about the ASCII file formats that can be loaded into Octave's workspace.
- ◆ How you can use Octave to perform simple descriptive statistics.
- ◆ About fitting different functions to data.
- ◆ How to use Octave to perform Fourier analysis.

Loading data files

When performing a statistical analysis of a particular problem, you often have some data stored in a file. In *Chapter 4*, it was shown how you can save your variables (or the entire workspace) using different file formats and then load them back in again. Octave can, of course, also load data from files generated by other programs. There are certain restrictions when you do this which we will discuss here. In the following matter, we will only consider ASCII files, that is, readable text files.

When you load data from an ASCII file using the `load` command (see *Chapter 4*), the data is treated as a two-dimensional array. We can then think of the data as a matrix where lines represent the matrix rows and columns the matrix columns. For this matrix to be well defined, the data must be organized such that all the rows have the same number of columns (and therefore the columns the same number of rows). For example, the content of a file called `series.dat` can be:

```
1      232.1     334

2      245.2     334

3      456.23    342

4      555.6     321
```

In *Chapter 4*, we learned how to load this into Octave's workspace:

octave:1> load -ascii series.dat;

whereby the data is stored in the variable named `series`. In fact, Octave is capable of loading the data even if you do not specify the ASCII format. The number of rows and columns are then:

octave:2> size(series)

ans =
```
   4      3
```

I prefer the file extension `.dat`, but again this is optional and can be anything you wish, say `.txt`, `.ascii`, `.data`, or nothing at all.

In the data files you can have:

- Octave comments
- Data blocks separated by blank lines (or equivalent empty rows)
- Tabs or single and multi-space for number separation

Thus, the following data file will successfully load into Octave:

```
# First block

1      232     334

2      245     334

3      456     342

4      555     321
```

```
# Second block

1            231           334

2            244           334

3            450           341

4            557           327
```

The resulting variable is a matrix with 8 rows and 3 columns. If you know the number of blocks or the block sizes, you can then separate the blocked-data.

Now, the following data stored in the file `bad.dat` will not load into Octave's workspace:

```
1     232.1      334

2     245.2

3     456.23

4     555.6
```

because line 1 has three columns whereas lines 2-4 have two columns. If you try to load this file, Octave will complain:

```
octave:3>  load -ascii bad.dat

error: load: bad.dat: inconsisitent number of columns near line 2

error:load: unable to extract matrix size from file 'bad.dat'
```

Simple descriptive statistics

In *Chapter 5*, we implemented an Octave function `mcintgr` and its vectorized version `mcintgrv`. This function can evaluate the integral for a mathematical function f in some interval $[a; b]$ where the function is positive. The Octave function is based on the Monte Carlo method and the return value, that is, the integral, is therefore a stochastic variable. When we calculate a given integral, we should as a minimum present the result as a mean or another appropriate measure of a central value together with an associated statistical uncertainty. This is true for any other stochastic variable, whether it is the height of the pupils in class, length of a plant's leaves, and so on.

In this section, we will use Octave for the most simple statistical description of stochastic variables.

Histogram and moments

Let us calculate the integral given in Equation (5.9) one thousand times using the vectorized version of the Monte Carlo integrator:

```
octave:4> for i=1:1000

> s(i) = mcintgrv("sin", 0, pi, 1000);

> endfor
```

The array s now contains a sequence of numbers which we know are approximately 2. Before we make any quantitative statistical description, it is always a good idea to first plot a histogram of the data as this gives an approximation to the true underlying probability distribution of the variable s. The easiest way to do this is by using Octave's hist function which can be called using:

```
octave:5> hist(s, 30, 1)
```

The first argument, s, to hist is the stochastic variable, the second is the number of bins that s should be grouped into (here we have used 30), and the third argument gives the sum of the heights of the histogram (here we set it to 1). The histogram is shown in the figure below. If hist is called via the command hist(s), s is grouped into ten bins and the sum of the heights of the histogram is equal to sum(s).

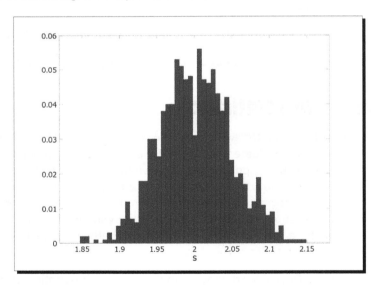

From the figure, we see that mcintgrv produces a sequence of random numbers that appear to be normal (or Gaussian) distributed with a mean of 2. This is what we expected. It then makes good sense to describe the variable via the sample mean defined as:

$$\bar{s} = \frac{1}{N} \sum_{i=i}^{N} s_i, \qquad (7.1)$$

where N is the number of samples (here 1000) and s_i the i'th data point, as well as the sample variance given by:

$$\mathrm{var}\,(s) = \frac{1}{N-1} \sum_{i=i}^{N} (s_i - \bar{s})^2. \qquad (7.2)$$

The variance is a measure of the distribution width and therefore an estimate of the statistical uncertainty of the mean value. Sometimes, one uses the standard deviation instead of the variance. The standard deviation is simply the square root of the variance $\sigma = \sqrt{\mathrm{var}\,(s)}$.

To calculate the sample mean, sample variance, and the standard deviation in Octave, you use:

```
octave:6> mean(s)
```

```
ans = 1.9999
```

```
octave:7> var(s)
```

```
ans = 0.002028
```

```
octave:8> std(s)
```

```
ans = 0.044976
```

In the statistical description of the data, we can also include the skewness which measures the symmetry of the underlying distribution around the mean. If it is positive, it is an indication that the distribution has a long tail stretching towards positive values with respect to the mean. If it is negative, it has a long negative tail. The skewness is often defined as:

$$\mathrm{skew}\,(s) = \frac{1}{N} \sum_{i=1}^{N} \left(\frac{s_i - \bar{s}}{\sigma}\right)^3. \qquad (7.3)$$

We can calculate this in Octave via:

```
octave:9> skewness(s)
```

```
ans = -0.15495
```

This result is a bit surprising because we would assume from the histogram that the data set represents numbers picked from a normal distribution which is symmetric around the mean and therefore has zero skewness. It illustrates an important point—be careful to use the skewness as a direct measure of the distributions symmetry—you need a very large data set to get a good estimate.[1]

---

[1]Also see discussion in "Numerical Recipes: The Art of Scientific Computing, 3rd Edition", Press et al., Cambridge University Press (2007).

You can also calculate the kurtosis which measures the flatness of the sample distribution compared to a normal distribution. Negative kurtosis indicates a relative flatter distribution around the mean and a positive kurtosis that the sample distribution has a sharp peak around the mean. The kurtosis is defined by the following:

$$\text{kurt}(s) = \frac{1}{N} \sum_{i=1}^{N} \left(\frac{s_i - \bar{s}}{\sigma}\right)^4 - 3. \tag{7.4}$$

It can be calculated by the `kurtosis` function.

```
octave:10> kurtosis(s)

ans = -0.02310
```

The kurtosis has the same problem as the skewness—you need a very large sample size to obtain a good estimate.

Sample moments

As you may know, the sample mean, variance, skewness, and kurtosis are examples of sample moments. The mean is related to the first moment, the variance the second moment, and so forth. Now, the moments are not uniquely defined. One can, for example, define the k'th absolute sample moment p_a^k and k'th central sample moment p_c^k as:

$$p_a^k = \frac{1}{N} \sum_{i=1}^{N} s_i^k \quad \text{and} \quad p_a^k = \frac{1}{N} \sum_{i=1}^{N} (s_i - \bar{s})^k. \tag{7.5}$$

Notice that the first absolute moment is simply the sample mean, but the first central sample moment is zero. In Octave, you can easily retrieve the sample moments using the `moment` function, for example, to calculate the second central sample moment you use:

```
octave:11> moment(s, 2, 'c')

ans = 0.002022
```

Here the first input argument is the sample data, the second defines the order of the moment, and the third argument specifies whether we want the central moment `'c'` or absolute moment `'a'` which is the default. Compare the output with the output from Command 7—why is it not the same?

Comparing data sets

Above, it was shown how you can use Octave to perform the very simplest statistical description of a single data set. In this section, we shall see how to statistically compare two data sets. What do we exactly mean by a statistical comparison? For example, we could test if two data sets statistically have the same means (this is known as the student's t-test), or if they have the same underlying probability distribution (the x^2 – test).

In Octave, you can perform almost all known statistical tests: the student's t-test, z-test, the Kolmogorov-Smirnov test, and many more. Here I will only show you how to perform one variance of the t-test and how to compute the Pearson correlation coefficient.

The correlation coefficient

The following table shows the height and weight of boys from age 2 to 15:

Age (Years)	Weight (Kilograms)	Height (Centi-metres)	Age (Years)	Weight (Kilograms)	Height (Centi-metres)
2	12.5	85.5	9	24.9	129.0
3	13.2	93.2	10	27.3	134.6
4	15.2	102.3	11	31.3	139.8
5	17.8	102.4	12	35.0	146.3
6	19.7	113.9	13	39.6	152.1
7	20.9	119.8	14	43.8	158.1
8	22.5	123.7	15	53.0	162.8

One can easily see that both height and weight are increasing with respect to age. To see if the two data sets are actually correlated, we need to be a bit more careful. Usually the correlation between two data sets is quantified by using the Pearson's correlation coefficient which is given by:

$$r_p = \frac{\sum_{i=1}^{N} (x_i - \bar{x})(y_i - \bar{y})}{(N-1)\,\sigma_x \sigma_y} \, , \qquad (7.6)$$

where σ_x is the standard deviation of the data set x_i and σ_y is the standard deviation of y_i. Values of r_p around one indicates good correlation between the two data sets. The Peason correlation coefficient is easily calculated in Octave using cor (or corrcoef). This function has the syntax:

```
r = cor(x, y)
```

No need to explain, I guess.

Assume that we have stored the data in an ASCII file called boys.dat like this:

```
# Age    weight    Height
  2      12.5      85.5
  3      13.2      93.2
```

. . .

```
octave:12> load -ascii boys.dat;
```

We then need to find the correlation between the second and the third column:

```
octave:13> cor(boys(:,2), boys(:,3))
```

```
ans = 0.97066
```

That is, the two data sets are indeed correlated, which we would expect.

The student t-test

The following sequence of numbers shows the height of the pupils in a class of 21 children (in centimetres):

156.92 140.00 163.20 167.24 149.84 149.21 166.86 152.01 147.53 157.56 154.48 170.33 155.82 162.24 161.43 174.94 146.30 151.08 150.82 154.49 165.98

The mean is 157.07 centimetres. The national average height is 161.11 centimetres. Under the assumption that the height of the pupils is normal distributed around the mean, can we show that the mean is statistically the same as the national average? Octave's t_test can help. A simple version of the syntax is:

```
pvalue = t_test(x, m)
```

Here pvalue is the probability that the null hypothesis (that the two means are the same) is true, x is the data, and m is the mean that we test against.

Suppose we have the heights stored in an array called heights. To perform the test, we use:

```
octave:14> t_test(heights, 161.11)
```

```
ans = 0.0508369
```

which means that we cannot definitely conclude that the mean height in the class is the same as the national average height assuming no variance in the latter. Usually one accepts the null hypothesis for pvalue > 0.05, so here we have a border-line situation.

The table below lists some of the most common statistical test functions:

Function name	Description
t_test(x, m, opt)	Tests the null-hypothesis that the normal distributed sample data x has mean m.
t_test2(x, y, opt)	Tests the null-hypothesis that the normal distributed sample data x and y has same mean.

Function name	Description
`kolmogorov_smirnov_test(x, dist)`	Tests the null-hypothesis that the sample data x comes from the continuous distribution `dist`.
`kolmogorov_smirnov_test_2(x, y, opt)`	Tests the null-hypothesis that the sample data x and y come from the same continuous distribution.
`var_test (x, y, opt)`	Tests the null-hypothesis that the normal distributed sample data x and y have same variance (F-test).
`chisquare_test_homogeneity(x,y,c)`	Tests the null-hypothesis that x and y come from the same probability distribution using the bins given via c.

Function fitting

In many areas of science, you want to fit a function to data. This function can represent either an empirical or a theoretical model. There are many reasons to do this, for example, if the theoretical model agrees with the observed data values, the theory is likely to be right and hopefully you have gained new insight into the phenomenon you are studying.

In this section, we will discuss some of Octave's fitting functionality. I will not go into details with the algorithms that are behind the fitting functions—this will simply take up too much space and not be of much relevance for the points.

Polynomial fitting

Suppose we want to investigate the length of the leaves in two different families of trees at different heights. Normally the leaves are largest near the ground, in order to increase the photosynthesis. The figure below shows fabricated data of the leaf length as a function of height from the ground for two imaginary families of trees called tree A (red squares) and tree B (blue triangles). For some reason, we have the idea that the leaf length for tree A, we denote this by y^A, is a linear function with respect to height x, but for tree B, the leaf length y^B follows a third order polynomial with respect to height. That is, we should test if the models:

$$y^A(x) = c_1 x + c_0 \text{ and } y^B(x) = c_3 x^3 + c_2 x^2 + c_0 \tag{7.7}$$

can fit the data well if we use the polynomial coefficients as fitting parameters.

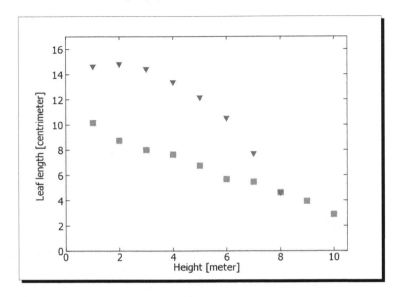

In Octave this is straightforward using `polyfit`. This function can be called via the following syntax:

```
[cfit s] = polyfit(x, y, n)
```

where `x` is the independent/free variable (in this case the height), `y` is the measured data (leaf length), and `n` is the degree of the polynomial. The first output is an array with the polynomial coefficients and therefore has length `n+1`, and the second is a structure that contains information about the fit. We shall study some the important structure fields below.

Time for action – using polyfit

1. Assume that we have loaded the relevant data into Octave and stored the leaf lengths of tree A and B in variables `yA` and `yB`. The corresponding heights are stored in `xA` and `xB`.

2. To fit the linear model to the data in `yA`, we do the following:

   ```
   octave:15> [cA sA] = polyfit(xA, yA, 1);
   ```

3. We must check if the fit made any sense at all. First, we can plot the resulting linear fit together with the data:

   ```
   octave:16> plot(xA, yA, 'rs', xA, sA.yf, 'r');
   ```

   and is shown in the figure below with red squares and a red line.

4. The fit of y^B to the third order polynomial follows the same procedure:

```
octave:17> [cB   sB] = polyfit(xB, yB, 3);

octave:18> hold on; plot(xB, yB, 'bv', xB, sB.yf, 'b');
```

The plot is shown in the figure below:

Notice that I have used the plotting style format `'rs'` and `'bv'`. Depending on your plotting backend, this may not be supported. You can change it to, for example, `'ro'` and `'b+'`

What just happened?

`polyfit` finds the polynomial coefficients $c_n, c_{n-1}, ..., c_1, c_0$ such that the difference between the polynomial (our statistical model) $y = y(x_i, c_n, c_{n-1}, ..., c_1, c_0)$ and the data points y_i is minimized by some measure. This measure is the sum of the residuals, $r_i = y_i - y$, that is:

$$\text{find } c_n, c_{n-1}, ..., c_1, c_0 \text{ to minimize } \sum_{i=1}^{N} r_i^2 = \sum_{i=1}^{N} (y_i - y)^2,$$

where N is the number of fitting points. This fitting procedure is called a least squares fit.

As mentioned above, `polyfit` returns a structure that stores information about the fit. In Command 16, we use one of the structure fields `yf` that contains the fitted values $y(x_i, c_n, c_{n-1}, ..., c_1, c_0)$ to plot the resulting fit. We could alternatively have used the polynomial coefficients returned in `cA`:

```
octave:19> cA
cA =
    -0.75172      10.52164
```

Using `polyval` (from *Chapter 3*):

```
octave:20> plot(xA, yA, 'rs', xA, polyval(cA, xA), 'r');
```

Goodness of the fit

From the figure above, it looks as if the fits represent the data quite well, that is, the polynomials seem to be good models of the leaf length variation. A visual verification of the fits and models in general is not really enough. Scientists often prefer some objective quantity to indicate whether the fit is satisfactory or not.

`polyfit` stores a quantity in the structure field `normr`, namely the 2-norm of the residuals. This is given by:

$$\text{norm}(r_i, 2) = \sqrt{\sum_{i=1}^{N} r_i^2}. \tag{7.8}$$

This is however not of much help here because this quantity depends on the absolute values of the residuals. One can instead use the correlation coefficient:

$$r_{\text{cor}} = 1 - \frac{\text{norm}(r_i, 2)^2}{(N-1)\sigma^2}, \quad 0 \le r_{\text{cor}} \le 1. \tag{7.9}$$

You can see that for small residuals (and possibly a good fit), the correlation coefficient is close to 1; if the fit is poor, it is close to 0. Unfortunately, `polyfit` won't calculate the quantity for you, but you can easily do it yourself.

Time for action – calculating the correlation coefficient

Let us try to calculate the correlation coefficient for the fit of the leaf length for tree A. We just need to follow Equation (7.9):

```
octave:21> denom = (length(yA) -  1)*var(yA);

octave:22> rcor = 1 - sA.normr^2/denom
rcor =   0.96801
```

This gives an indication that the fit is good as we expected.

What just happened?

In Command 21, we calculated the denominator in Equation (7.9). Notice that instead of calculating the square of the standard deviation, we simply use the variance found with `var`. From Equation (7.9), we see that the 2-norm of the residuals enters the nominator. This is already calculated in `polyfit` and stored in the structure field `normr`, so we use this in the evaluation of the correlation coefficient.

Residual plot

If there is a systematic deviation between the fit and the data, the model may have to be rejected. These deviations can be sufficiently small and are therefore not captured by the correlation coefficient. They can, however, be seen via residual plots. In Octave, it is straightforward to do, and I leave this to you to do as an exercise.

Non-polynomial fits

Of course, not everything can be described via simple polynomial models. Phenomena related to growth are for example often described via an exponential function or a power law. These two examples are trivial to solve with the polynomial fitting technique discussed above, but you may have particular fitting models that need a more general fitting procedure. Octave can help you with this as well.

Transforms

Before we discuss how to fit more general functions to data, it is worthwhile to see if we can transform the fitting function into a different form that allows us to use the polynomial fitting procedure above.

A very simple example of such a transform is if the data set follows a power law function, say:

$$y(x) = bx^a. \tag{7.10}$$

We can transform this into a linear equation by taking the logarithm on both sides:

$$\ln(y) = \ln(b) + a \ln(x). \tag{7.11}$$

In this way, the new variable $y' = \ln(y)$, is a linear function of $x' = \ln(x)$, that is, we can write $y' = ax' + b'$ with $b' = \ln(b)$. We then fit Equation (7.11) to the transformed data using the `polyfit` function. Remember to transform the fitted parameter b back using the inverse transform, $b = e^{b'}$.

In the example above, the transform is trivial. You could consider other possible ways of transforming your model. For example, if it is possible to Fourier transform the data and the model it could perhaps be a better choice to perform the fit in Fourier space. We will discuss the Fourier transform later in this chapter.

General least squares fitting

In case you cannot transform the model into a proper form that allows you to use `polyfit`, you can use `leasqr`. This function comes with the optimization package **optim** which can be downloaded from the Octave-Forge web page. See *Chapter 1* on how to install and load packages. `leasqr` is a really powerful function that allows you to perform even the most complicated fits—if I must choose my favorite Octave function, I think this would be it.

The syntax is as follows:

```
[yfit pfit cvg iter ...] = leasqr(x, y, p, fun, opt)
```

Describing all the inputs and outputs in sufficient detail would take a great deal of effort, so we shall only discuss a limited number of features, but these will take us quite far. If you are interested in knowing more about the function simply type: `help leasqr`.

The inputs are:

> `x`: the independent variable
>
> `y`: the measured/observed data
>
> `p`: an initial parameter guess
>
> `fun`: the model (fitting function)
>
> `opt`: up to six optional arguments specifying the weights of each data point, maximum number of iterations the algorithm can perform, and so on

`leasqr` can return 10 outputs, the first four are:

> `yfit`: the fitted function values
>
> `pfit`: the fitted parameter values
>
> `cvg`: is 1 if the fit converged (likely to be successful), 0 if not
>
> `iter`: number of iterations done

The crucial point when using `leasqr` is that you must provide the model in the form of an Octave function that can be fitted to the data set. This function must be dependent on at least one parameter and follow the syntax:

```
y = fun(x,p)
```

Again, `x` is the free variable, and `p` is the parameter list.

Let us illustrate `leasqr` by fitting the following two parameter model:

$$y(x) = \frac{1}{1 + \alpha x^{\beta}}$$

(7.12)

to some data that we simply generate ourselves. Note, α and β are the fitting parameters.

Time for action – using leasqr

1. Let us generate data with normally distributed random noise:

```
octave:23> x=linspace(0, 5); y = 1./(1 + 1.2*x.^1.8) + \
        > randn(1,100)*0.03;
```

2. Then we specify the model using the following function definition:

```
octave:24>  function y = ffun(x, p)

> y = 1./(1+p(1)*x.^p(2));

> endfunction
```

3. Give an initial guess of the parameters α and β:

```
octave:25> p = [0.5 0.0];
```

4. We can now fit the model to data:

```
octave:26> [yfit pfit cvg iter] = leasqr(x, y,  p, "ffun");
```

Easy!

5. We can check whether the fitting algorithm converged or not, and how many iterations it used:

```
octave:27> cvg, iter

cvg = 1
iter = 6
```

6. The values of the fitted parameters are of course important:

```
octave:28> pfit

p =
   1.1962
   1.7955
```

This is very close to the values that we would expect from Command 24. The fit is plotted together with the data in the figure below.

What just happened?

In Command 23, we instantiated the free variable x, and set it to be a vector with element values between 0 and 5 and consisting of one hundred elements. The variable y then plays the role of the dependent data set. We added a little noise with low amplitude to make it more realistic, hence the call to `randn`. In Command 24, we defined the model through an Octave function and we then set our initial guess in Command 25. This guess needs to be reasonable—how far from the true parameter value it can be depends on the model and the data. Sometimes the algorithm may not converge, and you must then use another (a better) initial guess. It should be clear what Commands 26 to 28 do.

 Always have a valid reason to use a specific functional form as a model. A fit of a model with too many or too few free parameters will fail to converge to the data set even though the function has the correct form.

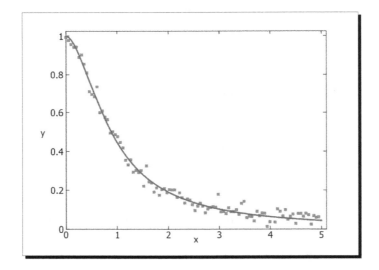

Note that if you follow the commands above, your fitted parameters may be a bit different and the number of iterations may be six plus or minus one depending on what random numbers your machine generated.

Have a go hero – calculating the deviation of the Monte Carlo integrator

In Command 4, we calculated the standard deviation of the Monte Carlo integration scheme for the integral $\int_0^\pi \sin(x)\, dx$. Here we used 1000 Monte Carlo loops. Calculate the standard deviation when the number of loops is, say 50, 70, ... , 1990, 2010. You can still use 1000 samples as the sample size. Determine the functional form of the standard deviation as a function of Monte Carlo loops.

Fourier analysis

The figure below shows the monthly average exchange rate between the Australian dollar and Danish kroner starting from January 1, 1991, and ending on March 2010. The y axis is the price in kroners for 100 dollars and the x axis is the month index after Janary 1, 1991. It is clearly seen that there exists an underlying oscillatory behavior. This could motivate us to buy dollars paying with kroners whenever the exchange rate is low, and then make an exchange back to kroners whenever the rate is high, thereby making a net earning. The exchange rate data are a bit hard to read because of the superimposed noise and by the fact that the periodicity is not strictly a constant. It would therefore be desirable to have a way to extract the main periods or frequencies before we make large investments. A Fourier (or spectral) analysis can help you with this.

Before we analyse the exchange rate data, however, we should try to get an understanding of how the Fourier transform works in Octave using a simple example.

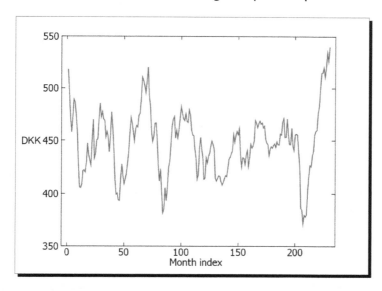

The Fourier transform

The fundamental principle behind Fourier analysis is the Fourier transform. If the function f is dependent on time t and is integrable, the Fourier transform of f is defined as:

$$F(\omega) = \int_{-\infty}^{\infty} f(t)\, e^{i\omega t} dt. \tag{7.13}$$

Note that the function F is a function of the angular frequency, ω, and that it is in general a complex valued function. In general, f is also a complex valued function, but we shall not consider this case here.

Now, suppose we have a set of N discrete data points $f_1, f_2, \ldots, f_N$ that are sampled at constant sampling interval Δt at times $t_1, t_2, \ldots, t_N$. In this situation, the integral form of the Fourier transform given above can be approximated by the discrete Fourier transform (DFT):

$$F_n = \sum_{k=1}^{N} f_k e^{i\omega_n t_k} \Delta t. \tag{7.14}$$

I will explain the index n in the following matter. According to the sampling theorem (or Nyquist-Shannon theorem), we cannot choose the frequencies ω_n at random in order to perform a correct Fourier analysis, but they are given by:

$$\omega_n = \frac{2\pi n}{N\Delta t}, \quad n = -\frac{N}{2}, \ldots, \frac{N}{2}. \tag{7.15}$$

This means that to retrieve large frequency modes, we must have sufficient frequent sampling which makes good sense. Substituting Equation (7.15) into Equation (7.14) and assuming $t_k = (k-1)\Delta t$ such that $t_1 = 0$, we arrive at:

$$F_n = \Delta t \sum_{k=1}^{N} f_k e^{i\pi n (k-1)/N}. \tag{7.16}$$

In principle we could just code Equation (7.16) directly. Octave even supports complex numbers, so it could be done in a few lines. As it stands, however, this will lead to what is called an order N^2 algorithm which means that the number of operations we need to perform is proportional to N^2 and thus the execution time increases dramatically for large sample sizes[2]. For a large data set, it would therefore not be a clever approach. Out of pure curiosity, we will try it out later in an exercise.

Time for action – using the fft function

1. Let us try to Fourier transform the function:

$$f(t) = \sin(2t) + 2\sin(5t), \tag{7.17}$$

where $t \in [0; 2\pi]$ using 150 data points. This function is characterized by two different frequencies (or modes) that will show in the Fourier transformation as two distinct peaks.

---

[2] *This is also referred to as an O(N²) algorithm. O is pronounced 'big-O'.*

2. To generate the data we use:

```
octave:29> N=150; t = linspace(0,2*pi, N);

octave:30> f = sin(2*t) + 2*sin(5*t);
```

3. Then we simply transform those data via:

```
octave:31> F = fft(f);
```

4. The complex vector F is not really of much information itself, so we often display the absolute value (or magnitude) of the elements in the array:

```
octave:32> plot(abs(F), "o-")
```

which produces the plot seen in the figure below:

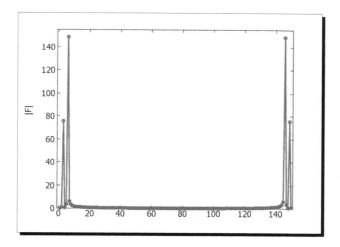

What just happened?

In Commands 29 and 30, we generated the data set. I strongly recommend that you try to plot f versus t to see the function that we are transforming. We then call fft and plot the absolute value of the transformed data.

Things look a bit odd though. We expected two peaks representing the two different modes in Equation (7.17), but the figure above shows four peaks that seem like mirror images of each other. This actually makes sense. From Equation (7.15), we see that the frequencies go from:

$$-\frac{\pi}{\Delta t} \leq \omega_n \leq \frac{\pi}{\Delta t}. \tag{7.18}$$

This explains that there is a mirroring taking place because $|F(-\omega)| = |F(\omega)|$. Note, the maximum frequency $\pi / \Delta t$ is denoted the Nyquist frequency ω_N.

`fft` organizes the output in two halves. The first half corresponds to the frequencies from 0 to $\pi/\Delta t$, the second half from $-\pi/\Delta t$ to 0. This is easily fixed with `fftshift` such that the values of F correspond to frequencies in the interval $-\pi/\Delta t \leq \omega_n \leq \pi/\Delta t$.

```
octave:35> F = fftshift(F);
```

Before we plot the magnitude of F again, we should also generate the frequencies we plot against. First, the sampling interval:

```
octave:34> dt = t(2);
```

then we define n in Equation (7.15) via:

```
octave:35> n=[-N/2:1:N/2];
```

But hold on, this array has length $N+1$! To fix this problem, we can simply remove the last and highest frequency point:

```
octave:36> n(N+1)=[];
```

According to Equation (7.15), the frequency is calculated as:

```
octave:37> freq = 2*pi*n./(N*dt);
```

We are now ready to plot the magnitude of F as a function of frequency—this is sometimes referred to as the magnitude spectrum:

```
octave:38> plot(freq, abs(F), 'o-')
```

The result from Command 38 is shown in the left-hand side figure below. In the right-hand side figure, only positive frequencies are shown. We now see that the two frequencies appear where we expect. The fact that the higher frequency component also has larger amplitude is also captured in the magnitude spectrum.

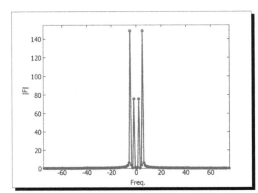
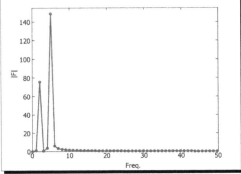

In the example above, we transformed a data set composed of 150 points. If you change this number, you will see that the magnitude of F will change too: the more the points, the larger the magnitude. The reason for this is that fft excludes the multiplication with Δt, see Equation (7.16). Thus to get a spectrum that is independent of the number of data points, we can simply multiply the output from fft with Δt.

Changing the number of data points also means changing the Nyquist frequency, ω_N, according to Equation (7.18). It is very important to remember when you perform fast Fourier transforms that the frequency is not a freely variable parameter, but is determined by the sample size and sampling interval. Also, the Nyquist frequency must be sufficiently large for the Fourier transform to capture all the frequencies embedded in the data. In fact, if ω_N is not large enough (that is, if the sampling interval is too large), the high-end frequencies will not show up correctly in the spectrum. This is known as aliasing. To be sure that there is no aliasing problem, the spectrum for the largest frequencies should be zero. We shall soon see that it is not always possible to have the necessary sample rate.

Fourier analysis of currency exchange rate

Let us return to the problem of the currency investment. We now know how to perform a Fourier analysis of data using Octave's fft function, so should we just dive into it? Well, we are not quite there yet. If we simply made a Fourier transform of the data, there will be a large peak at very low frequencies. This peak comes from the fact that the average exchange rate is not zero and that there exists an overall trend of increasing price. If we want to make shorter term investments, we are mainly interested in knowing about the higher frequency behavior and we should therefore remove these trends.

Time for action – analysing the exchange rate

1. Assume that we have loaded the currency exchange rate data into a variable curr and that we have 230 data points. The month index is given by:

   ```
   octave:39> m_index = [0:229];
   ```

2. The increasing trend is given by the end-points in the data:

   ```
   octave:40> a = (curr(230)-curr(1))/229; b = curr(1);
   ```

3. Subtracting the trend from the data:

   ```
   octave:41> curr1 = curr - a*m_index - b;
   ```

4. To ensure a data set with zero-mean, we use:

   ```
   octave:42> curr2 = curr1-mean(curr1);
   ```

5. We can then perform a Fourier analysis on the "trend-free" data using the ordinary frequency $f = \omega / 2\pi$:

```
octave:43> N=230; n=[-N/2:N/2]; n(N+1) = []; freq = n./N;

octave:44> acurr = abs( fftshift( fft(curr2) ) );
```

6. To plot the result, we use:

```
octave:45> plot(freq, acurr)
```

The result is shown below for positive frequencies. Note that we may have an aliasing problem!

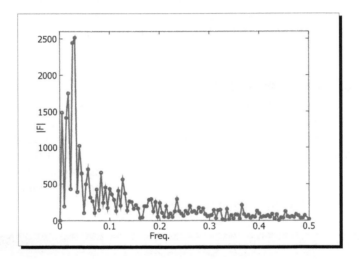

7. Now the ordinary frequency of the main mode is:

```
octave:46> i = find( acurr==max(accur) ); freq(i)

ans = 0.030434
```

What just happened?

In Command 39, we define the month index to go from zero (first month of 1991) to 229 (the second month in 2010). To remove the overall increasing trend, we simply subtract the line that goes through the end-points in the data set, here represented via the linear function $y = ax + b$, where x is the month index. a is calculated to 0.096. This will lead to a new data set where the end points are zero, but all others will be negative, which is also unwanted since this gives a non-zero mean which also shows in the Fourier spectrum. This bias is then removed in Command 42. It should be clear what Commands 43 to 45 do, but note that we use the ordinary frequency rather than the angular frequency.

The main frequency mode is computed in Command 46 by using the `find` function. This frequency corresponds to a period $T = 1/f$, that is, if we sell and reinvest every sixteen and a half months we could expect a net earning.

It is worth noting that since we have a possible aliasing problem, we cannot make any conclusions about the high frequency modes.

To sum up, the Fourier analysis using `fft` can be done in the following six steps:

1. Consider if you should remove any trends in the data set and do so if needed.
2. Fourier transform your data using `fft`.
3. Rearrange the output via `fftshift`.
4. Generate the sample frequency. Remember to remove the last high-end frequency component.
5. Plot the spectrum for positive frequencies.
6. Is the spectrum for high frequencies zero? If not, be aware of any aliasing problems.

Inverse Fourier transform and data smoothing

It would be very useful to somehow remove the "noise" that we see in the currency plot because it hides the underlying characteristics of the data and it brings no useful information. Such noise shows up in the high frequency end in the spectrum. Can we use this for anything? The answer is yes and the idea goes as follows: if we can somehow set the high frequencies to zero and then make an inverse Fourier transform, we should still see all the slowly varying modes, but no high frequency ones. The only thing we should be careful about is how we remove the unwanted frequencies—Octave takes care of the inverse Fourier transform.

Analogous to Equation (7.14), the discrete inverse Fourier transform is given as:

$$f_k = \frac{1}{2\pi} \sum_{n=1}^{N} F_n e^{-i\omega_n t_k} \Delta\omega. \tag{7.19}$$

Octave's inverse fast Fourier transform function `ifft` has the same syntax as `fft`. In its simplest form:

```
f = ifft(F)
```

Before we try it out, we should briefly discuss how to pick out the low frequencies in the spectrum.

The Butterworth filter

The following function is called a Butterworth function of order n:

$$h(\omega) = \sqrt{\frac{1}{1 - (\omega/\omega_c)^{2n}}}, \tag{7.20}$$

where ω_c is called the critical frequency. A fifth order Butterworth function is plotted below for different critical frequencies in the range from 1 to 5: the leftmost graph with the steepest descent is for $\omega_c = 1$, and the rightmost is for $\omega_c = 5$. Note that the Butterworth function is 1 for $\omega = 0$ and goes smoothly to zero for large ω. Now, if we multiply the Butterworth function with the Fourier transform of the data, we can pick out all the low frequencies and set the high frequencies to zero. This is exactly what we want. This is called a low pass filtering.

You can apply any other type of filter, however, you should be extremely careful with the particular choice. The Butterworth filter is a smooth varying function that prevents so-called edge effects, effects that show up in step-type filters.

 You can also apply the Butterworth filter for medium and high band filtering by simple function shifts.

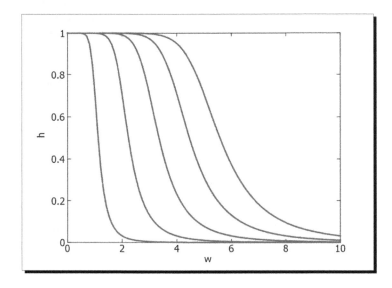

 In Octave you can also perform smoothing directly in the time domain using piecewise polynomial fits – this will usually be a low pass filter. Type `help spline` to see how.

Time for action – applying a low pass filter

1. Continuing from Commands 39-46, let us apply a tenth order Butterworth filter with $\omega_c = 0.1$ to smooth the "trend-less" data set stored in curr2, see Command 42:

```
octave:47> b_order = 10; w_c = 0.1;
```

2. The Butterworth function is simply given as:

```
octave:48> w = sqrt(1./(1 + (freq./wc).^(2*b_order)));
```

3. We can choose to rearrange either the Butterworth window function or the data before multiplying them together —we will rearrange the window function:

```
octave:49> w = fftshift(w);
```

4. In order to apply the filter to the Fourier transform of `curr2` and then perform the inverse Fourier transform, we use:

```
octave:50> plot(m_index, ifft(fft(curr2).*w), 'r', \
> m_index, curr2, 'b')
```

5. The result is given below, where the smoothed data is given by the red curve:

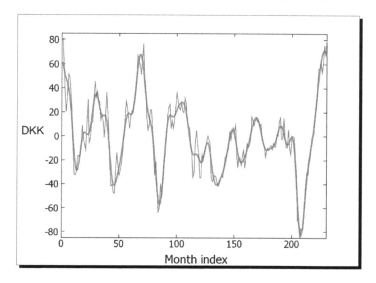

What just happened?

In Command 47, we specified the critical frequency and the Butterworth order parameter. There is no recipe on how to choose the particular parameters, but it is always a good idea to plot the resulting Butterworth filter to see if it actually picks out the frequencies we are after and removes the ones we wish to suppress. It is also important to be sure that the Butterworth function is arranged in the same manner as the output from `fft`. We do this in Command 49. In Command 50, we then apply the filter to the Fourier transformed data, inverse Fourier transform the filtered data back into the time domain, and plot it together with the unfiltered data.

Notice that the Butterworth filter and many other types of filters are available from the **signal** toolbox.

Have a go hero – implementing your own Fourier transform function

In this exercise, you are to code your own Fourier transform function. The syntax should be:

```
[F freq] = sft(f, dt)
```

where `F` is the Fourier transformed data, `freq` is a vector with the corresponding frequencies, `f` is the input data, and `dt` is the constant sampling interval. The function must use Equations (7.14) and (7.15) and not `fft`. `sft` should be vectorized to some degree.

Test `sft` with the function given in Equation (7.17) and compare with the corresponding figures in the section. By the way, why the name `sft`?

Summary

In this chapter we learned:

- About the file formats that Octave can load.
- How to calculate different sample moments in Octave for simple descriptive statistics.
- How to compare data sets using `cor` and `t_test`.
- How to use `polyfit` and `leasqr` to fit different functions to data.
- About the fast Fourier transform function `fft`.
- How to use the inverse Fourier transform function `ifft`.

We will now proceed with the last chapter where you will learn about optimization techniques and dynamically linked functions.

8

Need for Speed: Optimization and Dynamically Linked Functions

As we have seen a few times already, as long as you vectorize your code[1] and use Octave's built-in functionality, there is little you can do to make your code run significantly faster. This is the way it should be. Octave is primarily designed for scientists and engineers, and they should worry about the science, not how to tweak the code for it to perform better. Sometimes, however, you can end up with numerical problems that are not easy or even impossible to vectorize or where no built-in functionality exists. In this chapter, you will see what possibilities you have in these situations.

The chapter is divided into two parts explaining the two main approaches you can consider, namely:

1. Optimizing the Octave code.
2. Implementing the code in a lower level programming language like C or C++ and linking this to Octave's workspace using Octave's C++ library and interface.

It should be mentioned that Octave has no profiler yet. (A profiler is a tool that can detect the parts of the code that perform poorly). There are some indications that a profiler may be available in future versions of Octave, but until then we have to rely on experience and simpler profiling strategies.

In detail, we will discuss:

◆   How you can time your functions and scripts using the function pair `tic` and `toc`.

---

[1] *In the Octave sense of vectorization*

◆ A few techniques that you can apply to your Octave code in order to improve performance.

◆ How to use the Octave C++ library and interface with the Octave C++ functions, rather than in Octave's own programming language.

◆ How to compile the C++ code and how to call the function from the Octave command prompt.

◆ Different C++ classes that come with the library.

◆ A few ways to optimize the C++ code.

Most importantly, however, we shall see that the built-in functionality and operators that come with Octave are very fast and usually perform much better than what we (well at least what I) can manage with simple algorithms and C++ code.

For the second part of the chapter, I assume you have working knowledge of C++.

A few optimization techniques

There are a few things you should consider when you wish to optimize your Octave code. Some of these are:

1. Avoid loops, especially nested loops, whenever possible. Always try to vectorize your code!

2. Use Octave's built-in functionality. For example, do not try to implement your own linear equation solver because it is unlikely that you can do better than Octave.

3. Instantiate your array variables before entering a loop in order to minimize memory reallocation and therefore communication overhead with the operating system.

4. If you do partial vectorization, loop column-wise.

5. Clear large arrays whenever you are finished using them. In this way, you avoid using the slower parts of the chip memory.

6. In some situations, functions can execute faster than scripts. So it can be helpful to convert a large script to a function if it is called many times. This is because functions are read only once per Octave session (when they are called for the first time), whereas scripts are read every time they are called.

Item 6 is really only for the desperate ones. Let us illustrate the more important points above through a simple matrix addition, that is:

$$\mathbf{C} = \mathbf{A} + \mathbf{B}. \tag{8.1}$$

Before we jump into it, we need some sort of timer that can actually time the commands or blocks of code for us. Naturally, this is also implemented in Octave.

tic, toc

The functions tic and toc usually come in pairs and give you the time elapsed between the call to tic and the call to toc. This is also referred to as a wall-time. Basically, tic starts or restarts a timer and toc then returns the wall-time. You can therefore have several calls to toc using the same timer start. If you have many processes running on your computer at the same time, this will slow down the execution speed of your commands and increase the wall-time. You can measure the actual time spent by the CPU to execute the commands using the cputime function. In this chapter we will simply use the wall-time since this is a good approximation to the actual CPU-time.

Time for action – using tic and toc

Let us first use tic and toc to get the wall-time for adding two matrices together the usual vectorized way:

```
octave:1> A=rand(1000,1000); B=rand(1000,1000);

octave:2> tic(); C=A+B; toc()

Elapsed time is 0.015 seconds.
```

It took 15 milliseconds to add two 1000 x 1000 matrices together, that is, to perform 1 million addition operations.

What just happened?

In Command 1, we declared two 1000 x 1000 matrices with elements picked from a uniform distribution having values between 0 and 1. In Command 2, we started the timer using tic, added the two matrices, and returned the elapsed time. We can assign the output from toc to a variable for later use. For example, Command 2 could have been:

```
octave:2> tic(); C=A+B; add_time = toc()

add_time = 0.015
```

 toc returns the wall-time in resolution of milliseconds.

Vectorization

Let us, once more, illustrate the importance of vectorization. Instead of using the + operator between the two matrices, we can add the elements together in nested loops in the "traditional" manner:

```
octave:3>tic(), for i=1:1000, j=1:1000, C(i,j) = A(i,j)+B(i,j); end,
   end, toc()
```

```
Elapsed time is 26.53069
```

This is around 2000 times slower compared to the analogous vectorized addition! Also, in Command 3, you need to do much more coding which is always more error prone[2].

Initialization of variables

Let us add the matrices together again like in Command 3, but now we first delete the variable C from the workspace:

```
octave:4> clear C
```

```
octave:5>tic(),   for i=1:1000, j=1:1000, C(i,j) = A(i,j)+B(i,j); end,
   end, toc()
```

```
elapsed time is 30.2649 seconds
```

Command 5 was executed around 4 seconds slower than Command 3, even though these two commands are exactly the same. Why is that? In Command 5, the variable C is not defined in the workspace contrary to Command 2. This means that when we loop through the elements in A and B, Octave will have to allocate memory at runtime in order to store the sums in the elements of C. This means that Octave has to communicate with the operating system (perhaps one million times) during the command. This of course, takes time.

If you work with large arrays and know the sizes in advance, it is therefore a good idea to initialize the arrays using the function `zero` before entering the loop. For example, assuming that C is not declared, we can use:

```
octave:6> C = zeros(1000,1000);
```

```
octave:7> tic(),   for i=1:1000, j=1:1000, C(i,j) = A(i,j)+B(i,j); end,
   end, toc()
```

```
Elapsed time is 27.1714 seconds
```

In this case, only one memory allocation is needed.

---

[2]*It is not always true that vectorized code is less error prone that non-vectorized code!*

Looping row-wise versus looping column-wise

In the case of matrix addition, we can also find the matrix sum using row-wise or a column-wise looping. This is sometimes referred to as partial vectorization. Code Listings 6.1 and 6.2 are examples of partial vectorization using row-wise looping. In Octave, there is a performance difference when we use row-wise or column-wise loops. The following two examples illustrate this.

First, we loop over the rows (thereby performing a column-wise vectorization):

```
octave:8> tic(),   for i=1:1000, C(i,:) = A(i,:)+B(i,:); end, toc()

elapsed time is 0.109201 seconds
```

We then loop column-wise:

```
octave:9> tic(),   for i=1:1000, C(:,i) = A(:,i)+B(:,i); end, toc()

elapsed time is 0.0400001 seconds
```

That is, looping column-wise is about twice as fast as the row-wise looping for this particular example. The reason for this time difference is related to the way the arrays are stored in the chip memory. Commands 8 and 9 highlight the rule of thumb—if you do `for` or `while` loops, consider doing it column-wise if possible.

Have a go hero – revision of cmat_1d

In Code Listing 6.1, coefficient matrix is generated by looping row-wise. Re-implement the function by using column-wise looping. Do you observe any difference in execution speed?

Dynamically linked functions

In some situations, you may not be able to avoid heavy looping. For example, you may wish to use a particular numerical differential equation solver which does the job better than Octave's `lsode`. First, have a very good argument why `lsode` does not fulfil your criterion. Secondly, there already exists a differential equation solver package called **odepkg** that includes many different solvers. In the situation where you must implement your own function, you can do this in lower level programming languages like C or C++ and then link this to Octave. The linking enables you to use other libraries in your C/C++ code thereby making the possible extensions to Octave almost infinite.

There must be an interface between the lower level code and the Octave interpreter. Octave's native interface is based on C++, but you can also use MATLAB's MEX (MATLAB EXecutable) interface. We shall limit the discussion to the former. As mentioned in the introduction to the chapter, I expect that you have basic knowledge of C++.

The DEFUN_DLD function macro

The C++ interface is based on a function macro with name DEFUN_DLD (the name comes from the GNU dynamic linker dld). DEFUN_DLD has the interface:

```
DEFUN_DLD(function name, input argument list, number of ouputs,
  help string)
```

where the arguments are:

function name	Simply states the name of the function. The name *must* be the same as the filename without the extension.
input argument list	Variable containing the input arguments. This variable type is octave_value_list, which is a C++ class. We can think of it as an array of type octave_value, which is also a class. We shall discuss this in greater detail soon.
number of outputs	Contains the number of outputs the function is called with. This is an optional argument and can be left out.
help string	A string containing a simple help text.

The function macro always returns a variable of type octave_value_list even though this is not specified explicitly in the interface.

Time for action – writing a "Hello World" program

1. Let us try to implement the classical "Hello World" program. Open your editor and type in the following lines of code:

Code Listing 8.1

```
#include <octave/oct.h>                              #1
                                                      #2
DEFUN_DLD(hello, argv, , "Usage: hello()"){          #3
  octave_value_list retval;                          #4
                                                      #5
  octave_stdout << "Hello World\n";                  #6
                                                      #7
  return retval;                                      #8
}                                                     #9
```

2. Save the file as hello.cc in your working directory. At the Octave prompt, type in the following command:

octave:10> mkoctfile hello.cc

This compiles the C++ code.

3. Make a call to the function, which is then dynamically linked to the Octave environment:

```
octave:11> hello()

Hello World
```

What just happened?

To use the C++ interface and library, we need to include the header `oct.h`, which is done in line 1 in Code Listing 8.1. In line 3, we set the function name to `hello` and name the input argument list `argv`. We do not specify the number of outputs as this is not used and write a small help text string. The help text is shown if we use the usual `help` command:

```
octave:12> help hello

Usage: hello()
```

In line 4, we instantiate an object of type `octave_value_list` with the generic name `retval`. As mentioned above, `DEFUN_DLD` must always return a variable of this type. In line 5, we pipe the string `Hello World` to the Octave standard output and in line 8 we return `retval` and exit the function.

Per default, the filename must be the same as the function name, so here we save the file as `hello.cc`. Command 8 compiles the file and generates a binary object file called `hello.oct`, hence, the command name `mkoctfile`, which is an abbreviation for "make oct file". It is this object file that links to the Octave interpreter.

 Often, the dynamically linked object file is referred to as an oct-file or an oct-function. Functions written in Octave's own programming language are referred to as m-functions.

Managing input arguments and outputs

Just like an m-function, you should be able to call the oct-function with a different number of arguments and these can be of any type. In the function, we should then check how it is called and if it is not called correctly, we should issue a warning or error.

Fortunately, this is rather simple using Octave's C++ library. As we saw above, the arguments to the function are passed to the function via the class `octave_value_list`. This is practically an array `octave_values`. An object of type `octave_value` can be, for example, a matrix, a vector, or a scalar.

Time for action – checking user inputs and outputs

1. Code Listing 8.2 shows an example of a function called `args`. This function takes any number of inputs, checks what type they are, and writes this to the Octave command prompt. It returns a sequence of numbers going from 1 to the number of input arguments:

Code Listing 8.2

```
#include <octave/oct.h>                                          #1
                                                                #2
#define HELP_TEXT "Usage:[out1,out2,...]=args(in1,in2,...)"     #3
                                                                #4
DEFUN_DLD(args, argv, nargout, HELP_TEXT){                      #5
  octave_value_list retval;                                     #6
                                                                #7
  int nargs = argv.length();                                    #8
  octave_stdout<<"You've entered "<< nargs << " argument(s)\n"; #9
                                                                #10
  if ( nargout > nargs ){                                       #11
    error("Number of output variables is too large");           #12
    return retval;                                              #13
  }                                                             #14
                                                                #15
  for ( int n=0; n<nargs; n++ ){                               #16
    octave_stdout << "Argument " << n+1 << " is ";              #17
    if ( argv(n).is_string() )                                  #18
      octave_stdout << "a text string ";                       #19
    if ( argv(n).is_real_scalar() )                             #20
      octave_stdout << "a real scalar ";                       #21
    if ( argv(n).is_real_matrix() )                             #22
      octave_stdout << "a real matrix ";                       #23
    if ( argv(n).is_complex_matrix() )                          #24
      octave_stdout << "a complex matrix ";                    #25
                                                                #26
    octave_std << "\n";                                         #27
    retval.append(octave_value(n+1));                           #28
  }                                                             #29
                                                                #30
  return retval;                                                #31
}                                                               #32
```

2. We, of course, compile this with `mkoctfile`. After compiling, try out the command:

```
octave:13> [a b c] = args([1 1], "string", zeros(10) + I*ones(10))
```

```
You've entered 3 arguments

Argument 1 is a real matrix

Argument 2 is a text string a real matrix

Argument 3 is a complex matrix

a = 1

b = 2

c = 3
```

3. We can try a complex scalar input argument:

```
octave:14> args(I)

You've entered 1 argument(s)

Argument 1 is

ans = 1
```

What just happened?

The first 7 lines in Code Listing 8.2 should be straightforward. In line 8, we call the method `length` which returns the length of the argument list, that is, the number of input arguments that the user called the function with. We print this to the command prompt.

In lines 11-14, we check if the number of output variables is larger than the number of inputs. If this is the case, we print an error message and return from the function. Such a check is necessary if you want to avoid a warning message in calls like `[a b] = args(1)`.

In the loop in lines 16-29, we then check the type of each argument. You may have been puzzled; one accesses the array elements in the variable `argv` via parenthesis! This is different from the usual square brackets `[]`. The parentheses are operators in the C++ sense and do additional checking for you when called. Also notice, the interface follows the usual C++ convention, so the first index in an array is 0.

The list of possible types is exhausting and here we only check for 4 different types: strings, real scalars, real matrices, and complex matrices. These checks are done through the methods `is_string`, `is_real_scalar`, `is_real_matrix`, and `is_complex_matrix`. All these methods return Booleans (true or false) depending on the type of the variable.

In line 28, we append the argument number to the return value which is of type `octave_value_list`. We use the `append` method for this. It's argument is an `octave_value` and we therefore convert the integer `n+1` into the appropriate type using `octave_value(n+1)`.

The output from Command 13 may surprise you:

- ◆ The function claims that the first argument is a real matrix, but the input is a row vector. This is, of course, because Octave does distinguish between a $1 \times N$ matrix and a row vector.

- ◆ The second argument is recognized as a string, which is fine, but also as a matrix. Octave simply interprets the string array as a matrix of characters.

In Command 14, we call args with a complex scalar. Since we do not check for this with the method is_complex_scalar, the type is not printed to the screen.

Retrieving the inputs

We still need to retrieve the inputs somehow in order to perform actual computations. To illustrate how this is done, let us implement a matrix addition function, doing what the + operator does already.

```
Code Listing 8.3
#include <octave/oct.h>                                    #1
#define HELP_TEXT "Usage C = madd(A, B)"                   #2
                                                           #3
DEFUN_DLD(madd, argv, nargout, HELP_TEXT){                 #4
  octave_value_list retval;                                #5
                                                           #6
  int nargs = argv.length();                               #7
  if ( nargs>2 || nargout>1 ){                             #8
    error(HELP_TEXT);                                      #9
    return retval;                                         #10
  }                                                        #11
                                                           #12
  Matrix A(argv(0).matrix_value());                        #13
  Matrix B(argv(1).matrix_value());                        #14
                                                           #15
  size_t nr = A.rows();                                    #16
  size_t nc = A.columns();                                 #17
                                                           #18
  Matrix C(nr, nc);                                        #19
                                                           #20
  for ( size_t i=0; i<nr; i++ )                            #21
    for ( size_t j=0; j<nc; j++ ) C(i,j) = A(i,j)+B(i,j);  #22
                                                           #23
  retval.append(C);                                        #24
                                                           #25
  return retval;                                           #26
}                                                          #27
```

In lines 13 and 14, we instantiate two objects of type `Matrix`, which is a class defined in the Octave C++ library. The constructor can be called with a `Matrix` type argument, for example, line 13 instantiates the object A of type `Matrix` with the same number of rows, columns, and element values as the first input argument. The constructor can also be called with two input arguments specifying the dimensions of the matrix leaving the value of the elements uninitialized as seen in line 19.

The `Matrix` class has two very useful methods, namely, `rows` and `columns`, that return the number of rows and columns in the matrix. We call these two methods in lines 16 and 17.

In lines 21-22, we perform the actual matrix addition and we then return the values through the matrix object C.

We would expect this function to be almost as fast as the usual + operator. Let's check that. After compiling (recall that A and B are two 1000 x 1000 matrices with random numbers).

```
octave:13>  tic(),  C=madd(A,B);  toc()
Elapsed time is 0.0825 seconds.
```

This is around 5 times slower than Command 2, where the + operator is used.

One reason for this is that accessing the matrix elements through the parenthesis operator, (), results in substantial overhead. In fact, rather than performing element-wise operations inside the C++ function, you should use the functions and operators available in the C++ library. For example, lines 21 and 22 can be replaced with one single line, namely,

```
C = A + B;
```

If you use this operator instead of adding the matrix elements individually, you will see that the `madd` function performs just as well as the ordinary Octave + operator.

 As for m-functions, the rule of thumb for oct-functions is: use the vectorized operators and built-in functions in the code whenever possible.

If you are in a situation where you must access the array elements, you can let a simple pointer to doubles point to the memory location of the array, and thereby access these the usual way. The way to declare this pointer is through the `fortran_vec` method. In the matrix addition example above, lines 21-22 can be replaced with:

```
const double *Aval = A.fortran_vec();
const double *Bval = B.fortran_vec();
double *Cval = C.fortran_vec();

for ( size_t i=0; i<nr*nc; i ++)
  Cval[i] = Aval[i] + Bval[i];
```

Class types

Code Listing 8.3 shows how you can access and work with real matrices, that is, with matrices where each element is a real scalar. If you try to add two complex matrices using `madd`, you will see that only the real part is added together and returned. You can also add complex matrices—here you will have to use the `ComplexMatrix` class. Likewise, if you work with vectors, you should specify the type as row or column vector and if it is complex. Below are listed a few of the most important (and high-level) classes that come with Octave's C++ interface:

```
RowVector            ColumnVector           Matrix
ComplexRowVector     ComplexColumnVector    ComplexMatrix
SparseMatrix         SparseComplexMatrix
```

As we saw above, you can instantiate an object of any of these classes in many different ways. The most common ones are:

Constructor	Examples
`classname A(dim1, dim2);`	`RowVector a(length);`
	`Matrix A(nrows, ncols);`
`classname A(dim1, dim2, value);`	`RowVector a(length, 42.0);`
	`Matrix A(nrows, ncols, 0);`
`classname A(classname);`	`RowVector a(argv(0).vector_value());`
	`Matrix A(argv(0).matrix_value());`
`classname A;`	`RowVector a;`
	`Matrix A;`

The last type of instantiation will not allocate memory to the array elements, so this must be done at a later stage.

An object of `SparseMatrix` or `SparseComplexMatrix` type can also be instantiated with the following constructor:

Constructor	Example
`classname A(dim1, dim2, nz)`	`SparseMatrix A(nrows,ncols, 20)`

Here, `nz` is the number of non-zero elements in the matrix. I strongly recommend you use this whenever you know the number of non-zero elements in advance in order to reduce the memory reallocation overhead.

In Code Listing 8.3, we saw how to access the input arguments via the method `matrix_value`. The table below summarizes what you can use in order to access the arguments to `DEFUN_DLD`:

Method	Return type	Corresponding check method (returns a Boolean)
`string_value`	`std::string` (standard string)	`is_string`
`int_value`	`int`	`is_integer_type`
`long_value`	`long int`	`is_integer_type`
`scalar_value`	`double`	`is_real_scalar` / `is_scalar_type` / `is_double_type`
`row_vector_value`	`RowVector`	`is_matrix_type`
`column_vector_value`	`ColumnVector`	`is_matrix_type`
`matrix_value`	`Matrix`	`is_matrix_type` / `is_real_matrix`
`complex_row_vector_value`	`ComplexRowVector`	`is_complex_matrix`
`complex_column_vector_value`	`ComplexColumnVector`	`is_complex_matrix`
`complex_matrix_value`	`ComplexMatrix`	`is_complex_matrix`
`sparse_matrix_value`	`SparseMatrix`	`is_sparse_type`
`sparse_complex_matrix_value`	`SparseComplexMatrix`	`is_sparse_type` / `is_complex_matrix`

If you wish to work with Octave's C++ library and interface, I recommend that you browse through the Application Programming Interface (API), which is available via the Octave-Forge: `http://octave.sourceforge.net/doxygen/html/index.html`.

Functions as input argument

In *Chapter 5*, we saw how to write an Octave m-function that calls a user-supplied function. You can also do this in oct-functions of course. As is the case for m-functions, you need to call the user-supplied function via a C++ version of the `feval` function.

The first argument to `feval` is the name (a string) specifying the user-supplied function, the second argument is of type `octave_value_list`, and the third argument gives the number of outputs from the function. `feval` returns a variable of type `octave_value_list`. For example, to create a 2 x 2 a matrix with random numbers picked from a uniform distribution we can use:

```
#include <octave/oct.h>
#include <octave/parse.h>

. . .

octave_value_list r = feval("rand", octave_value(2), 1);

. . .
```

Note that we need to include the `parse.h` header where `feval` is declared. The first argument to `feval` is a string giving the function name `rand`, which is the built-in random number generator and the second argument is the number 2 (since we want a 2 x 2 matrix). This integer is converted into the appropriate `octave_value_list` or equivalent `octave_value` class type using `octave_value(2)`. The third argument states the number of outputs from `rand`. Here it is 1.

Let us try something more advanced. In *Chapter 5*, we programmed a Monte Carlo integrator to evaluate the integral of a scalar function f in some interval $[a; b]$, where f is positive. We made two versions of the integrator: (i) One that followed the programming flowchart called `mcintgr` and (ii) A much faster vectorized version called `mcintgrv`. Let us try to implement this integrator using the C++ interface and see if we can get an improved performance compared to the vectorized m-function version.

As noted above, we should make an effort to vectorize the C++ code as well. When we do this we can actually follow the method used in `mcintgrv`. Before we go ahead though, we need to find the maximum value of f in the interval. We will do this in a separate function called `findmax` as shown in Code Listing 8.4 together with the rest of the code.

The oct-function is called in the exact same way as `mcintgr` and `mcintgrv`, that is:

```
I = mcintgro(fun, a, b, mcloops)
```

where `fun` is the user-supplied function, `a` and `b` give the interval, and `mcloops` is the number of Monte Carlo loops the function should perform.

Code Listing 8.4

```
#include <octave/oct.h>                                        #1
#include <octave/parse.h>                                      #2
                                                               #3
#define NINTERVAL 100                                          #4
#define HELPTEXT "Usage s = mcintgro(fun, a, b, mcloops)"      #5
                                                               #6
```

```
double findmax(std::string fun, double a, double b){          #7
                                                              #8
  double dx = (b - a)/(NINTERVAL-1);                          #9
  ColumnVector v(NINTERVAL);                                  #10
  for ( int n=0; n<NINTERVAL; n++ ) v(n) = n*dx + a;          #11
                                                              #12
      octave_value_list f = feval(fun, octave_value(v), 1);   #13
                                                              #14
      return ColumnVector(f(0).vector_value()).max();         #15
                                                              #16
}                                                             #17
                                                              #18
DEFUN_DLD(mcintgro, args, , HELPTEXT){                        #19
  octave_value_list retval;                                   #20
                                                              #21
  std::string fun = args(0).string_value();                   #22
  double a = args(1).double_value();                          #23
  double b = args(2).double_value();                          #24
  long int mcloops = args(3).long_value();                    #25
                                                              #26
  double maxy = findmax(fun, a, b);                           #27
  double l = b-a;                                             #28
                                                              #29
  long int counter = 0, nloops = 0;                           #30
                                                              #31
  octave_value_list rargs;                                    #32
  rargs.append(octave_value(mcloops));                        #33
  rargs.append(octave_value(1));                              #34
                                                              #35
  octave_value_list tmp = feval("rand", rargs, 1);            #36
  ColumnVector r1( tmp(0).vector_value() );                   #37
                                                              #38
  tmp = feval("rand", rargs, 1);                              #39
  ColumnVector r2( tmp(0).vector_value() );                   #40
                                                              #41
  ColumnVector x(a+r1*l)                                      #42
  ColumnVector y(maxy*r2);                                    #43
                                                              #44
  tmp = feval(fun, octave_value(x), 1);                       #45
  ColumnVector fx( tmp(0).vector_value() );                   #46
                                                              #47
  while ( nloops < mcloops ){                                 #48
    if ( y(nloops)<fx(nloops) ) counter ++;                   #49
    nloops ++;                                                #50
```

```
    }                                                           #51
                                                                #52
    double s = (double)counter/mcloops*maxy*1;                  #53
    retval.append(octave_value(s));                             #54
                                                                #55
    return retval;                                              #56
}                                                               #57
```

To save space, I have left out any checking and validation of the input arguments.

Let us go through the DEFUN_DLD function macro first. In line 22-25, we extract the input arguments. For example, the first argument is a string containing the name of the user-supplied function. There should be a check whether the argument really is a string—one can use the is_string method here. See the table that lists the methods above. Let us jump down to line 32. We need to generate two sequences of random numbers, r1 and r2. To do this, we use Octave's built-in rand function. We must call this function with two arguments—the corresponding Octave command is rand(mcloops, 1). In our C++ code, these two arguments are provided through the variable rargs of type octave_value_list, where the first element has value mcloops and the second element has value 1.

In line 36, we then call rand with the arguments stored in rargs using feval. The return value is stored in the variable tmp and finally the random number sequence is stored in a column vector in line 37. The second sequence is generated in the same manner.

Lines 42 and 43 make use of the vectorized operators + and *. Of course, we could have carried out these arithmetic operations in a loop, but since Octave provides this nice and fast functionality we should use it. It should be clear what happens in lines 45-57.

Returning to the function findmax, in lines 9-11 we generate a vector with points equally spaced in the interval between a and b. The number of points is given by the macro NINTERVAL. The vector v is used as the argument for the user-supplied function from which we can then find the maximum in the interval. Note that we have used the method max in the ColumnVector class to calculate the maximum of the function output.

If we compile this code and test it against mcintgrv, we will see it does not perform any better. Again this illustrates the important point that you can do little to optimize vectorized Octave code.

Optimization with oct-files

You may start to wonder if one can use the C++ interface for optimization at all. There are at least two good reasons why you will want to use oct-files for optimization:

1. If you need to implement a new algorithm which cannot be vectorized, you can gain a significant speed-up by implementing the algorithm using a lower-level programming language and using Octave's C++ interface to link to Octave's interpreter. You may even have access to a library that does the job for you, so you only need to make an Octave interface.

2. If your problem involves a user-supplied function, you can program this function via Octave's C++ library and interface potentially gaining a significant speed-up.

Item 1 is discussed in the exercises, so let us move on to item 2.

Time for action – revisiting the Sel'kov model

1. In *Chapter 5*, we discussed how to solve a differential equation system using lsode. Specifically, we used lsode to solve the Sel'kov model. There the differential equation system was specified in an m-function, but we can also implement it using the C++ interface. Recall that in the original function, we used the global variable global_b in the function, so the C++ implementation needs to retrieve this variable from the Octave workspace as well.

Code Listing 8.5

```
#include <octave/oct.h>                                      #1
                                                             #2
DEFUN_DLD(selkovo, argv, , "Usage: y = selkovo(x)"){         #3
  octave_value_list retval;                                  #4
                                                             #5
  octave_value boct = get_global_value("global_b");          #6
  double b = boct.scalar_value();                            #7
                                                             #8
  ColumnVector x( argv(0).vector_value() );                  #9
  ColumnVector f(2);                                         #10
                                                             #11
  const double *xval = x.fortran_vec();                      #12
  double *fval = f.fortran_vec();                            #13
                                                             #14
  double xt = 0.1*xval[1] + xval[0]*xval[0]*xval[1];         #15
                                                             #16
  fval[0] = -xval[0] + xt;                                   #17
  fval[1] = b - xt;                                          #18
                                                             #19
  retval.append( octave_value(f) );                          #20
                                                             #21
  return retval;                                             #22
}                                                            #23
```

2. If we compile the code with mkoctfile, we can compare the execution speed with the m-function implementation selkov.m. Be sure that both functions can be found by Octave. For example, copy selkov.m to the current working directory:

```
octave:16> global global_b = 0.5;

octave:17> t=linspace(0, 10000, 500); init=[0.4 0.2];

octave:18> tic(), x=lsode("selkov", init, t); toc()

Elapsed time is 7.40625 seconds.

octave:19> tic(), x=lsode("selkovo", init, t); toc()
Elapsed time is 1.25 seconds.
```

This shows a significant speed-up[3].

3. Let us try with a different value of global_b:

```
octave:20> global_b = 1.0;

octave:21> tic(), x=lsode("selkov", init, t); toc()

Elapsed time is 0.07816 seconds.

octave:22> tic(), x=lsode("selkovo", init, t); toc()

Elapsed time is 0.03125 seconds.
```

What just happened

The value of the global_b variable is copied to the function using get_global_value in line 6. This function returns an octave_value type, and we can retrieve the value by calling the method scalar_value defined in the octave_value class.

In order to optimize the code as much as possible, we access the values in the vectors x and f directly through the pointers xval and fval, rather than using the () operator. In this particular case, however, there is hardly any measurable performance difference.

From the outputs in Commands 18 and 19, we observe a speed-up of around 6, which makes the extra effort all worth it. You may think that you can wait 7 seconds. But what if you have a very large differential equation system that you need to solve for many different parameter values? Then it matters if you have to wait 1 day or 6 days for the results.

---

[3]*Again, it is to be noted that my computer is not running any other programs, so the wall-time from toc is a good estimation of the true cpu-time.*

In Commands 21 and 22, the speed-up is reduced to around a factor of 2. The reason for this is that the system falls into the steady state with this value of `global_b`, that is, the elements in the vector `x` do not change. `lsode` is capable of changing its time step such that if the system is steady, it can take arbitrary long steps and reduce the calls to the user-supplied function significantly. The point here is that the actual seed-up you can gain from the C++ implementation depends on the specific problem at hand.

Have a go hero – implementing the Euler integrator

In this exercise, you are to implement an Euler integrator. In general, we can write an ordinary differential equation as:

$$\frac{d\mathbf{x}}{dt} = \mathbf{f}(\mathbf{x}).$$ (P.1)

The derivative on the left-hand side can be approximated by a first order finite difference scheme:

$$\frac{d\mathbf{x}}{dt} = \frac{\mathbf{x}^{n+1} - \mathbf{x}^{n}}{\Delta t}.$$ (P.2)

Substituting Equation (P.2) into Equation (P.1) and rearranging a bit, we obtain a simple difference equation:

$$\mathbf{x}^{n+1} = \mathbf{x}^{n} + \mathbf{f}(\mathbf{x}^{n})\Delta t.$$ (P.3)

This is called the Euler integration scheme. The scheme is an iterative and approximate solution to the differential equation system, for sufficiently small time steps, Δt.

1. Implement the Euler scheme in an m-function. The syntax should be:

   ```
   x = euler(fun, x0, dt, nsteps)
   ```

   where `fun` defines the right hand of Equation (P.1), `x0` is the initial condition, `dt` the time step, and `nsteps` is the number of steps the integrator should perform. The solution is returned in `x`. Test your implementation against the Sel'kov model and compare the result with the solution from `lsode`. Use maybe 1000-10000 time steps. Change the size of the time step and number of time steps—when is the agreement between the two numerical solutions satisfactory?

2. Implement the Euler scheme using Octave's C++ interface. You can name the function `eulero`, for example. Compare the performance with the corresponding m-function and with `lsode`.

3. Use your Euler integrator to solve the Lotka-Volterra differential equation system:

$$\frac{dx_1}{dt} = x_1 - x_1 x_2$$

$$\frac{dx_2}{dt} = x_1 x_2 - x_2 \qquad\qquad (P.4)$$

(Use, for example, the initial condition $x_1 = 0.1$ and $x_2 = 0.4$). Compare the output with the result from `lsode`. Why is there a persistent difference even though you reduce the time step? ? (Hint: The Lotka-Volterra equation describes a conservative system, whereas the Sel'kov model is a dissipative system.)

Summary

In this chapter we learned:

◆ About `tic` and `toc`.

◆ How you can optimize your Octave code.

◆ To use the function macro `DEFUN_DLD`.

◆ About the most common high-level classes in the Octave C++ library like `Matrix`, `ColumnVector`, and `SparseMatrix`.

◆ To use the `feval` C++ function in order to call user-supplied functions.

◆ How to access global variables (defined in the Octave work space) inside your C++ function.

◆ That you should use the C++ functionality that comes with the library, that is, you should also vectorize your C++ code.

◆ How you can optimize your C++ code by accessing the data stored in the classes directly.

This chapter concludes the book. The book is meant to give you an introduction to Octave and you should now be able to move on and exploit the more advanced features of Octave. I recommend that you look through the official Octave manual where most of Octave's functionality is described in detail. If you have questions or problems, browse through the posts listed on the usergroup web page to see if it has been discussed earlier—if not, ask all the experts in the group.

Pop Quiz Answers

Chapter 2: Interacting with Octave: Variables and Operators

Working with arrays

1   e)   f)   i)

2   a) 11   b) 3   c) 4
                                         9
                                   14
                                   19
                                 24

    d) 1 2 3 4 5   e) 1 2 3   f) 5
                                   10
                                   15
                                 20

    g) 1 2 3   h) 1 3   5   i) 16 17 18 19 20
        6 7 8   11 13 15   21 22 23 24 25
      11 12 13   21 23 25

Understanding arrays

a) 3 3   b) 3   c) 3   d) 1   e) 0   f) 3   g) 3

Understanding simple operations

a)   b)   d)   e)   g)

Understanding precedence rules

a) -1.000   b) 2.0000   c) Non-conformant
   1.000   1.0000   arguments
   4.667   0.18182

d) -1.000 1.0000 4.667

e) 3.0000 2.5000 4.2222

Chapter 3: Working with Octave: Functions and Plotting

Using simple mathematical functions

1   a)   b)   c)   d)   e)   f)

2   c)   d)   Note that while e) is valid, it is not really
                       meaningful—why is that?

Understanding the plotting options

b)   c)   d)   f)

Chapter 4: Rationalizing: Octave Scripts

Understanding disp and input

b)   d)   e)   Note that c) will likely give an error later.

Understanding statements and Boolean operators

1   a)   f)   g)

2   1 1 1 3 1 5 2 1 2 3 2 5

3   Line 5 does not match the `while` statement
     Line 6 does not match the `for` statement
     `m` is not incremented which will lead to an infinite loop

4   Line 1: `input` must have the optional argument `'s'` for string inputs
     Line 3: is not a valid expression (use `strcmp` instead)
     Line 5: the `elseif` statement evaluates a Boolean

Printing with printf

1   a) blank   b) Hello Worl   c) Hello Worl
     d) 2   e) 2.000000   f) 2.000000e+000

Chapter 5: Extensions: Write Your Own Octave Functions

Understanding functions

1   a) Missing function keyword   b) Missing commas in the argument list
     e) The second output is undefined   f) The output variable not defined.
     Note that in d) the help text is misplaced

2   Number of input arguments, (Number of ARGuments IN)

     Number of output arguments (Number of ARGuments OUT)

Implementing mathematical functions as Octave functions

a)
```
function f = fun(x)

    f = x + sin(x);

endfunction
```

c)
```
function f = fun(x)

    f = x + y./z;

endfunction
```

b)
```
function f = fun(t)

    f = [sin(t), t.^2,  cos(t)];

endfunction
```

d)
```
function f = fun(t)

    global global_o;

    f =exp(-I.*global_o.* t);

endfunction
```

Notice that the functions are vectorized

Understanding vectorization

a)
```
b = A(:,1) + 1.0;
```

c)
```
n=length(a);   b = a(1:2:n);
```

b)
```
i=find(a>1.0);   s=sum(a(i));
```

d)
```
n=length(a);

    c = 0.5.*(a(2:n) - a(1:n-1));
```

Chapter 6: Making Your Own Package: A Poisson Equation Solver

Identifying the Poisson equation

b)   c)   e)   f)   e) is also a Laplace equation

Index

J

Jacobian matrix
  providing, to fsolve function 148, 149

K

Kolmogorov-Smirnov test 205
kolmogorov_smirnov_test_2() function 207
kolmogorov_smirnov_test() function 207
kurtosis function 204

L

LAPACK 78
Laplace equation 172
Laplace operator 173
leasqr function
  about 212
  syntax 212
  using 212-214
least squares fit 209
left division operator 54
legend
  adding, to graph 87
length method 233
limitations, Octave 9, 10
linear algebra 78
linear equation systems
  about 175-177
  solving 52, 53
line function 86, 92
lines
  adding, to plot 86
linewidth property 84, 93, 94
load command 200
local variable 42
log function 68
long_value method 237
low pass filter
  applying 223, 224
low pass filtering 222
lsode
  about 229
  used, for numerical integration 150, 151

M

madd function 235, 236
makersize property 93
markersize property 87
mathematical functions, Octave
  about 66
  cos 66, 67
  cot 68
  exp 68
  log 68
  power 68
  sin 68
  tan 68
MathWorksTM 10
MATLAB 10, 79, 82
MATLAB EXecutable. *See* **MATLAB's MEX interface**
MATLAB's MEX interface 229
matrix
  instantiating 27
matrix addition function
  implementing 234, 235
Matrix class 235
matrix multiplication
  performing 49, 50
matrix_value method 237
max function 73, 136
maxx argument 137, 139
mcintgr 154, 238
mcintgrv 238
mesh function 99
m-function 231
min function 73, 136
minimax function 137
minmax function 139
minx argument 137, 139
mkoctfile command 232
moment function 204
Monte Carlo integrator
  deviation, calculating of 214
  vectorized version, using 202-204
  vectorizing 160, 161
Monte Carlo loop 159
Monte Carlo method
  about 201
  integrals, computing 153, 154

msh package **21**
multi-core package **169**
multidimensional arrays **66**
multiple figure windows **90**
multiple function file **164**
multiple graphs
  plotting, in single window **89**
multiplication operations
  performing **49, 50**

N

nargin variable **142**
nargout variable **142, 143**
nested loops **120**
nested statements **116**
nested structures
  instantiating **38**
nnz variable **178**
non-polynomial fits
  about **211**
  general least squares fitting **212-214**
  transforms **211**
Number of ARGuments IN. *See* nargin variable
Number of ARGuments OUT. *See* nargout
     variable
number sequence
  generating **45, 46**
numerical integration
  lsode, using for **150, 151**
Nyquist-Shannon theorem **216**

O

oct2mat package **12, 16**
Octave. *See also* GNU Octave
Octave
  .octaverc file, creating **19**
  .octaverc file, editing **19**
  about **25, 159, 199**
  additional packages, installing **21-23**
  applications **9**
  arithmetic operations **47, 57**
  Boolean operators **113**
  building, from source **14**
  cell arrays **39, 40**
  comparison operators **58, 59**
  compatible, with MATLAB **10**

complicated mathematical functions **69, 70**
customizing **17, 19**
data files, loading **199-201**
data sets, comparing **204**
descriptive statistics **201**
eigenvalues, calculating in **79**
help utility **23**
higher-dimensional arrays **34**
inline functions, defining **151**
installation, checking with peaks **15, 16**
installing, on Windows **11, 12**
limitations **9, 10**
optimization techniques **226, 227**
package, uninstalling **23**
polynomials, handling **68, 69**
polynomials, plotting **83**
precedence rules **60, 61**
sample moments, retrieving **204**
sparse matrix, using in **177-179**
structures **35**
three-dimensional plotting **96, 97**
two-dimensional plotting **82-85**
using, for advanced linear algebra **78**
Octave code
  optimizing techniques **226, 227**
Octave command prompt **24**
Octave community **10**
Octave-Forge
  URL **10**
Octave functions
  about **65**
  complicated mathematical functions **69, 70**
  example **136-138**
  helper **66, 71-77**
  mathematical **66-68**
  operational **66, 78-80**
  syntax **135, 136**
Octave script
  behaviour, controlling with statements **111**
  commands, breaking **108**
  comments **107**
  exception handling **124**
  executing **104**
  fflush(stdout) command **107**
  for GNU/Linux users **110**
  for MacOS X users **110**
  improving, input and disp functions used **105**

prime_sequence variable, loading 131, 132
prime_sequence variable, saving 130, 131
statements, implementing 121-124
storing, in workplace 109
used, for plotting 110
user, interacting with 106, 107
writing 104
octave_value_list 230-233
oct-files
  optimizing with 240, 241
odepkg package 229
one-dimensional heat conduction
        example 170, 171
ones function 46, 71
operator functions, Octave
  about 66, 78
  det 78, 80
  eig 79
  inv 80
  inverse 80
  orth 80
optimization techniques 226, 227
orth function 80
outputs
  managing 231-234
output variables 136

P

package directory
  files, organizing into 193
packages 169
parametric curves
  plotting 100
partial vectorization 229
Pearson correlation coefficient 205
Peason correlation coefficient 205
pi argument 66, 67
pkg command 23, 193
plot
  lines, adding to 86
  saving 94
  text, adding to 86
plot function
  about 83, 92
  interface 84
pois_fd function 190, 192

pois-solv package
  about 193
  building 195, 196
  limitations 196, 197
Poisson equation
  about 170
  one-dimensional heat conduction
        example 170, 171
  requisites, for solving 179
  two-dimensional heat conduction example 172
Poisson solver
  implementing 179
polyfit function
  about 208, 210
  using 208, 209
polynomial fitting 207-210
polynomials
  handling, in Octave 68, 69
  plotting 83
  roots, finding for 80
polyval function
  about 69
  using 210
power function 68
precedence rules, for Octave operators 60, 61
prime gab
  investigating 133
prime_sequence variable 130
  loading 131, 132
  saving 130
printf function
  about 127-129
  format specifiers 128
print function
  about 94
  supported formats 94
prod function 76
properties
  modifying, for plot 84, 85

Q

quad function 159

R

rande function 72
rand function 72, 154, 240

randg function 72
randn function 72
random numbers
  generating 72
randp function 72
real function 65, 66, 71
real part
  retrieving, of complex number 32
rem function 112
residual plot 211
right division operator 54
roots
  finding, for polynomials 80
round function 76
row vector 26, 67
row_vector_value method 237
row-wise looping
  versus column-wise looping 229

S

sample mean
  cxalculating 203
sample moments
  retrieving 204
sample variance
  cxalculating 203
sampling theorem 216
scalar function 70
scalars 66
scalar_value method 237
scalar variable 26
script. *See* Octave script
scripts
  converting, into functions 145
  versus functions 138
Sel'kov function
  about 148, 149
Sel'kov model
  about 241
  revisiting 242, 243
series.dat file 200
series variable 200
setfield function 38, 41, 138
set function 84, 87, 92
short-circuit Boolean operators
  && 115
  about 115

signal toolbox 224
simple variables
  about 26
  instantiating 26, 27
sin function 68
single window
  multiple graphs, plotting in 89
sockets 9
sort function 73, 74
sparse_complex_matrix_value method 237
sparse function
  about 177
  usage, optimizing 192
sparse matrix
  instantiating 177-179
  using, in Octave 177-179
sparse_matrix_value method 237
spline package 21
spy function 185
standard deviation
  cxalculating 203
statements
  about 111
  Boolean operators 113
  elseif statement 112
  endif statement 112
  for statement 117
  if statement 112
  implementing 121-124
  loops 117
  nested loops 120
  nested statements 116
  switch statement 116
  try statement 125
  unwind_protect statement 125
  using 111
  while statement 118
statistical analysis
  performing 199
statistical test functions 206, 207
steady state temperature profile 170
stochastic variable 201
strcmp function 59
string_value method 237
struct function 37
structure fields
  accessing 37, 38
  operations 52

structures
  about 35, 66
  instantiating 36, 37
  working with 40
subplot function 91
subplots 91
subtraction operations
  performing 47, 48
sum function 76
supported formats, print function
  eps 94
  gif 94
  jpg 94
  pdf 94
  png 94
  ps 94
  pslatex 94
  tex 94
surface color
  modifying 98
surface plot
  creating 96, 97
switch statement 116

T

tan function 68
temperature profile 171
text
  adding, to plot 86
text function 84, 86, 92, 94
text string variables
  instantiating 32, 33
thermal conductance 171
three-dimensional parametric plots 100
three-dimensional plotting 96, 97
tic function
  about 227
  using 227
title property 87, 94
toc function
  about 227
  using 227
transform
  example 211
transpose operator 51
trapz function 159

trigonometric functions 68
t_test2() function 206
t_test() function 206
two-dimensional array 200
two-dimensional heat conduction equation 172
two-dimensional Laplace equation
  solving 187, 188
two-dimensional plotting, Octave 82

U

Ubuntu 13
unwind_project_cleanup statement 125
usage function
  about 141
  versus warning function 141
user-supplied function
  about 237
  validating 155-158
user-supplied functions
  applying 145-147
  writing 145-147

V

variable names 27
variables
  about 146
  deleting 44
  information, retrieving for 42, 43
  initializing 228
  listing 41, 42
variable type
  identifying 43, 44
var_test() function 207
vecmat_convert function 187
vector
  about 66
  tranposing 51
vectorization 226, 228
vectorized language 159
vectorized programming 159, 160
vectorized version
  using 202-204
viewer position
  modifying 98
view function 98

W

X

Y

Z

Thank you for buying
GNU Octave Beginner's Guide

About Packt Publishing

Packt, pronounced 'packed', published its first book "*Mastering phpMyAdmin for Effective MySQL Management*" in April 2004 and subsequently continued to specialize in publishing highly focused books on specific technologies and solutions.

Our books and publications share the experiences of your fellow IT professionals in adapting and customizing today's systems, applications, and frameworks. Our solution based books give you the knowledge and power to customize the software and technologies you're using to get the job done. Packt books are more specific and less general than the IT books you have seen in the past. Our unique business model allows us to bring you more focused information, giving you more of what you need to know, and less of what you don't.

Packt is a modern, yet unique publishing company, which focuses on producing quality, cutting-edge books for communities of developers, administrators, and newbies alike. For more information, please visit our website: www.packtpub.com.

About Packt Open Source

In 2010, Packt launched two new brands, Packt Open Source and Packt Enterprise, in order to continue its focus on specialization. This book is part of the Packt Open Source brand, home to books published on software built around Open Source licences, and offering information to anybody from advanced developers to budding web designers. The Open Source brand also runs Packt's Open Source Royalty Scheme, by which Packt gives a royalty to each Open Source project about whose software a book is sold.

Writing for Packt

We welcome all inquiries from people who are interested in authoring. Book proposals should be sent to author@packtpub.com. If your book idea is still at an early stage and you would like to discuss it first before writing a formal book proposal, contact us; one of our commissioning editors will get in touch with you.

We're not just looking for published authors; if you have strong technical skills but no writing experience, our experienced editors can help you develop a writing career, or simply get some additional reward for your expertise.

Sage ACT! 2011 Dashboard and Report Cookbook

ISBN: 978-1-849681-92-6   Paperback: 216 pages

Over 65 simple and incredibly effective recipes for creating and customizing exciting dashboards and reports from your ACT! data

1. Immediately access and fully understand the out-of-the-box ACT! reports and dashboards

2. Get to grips with filtering dashboard information

3. Customize existing reports and dashboards to make permanent changes

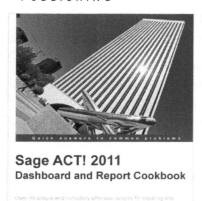

GlassFish Administration

ISBN: 978-1-847196-50-7   Paperback: 284 pages

Administer and configure the GlassFish v2 application server

1. Get GlassFish installed and configured ready for use

2. Integrate GlassFish with popular Open Source products such as Open MQ, Open DS, and Apache Active MQ, and get them working together in a loosely-coupled manner

3. Configure resource types like JDBC, Java Connector Architecture (JCA), JavaMail Sessions, and Custom JNDI supported in GlassFish to simplify resource access and integration

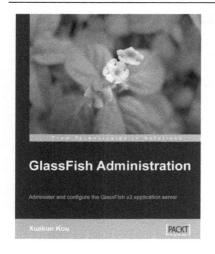

Please check **www.PacktPub.com** for information on our titles

 open source
community experience distilled

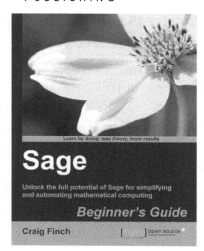

Sage Beginner's Guide

ISBN: 978-1-849514-46-0   Paperback: 364 pages

Unlock the full potential of Sage for simplifying and automating mathematical computing

1. The best way to learn Sage which is a open source alternative to Magma, Maple, Mathematica, and Matlab

2. Learn to use symbolic and numerical computation to simplify your work and produce publication-quality graphics

3. Numerically solve systems of equations, find roots, and analyze data from experiments or simulations

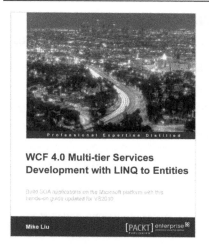

WCF 4.0 Multi-tier Services Development with LINQ to Entities

ISBN: 978-1-849681-14-8   Paperback: 348 pages

Master WCF and LINQ to Entities concepts by completing practical examples and applying them to your real-world assignments

1. Master WCF and LINQ to Entities concepts by completing practical examples and applying them to your real-world assignments

2. The first and only book to combine WCF and LINQ to Entities in a multi-tier real-world WCF service

3. Ideal for beginners who want to build scalable, powerful, easy-to-maintain WCF services

Please check **www.PacktPub.com** for information on our titles

phpBB: A User Guide

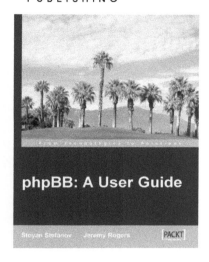

ISBN: 978-1-904811-91-6   Paperback: 176 pages

Set up and run your own discussion forum

1. Simple, practical steps to create and manage your own phpBB-powered online community

2. Learn from experienced phpBB administrators and enthusiasts to get the most from phpBB

WCF Multi-tier Services Development with LINQ

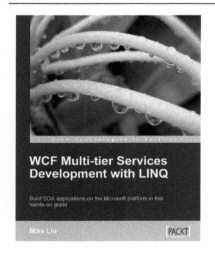

ISBN: 978-1-847196-62-0   Paperback: 384 pages

Build SOA applications on the Microsoft platform in this hands-on guide

1. Master WCF and LINQ concepts by completing practical examples and apply them to your real-world assignments

2. First book to combine WCF and LINQ in a multi-tier real-world WCF service

3. Ideal for beginners who want to build scalable, powerful, easy-to-maintain WCF services

Please check **www.PacktPub.com** for information on our titles

9 781849 513326